The Age of

SULTAN SÜLEYMAN

the Magnificent

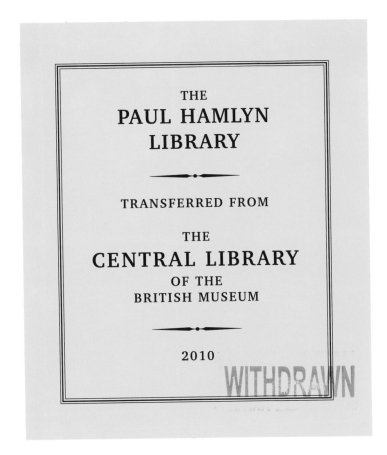

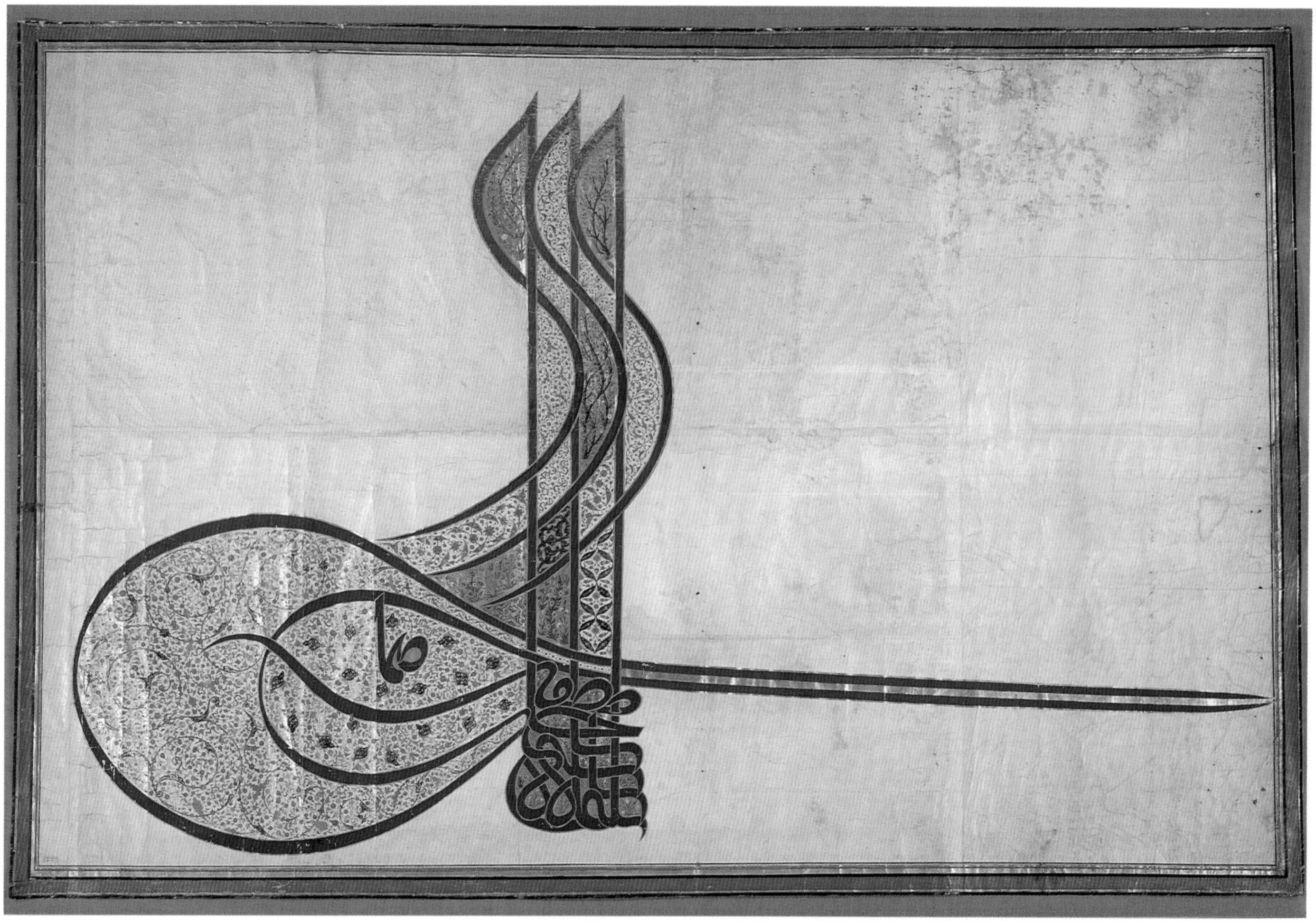

TUĞRA OF SULTAN SÜLEYMAN, after 1535, cat. no. 1 photograph by Jacqueline Hyde

The Age of

SULTAN SÜLEYMAN

the Magnificent

Organised by the

INTERNATIONAL CULTURAL CORPORATION OF AUSTRALIA LIMITED

in association with the

MINISTRY OF CULTURE, REPUBLIC OF TURKEY

PRODUCED BY THE BEAGLE PRESS FOR THE

INTERNATIONAL CULTURAL CORPORATION OF AUSTRALIA LIMITED

Published by the
International Cultural Corporation of Australia Limited,
12 Playfair Street, The Rocks, Sydney,
New South Wales, Australia 2000.

National Library of Australia
Cataloguing-in-Publication entry:

Bibliography
ISBN 1 875460 00 4
1. Süleyman I, Sultan of the Turks,
   1494 or 5-1566 — Art patronage — Exhibitions
2. Art, Ottoman — Exhibitions
3. Architecture, Ottoman — Exhibitions
4. Turkey — Civilisation — 16th century — Exhibitions
I International Cultural Corporation of Australia
II Turkey. Kültür ve Turizm Bakanliği.

First edition

Editorial assistance by
Marthe Bernus Taylor, David Alexander,
Edmund Capon, Jacqueline Menzies

Photography by
Jacqueline Hyde, Paris,
Art Gallery of New South Wales, Sydney,
and National Gallery of Victoria, Melbourne

Produced by The Beagle Press, Sydney
Designed by Catherine Martin

Typesetting by Savage Type, Brisbane
Colour separation by Laser Graphics NSW Pty Ltd
Printed by Bloxham and Chambers, Sydney

Cover: PORTRAIT OF SÜLEYMAN, c1579–80, cat. no. 2

This Exhibition is a gesture
of goodwill to Australia from
THE REPUBLIC OF TURKEY
and is provided by
THE DIRECTORATE-GENERAL OF
MONUMENTS AND MUSEUMS OF
THE MINISTRY OF CULTURE

Organised by the
INTERNATIONAL CULTURAL
CORPORATION OF AUSTRALIA LIMITED

Indemnified by
THE AUSTRALIAN GOVERNMENT
through the Department of the Arts,
Sport, the Environment, Tourism and Territories

Made possible by
LOUIS VUITTON AUSTRALIA

Sponsored by
SINGAPORE AIRLINES

Official domestic carrier
AUSTRALIAN AIRLINES

ART GALLERY OF NEW SOUTH WALES
27 June–26 August 1990

NATIONAL GALLERY OF VICTORIA
7 September–25 November 1990

ACKNOWLEDGEMENTS

The International Cultural Corporation of Australia thanks the many organisations and individuals who contributed to this exhibition, especially:

Topkapı Sarayı Müzesi, Istanbul
Türk ve Islam Eserleri Müzesi, Istanbul
Arkeoloji Müzesi Çinili Köşk, Istanbul
Musée du Louvre, Paris
Kunsthistorisches Museum, Vienna
Rifaat Sheikh El-Ard, Riyadh
National Gallery of Victoria, Melbourne

Marc-André Wagner, *Secrétaire-Général de l'Association Française d'Action Artistique, Paris*
Marthe Bernus Taylor, *Conservateur en chef, Section Islamique, musée du Louvre*
Thérèse Bittar, *Chargé de mission, Section Islamique, musée du Louvre*
David Alexander, *Puycelsi*
Dr Christian Beaufort-Spontin, *Director, Waffensammlung, Kunsthistorisches Museum, Vienna*
Bashir Mohammed, *London*
John Guy, *Assistant Keeper Indian Section, Victoria and Albert Museum, London*
Dr Michael Brand, *Curator Asian Art, Australian National Gallery, Canberra*
Robin Nair, *Chargé d'affaires, Australian Embassy, Ankara*

Jan Meek, *Public Relations Director, Art Gallery of New South Wales, Sydney*

Essays and catalogue entries for each object in the exhibition have been translated from the French catalogue, *Soliman le Magnifique*, published by Ministère des Affaires Étrangeres, Secrétariat d'Etat aux Relations Culturelles Internationales, Association Française d'Action Artistique (1990).

The Corporation particularly thanks Mr Francis Reiss of Brighton, Victoria, who first conceived the idea of this exhibition.

Contents

AUTHORS

M.B.T. MARTHE BERNUS TAYLOR *Conservateur en chef de la Section islamique, musée du Louvre*
A.B. ANNIE BERTHIER *Conservateur au Département des manuscrits orientaux, Bibliothèque nationale*
T.B. THERESE BITTAR *Chargé de mission à la Section islamique, musée du Louvre*
F.Ç. FILIZ ÇAĞMAN *Curator of the Library, Topkapı Sarayı Müzesi*
M.C. MARGUERITE CHARRITAT *Documentaliste à la Section islamique, musée du Louvre*
G.J. GUILLERMINA JOEL *Chargé de mission à la Section islamique, musée du Louvre*
L.K. LUDVIK KALUS *Directeur de recherche au CNRS*
A.L. ANNICK LECLERC *Chargé de mission à la Section islamique, musée du Louvre*
O.P. OLIVIA PELLETIER *Section islamique, musée du Louvre*
G.V. GILLES VEINSTEIN *Directeur d'Etudes à l'Ecole des Hautes Etudes en Sciences sociales*
S.Y. STEPHANE YERASIMOS *Professeur à l'Université de Paris VIII*
D.A. DAVID ALEXANDER

Ankara

MESSAGE FROM
HIS EXCELLENCY YILDIRIM AKBULUT
PRIME MINISTER
OF THE REPUBLIC OF TURKEY

It is very rare in the course of history that two nations so distant have come so close after having fought a battle in which they lost many thousands of lives. Yet, we each could deduce the best of it, whereby Australia found a national identity and we found a national hero.

It was only a few months ago that we hugged each other on the very shore of Gallipoli itself to commemorate the 75th anniversary of our "encounter" as noble "rival forces" of the past and as "mates" of today in the highest spirit of camaraderie.

That spirit found its highest tribute in the words of Mustafa Kemal Ataturk when, in 1934, he said for the Anzacs:

Having lost their lives on our soil, they have now become our sons as well.

This exhibition, which reflects yet another noble and rich period of our nation, is a gift of the Turkish people to the people of Australia as a memento of that lasting mutual respect.

During the period of Süleyman the Magnificent, one of the greatest figures on the world stage in the sixteenth century, the Ottoman Empire was politically, militarily and culturally a major power on the stages of three continents. This time, the Sultan, in the form of a travelling exhibition, after having mesmerized millions of people in three continents, is now launching an artistic "landing" in the new continent. Military victories of Süleyman the Magnificent may have faded into the past; but the art he so generously patronised survives in full splendour and glory.

I am sure visitors to this exhibition will understand why Thomas Dallam, the English traveller who visited Istanbul and the Sultan's Court in 1599 wrote:

What I did see was very wonderful unto me . . . the sight whereof did make me almost to think that I was in another world.

Not least of all, I hope this exhibition on a brief part of our past will entice you to go, not only a bit deeper into our history, but also to come and visit our beautiful country to see many other aspects of our life and cultural heritage. With these thoughts and sentiments, I believe that this exhibition will open a new and important avenue in the domain of ever-increasing closer bilateral relations between our nations.

YILDIRIM AKBULUT

MESSAGE FROM THE HONOURABLE R. J. L. HAWKE, AC, MP PRIME MINISTER OF AUSTRALIA

This outstanding historical exhibition, *The Age of Sultan Süleyman the Magnificent*, opens in a year of great historic significance for Australia and for the Republic of Turkey.

On Anzac Day, 1990, our two nations remembered those who fell in the Gallipoli campaign 75 years earlier.

The moving ceremonies, conducted on the Gallipoli Peninsula and attended by veterans from both sides of the conflict, helped to confirm the end of past enmity and to cement the present bonds between Turkey and Australia.

Since the 1960s, those bonds have been steadily strengthening through the establishment of diplomatic representation in both our countries, through an expanding trading relationship and especially through a continuing migration program producing a population of 60,000 Turkish Australians, most of whom live in Sydney and Melbourne, where the exhibition will be shown.

The generous provision of this collection by the Republic of Turkey will deepen Australians' appreciation of Turkish history and cultural achievements, a vivid impression of which I was able to form during my recent, all-too-brief visit to Turkey.

The priceless objects displayed date from the most prolific period of the Ottoman Empire, the reign of Sultan Süleyman, from 1520 to 1566. Sultan Süleyman earned his honorific title 'the Magnificent' through an extraordinary combination of talents as statesman, military leader, jurist, poet and patron of the arts. The imperial studios and workshops Sultan Süleyman personally founded and fostered created the highest standards of artistry and craftsmanship, building a new synthesis of Turkish, European and Islamic civilizations into a tradition which continues to inform Turkish culture today.

I hope this exceptional exhibition will be the first of many cultural exchanges, helping to extend the bridges of friendship between Australia and the Republic of Turkey.

R. J. L. HAWKE

UNDER THE PATRONAGE OF

Prime Minister of Australia
THE HONOURABLE R. J. L. HAWKE, AC, MP

Prime Minister of the Republic of Turkey
HIS EXCELLENCY YILDIRIM AKBULUT

COMMITTEE OF HONOUR

AUSTRALIA

Senator The Honourable Gareth Evans, QC
Federal Minister for Foreign Affairs and Trade

The Honourable David Simmons, MP
Federal Minister for the Arts, Tourism and Territories

His Excellency D. W. Witheford
Australian Ambassador to Turkey

James B. Leslie, AO, MC
Chairman, International Cultural Corporation of Australia Limited

Anthony S. Blunn, AO
Secretary, Department of the Arts, Sport, the Environment, Tourism and Territories

Cathy Santamaria
First Assistant Secretary, Arts, Film and Cultural Heritage Division, Department of the Arts, Sport, the Environment, Tourism and Territories

TURKEY

His Excellency Professor Dr Ali Bozer
Minister of Foreign Affairs

His Excellency Namik Kemal Zeybek
Minister of Culture

His Excellency Ergun Pelit
Turkish Ambassador to Australia

Acar Okan
Under-Secretary, Ministry of Culture

His Excellency Ismet Birsel
Ambassador, Director-General of Cultural Affairs, Ministry of Foreign Affairs

Mehmet Akif Isik
Deputy Director-General of Monuments and Museums, Ministry of Culture

NATIONAL PLANNING COMMITTEE

Robert Edwards (Chairman),
Chief Executive,
International Cultural Corporation of Australia Limited

Edmund Capon,
Director,
Art Gallery of New South Wales

Carol Henry,
General Manager,
International Cultural Corporation of Australia Limited

Jacqueline Healy,
Deputy Director Public Programs,
National Gallery of Victoria

Jacqueline Menzies (Exhibition Curator),
Curator of Asian Art,
Art Gallery of New South Wales

Ahmet Arda,
First Secretary,
Turkish Embassy in Australia

TURKISH ORGANISING COMMITTEE

Mehmet Akif Işik,
Deputy Director-General of Monuments and Museums,
Ministry of Culture

Metin Göker,
Minister-Plenipotentiary,
Assistant Director-General of Cultural Affairs,
Ministry of Foreign Affairs

Nimet Berkok,
Assistant Director-General of Monuments and Museums,
Ministry of Culture

Nilufer Ertan,
Assistant Head of Section,
Cultural Activities, Monuments and Museums,
Ministry of Culture

Gülhan Ulutekin,
Attaché, Director of Cultural Affairs,
Ministry of Foreign Affairs

MESSAGE FROM
HIS EXCELLENCY NAMIK KEMAL ZEYBEK
MINISTER OF CULTURE OF THE REPUBLIC OF TURKEY

Anatolia, straddling the continents of Asia and Europe, has been, by virtue of its geography, the cradle of many civilizations in the course of history. Born on this land, the Ottoman Empire, for 600 years, has amalgamated the eastern and western cultures by constituting a link in this chain of civilizations and creating an art form of its own.

The peak of this art form in the Ottoman Empire has been achieved, not only by the artists themselves, but also by the guiding role played by the administrators and rulers. The works of art exhibited in this gallery are from the Age of Sultan Süleyman the Lawgiver (known better in the west as Süleyman the Magnificent), one of the foremost of the Ottoman Sultans.

While he proved his military genius by victories in the battlefield, and his virtue of justice by enacting and implementing laws, he has also put his mark in his age as a patron of the arts and as an artist, thus promoting Ottoman art to its zenith.

An understanding of the art of a nation will give us an understanding of that nation and its history, and that is the basic idea behind this exhibition; to reach into the depths of history, fostering love and friendship among nations and cultures.

I am glad we could, after the USA, the UK, Germany, Japan and France, offer to the people of Australia this exhibition, which covers but a brief period in our history.

While expressing my trust that this exhibition, comprising 111 pieces selected from the Topkapı Palace and the Museums of Islamic art and archaeology in Istanbul, will be viewed with interest and help enhance the already existing friendly relations between our countries, I also extend my heartfelt thanks to those who have contributed so much to its realisation.

NAMIK KEMAL ZEYBEK

MESSAGE FROM
THE HONOURABLE DAVID SIMMONS, MP
MINISTER FOR THE ARTS, TOURISM AND TERRITORIES

Sultan Süleyman, during a reign of high achievement in all areas of government, fostered a rare flowering of art and architecture.

History speaks eloquently of the Sultan's great talents as ruler, law-maker and military campaigner.

But here, in this splendid exhibition, we see the concrete embodiment of his role as enthusiastic patron of the arts, giving opportunity and scope for the refinement of the exquisite skills of practitioners throughout his vast realm.

Australians are fortunate to be able to see and appreciate, for the first time, the fruits of such a rich heritage.

As we admire the glories displayed in this exhibition, we should recognise the parallel achievement of succeeding Turkish generations in devotedly preserving their endowment over more than five centuries to the present day.

The exercise of that responsibility reminds us that governments throughout the world now, as in Sultan Süleyman's time, play a crucial role in conserving our cultural inheritance and in fostering contemporary artistic endeavour.

In Australia, encouraging and facilitating significant cultural exchanges is high among our Government's priorities in a wide-ranging arts support program.

The International Cultural Corporation of Australia has a vital function in those exchanges as the expert manager of major exhibition tours.

The ICCA, established by the Federal Government in 1980 as an independent company, has proved to be a highly successful new form of arts management enterprise.

With minimal initial seeding capital, the ICCA has grown into a thoroughly professional, self-funding operation, attracting substantial corporate support for major exhibitions and developing unique expertise in the complex array of tasks involved in international cultural exchanges.

The Corporation is also the principal agency through which the Government administers the Commonwealth Indemnity Scheme, which provides insurance cover for cultural property of immense value and thereby makes the exhibition in Australia of some of the world's great artistic treasures a commercially viable undertaking.

I am sure this important exhibition, opening as the ICCA enters its second decade, heralds an expanding program of exchanges between Australia and nations such as the Republic of Turkey, the keepers of the world's cultural inheritance.

DAVID SIMMONS

MESSAGE FROM MR Y. CARCELLE CHAIRMAN, LOUIS VUITTON MALLETIER

It is my very great pleasure to be associated with the bringing of this wonderful exhibition, *The Age of Sultan Süleyman the Magnificent*, to Australia.

Sultan Süleyman was one of the greatest figures on the European stage of the sixteenth century. He was not only known for his political and military exploits but also as a patron of the arts. His court brought together treasures from all over Europe and Asia.

In this special year for Australians, the 75th anniversary of ANZAC, I hope this exhibition helps strengthen the bonds between Australia and Turkey in the same way that Sultan Süleyman built links between the East and West.

Louis Vuitton Australia is very proud to sponsor this exhibition and thanks the Australian Government and the Turkish Government for the opportunity.

Y. CARCELLE

Foreword

Australians are privileged to be able to view this exceptionally fine exhibition, *The Age of Sultan Süleyman the Magnificent.*

Only since 1983 has the Republic of Turkey again allowed objects from its priceless museum collections to tour abroad. Australia is thus among the first countries to see a selection of great treasures from the rich Turkish tradition, represented here by works from the reign of Sultan Süleyman, one of the most creative periods of the Ottoman civilization.

The exhibition has been made possible through the generosity of the Government of the Republic of Turkey, which gave permission for a collection, displayed earlier this year at the Grand Palais in Paris, to travel to Australia. In particular, we are grateful for the help and co-operation of the Turkish Ministry of Culture and the Directorate-General of Monuments and Museums.

I also wish specifically to thank the lending organisations which made available the 140 objects displayed in this exhibition. These include the Topkapı Sarayı Müzesi, Türk ve Islam Eserleri Müzesi and the Arkeoloji Müzesi Çinili Köşk, three of the most important national institutions in the Republic of Turkey. Works have also been loaned by the Musée du Louvre, Paris; the Kunsthistorisches Museum, Vienna; Rifaat Sheikh El-Ard of Saudi Arabia and the National Gallery of Victoria.

We are grateful for the generous financial support of our sponsors, without whom such valuable cultural exchanges could not take place.

The opening of such an important exhibition is highly appropriate in 1990, a year of particular significance for the International Cultural Corporation of Australia. The ICCA has completed ten years of successful exhibition management, organising cultural exchanges with countries around the world, ranging widely in depth and scope from Chinese archaeological treasures to challenging contemporary art.

It is extremely rewarding to have participated as Chairman in the birth and growth of the ICCA, which has earned the respect and confidence of foreign governments and lending bodies as well as the Australian Government and our exhibiting partners, the major national and State galleries and museums.

The ICCA has developed into a viable, professional management company, perfectly placed to plan and implement an exciting program of major international exhibitions over our next decade of successful operation.

JAMES B. LESLIE, AO, MC
Chairman
International Cultural Corporation of Australia Limited

Preface

When Süleyman succeeded to the throne of the Ottoman Empire in 1520, at the age of 26, he inherited an already extensive empire that extended from parts of present-day Yugoslavia, Bulgaria and the Crimea in the north to Syria and Egypt in the south. At that time he was perceived as a quiet and tranquil individual, perhaps ill-suited to serve as ruler. However, the measure of Sultan Süleyman's achievement is in the comparison of the Empire he inherited and the Empire he passed on to his successors.

In the 46 years of his reign, Sultan Süleyman expanded the Ottoman Empire into Central Europe, to Iraq, the Gulf, the Red Sea and along the North African coast to the border of Morocco. Under his aegis the Ottoman Empire reached its zenith, but more significantly, it was not a zenith determined by solely territorial gains so much as one determined by the successful expression of an emerging vision. That vision embraced the material and intellectual horizons of one of those extraordinary figures who quite justly become the ultimate symbol of the era. Sultan Süleyman, like others of his ilk, Philip of Macedonia and Alexander the Great for example, could not dissociate culture and its values and aspirations from his role as ruler. Thus he is known and honoured every bit as much for his military quests as he is for his achievements in defining and prescribing the processes of law in government and for his inspirational role in the patronage of the arts, from architecture to jewellery.

This exhibition naturally focuses upon the artistic achievements of the Ottoman Empire under Sultan Süleyman's reign, but such achievements must be seen as the expression, and indeed the exploitation, through Sultan Süleyman's vision, of the talents and craftsmanship of his subjects. It is an exhibition of a particular era of a distinctive culture; an exhibition of opulence, exquisite craftsmanship, cosmopolitan attitude and enduring quality. On behalf of the Art Gallery of New South Wales and the National Gallery of Victoria, the two fortunate Australian venues, we express our thanks to the authorities and individuals in Turkey, France, Austria and Australia who made *The Age of Sultan Süleyman the Magnificent* possible.

EDMUND CAPON
Director
Art Gallery of New South Wales

cat. no. 2

The Century of Sultan Süleyman the Magnificent

In the introduction to his work, *The Century of Louis XIV*, Voltaire, in order to justify the book title, reflects upon universal history, from amid a myriad of seemingly unconnected facts, that "all history is equal to those who only wish to retain facts in their memory"; he distinguished four great historical periods, each of which pertained to a century if not a ruler: these were the century of Philip and Alexander, that of Caesar and Augustus, that of the Medici in Italy and finally that of Louis XIV. With regard to the last, he notes: "There has been in our arts, in our minds, in our customs as in our government, a general revolution that serves to characterise the real glory of our country".

It was the blossoming of art, thought and attitude in general, the confirmation of great minds and exceptional talents in one time and place, that persuaded Voltaire to think of such periods as exemplary. Nevertheless, he stresses, "one must not think that these special centuries were exempt from misfortune and crime". He does not, however, note what his examples so strongly suggest: that cultural flowering is synonymous in those states with their attainment of the height of power, with the exception of Florence, of course, where we saw "a family of normal citizens assume monarchical power".

It was a similar coincidence of classical perfection and political power, associated with a reign of exceptional duration (1520–66), that characterised the Ottoman Empire under the rule of Sultan Süleyman the Magnificent. But Voltaire made no mention of this, indeed he could not. Not that the Turks were completely absent from his considerations; he mentioned Meḥmed II, the conqueror of Constantinople, but acknowledged his contribution to cultural history as only indirect and entirely involuntary thus: "The Medicis called to Florence the scholars that the Turks were driving away from Greece." Despite being the supreme philosopher, a free-thinker and among the most cultured individuals of his time, and although he did not eschew the styles and images of the Orient, it is clear that there was for Voltaire only a Western or European civilization. If the breath of the human spirit had filtered through the world throughout history, he thought that all this emanated from Europe.

Such prejudice was further encouraged by the decadence which had affected the Ottoman Empire since the death of the great Sultan; if there still existed a near-intact territory in the middle of the eighteenth century, its image had been greatly damaged since the time when the philosophers and thinkers of the Renaissance had observed that Ottoman Empire with fascination. They had convinced themselves, with a mixture of admiration and anxiety, that in this Moslem empire they were yoked to a fearful opponent, ruled by a supreme authority known as the "Grand Seigneur". It was an empire of power, wealth and unequalled splendour. They expressed their recognition of this in acknowledging Süleyman as "the Magnificent", and even sometimes in viewing him as a true reincarnation of the Roman emperors.

But the dominance of Sultan Süleyman in Istanbul was not the result of spontaneous generation. On his succession to the throne in 1520, at the age of 26, Sultan Süleyman inherited from his nine predecessors an already extensive empire. The small Turkish principality established at the end of the thirteenth century on the borders of the Seljuk Sultanate of Rum, in north-west Asia Minor, became for Byzantium something like an oil slick as it rapidly expanded under the aegis of a series of remarkable rulers.

The warriors of Osman and his descendants, the Osmani, progressively extended their territories over a large part of Asia Minor at the expense of their neighbours, and, crossing the Straits of the Dardanelles, entered Europe. Taking advantage of weaknesses and divisions within the Byzantine Empire they took possession of almost the entire Balkan peninsula. The capture of Constantinople in 1453 had been a decisive and symbolic step: this conquest which had for so long been delayed by the powerful walls of the Second Rome, rang the death knell of the Byzantine Empire, installed Mehmed II in the capital, now known as Istanbul, and made him heir to Caesar and Basil. Having for long lain dormant, the expansion of Islam underwent a regeneration under the initiative of the Osmani Turks.

However, their possessions lay on the fringes of the traditional domains of Islam, which had been defined by the Arab conquests during the early centuries of the Hijrī (the flight of Mohammed from Mecca to Medina in AD 622 from which the Islamic chronological era is calculated). In the sixteenth century the very heart of the Islamic world was struck by this irresistible force when in 1514 the grandson of the conqueror of Constantinople, Selim I "the grim" (*yavuz*), defeated the Shah of Persia and then in 1516–17 subdued Mamluk power by taking possession of Egypt and Syria. Following these victories the Ottoman Sultan secured large territories in the Middle

East and claimed suzerainty over Mecca and Medina, becoming the protector of the most holy places of Islam, all of which confirmed his pre-eminence among Muslim rulers.

A premature death interrupted the terrifying career of Selim "the grim"; Süleyman, his only son, was able to succeed him without difficulty.

In accordance with tradition, Süleyman had already served his apprenticeship in provincial government, but was considered to be of a tranquil nature and thus not well suited to the role of ruler. A pause in the expansion of the Ottoman Empire was therefore expected upon his succession. However, he contradicted all expectations by inaugurating his reign with two major coups which took on an added significance because in each case he succeeded where his grandfather, Mehmed II, the supreme conqueror, had failed. On 29 August 1521 he obtained the surrender of Belgrade, the formidable fortress at the confluence of the Danube and Sava rivers, the key to the plains of Hungary. On 21 December he evicted the Knights of Saint John (the Hospitallers) from the Island of Rhodes. The Knights had settled there following their departure from Jerusalem and, like eager pirates, menaced the maritime routes between the new provinces of Egypt and Syria and the capital of the Empire.

Sultan Süleyman's conquering zeal continued without abating for more than 30 years; he personally led his army on a dozen campaigns. Sultan Süleyman was imbued with the tradition of the great warriors of the house of Osman but his actions were distinguished as much by the evolution of his own character as by the expansion of his empire. He was involved in all the activities and operations of the "well-guarded countries" forming his empire. Naval activities assumed an ever-increasing importance (despite the Sultan's personal distrust of naval campaigns) alongside the land-based campaigns which were more familiar to the Turks.

Recognising the growing distances involved, Süleyman acknowledged early in his reign the limitations such journeys imposed and that it would be unrealistic to expand indefinitely the borders of the empire. Perhaps he had seen in some of those close to him, such as the Grand Vizier Ibrahim Paşa (?1493–1536), the dangers of submitting to temptation. He sought to consolidate existing borders even at the expense of possible territorial gains. Indeed we might even attribute "faint-heartedness and lack of courage" to the ruler, who nevertheless extended more than any other the domination of his dynasty.

In Central Europe these attitudes inclined Sultan Süleyman less to conquer Hungary, despite the conquest of Belgrade, than to make it a vassal state which could serve as a buffer with the powerful Habsburg Empire, always a disturbing rival. Allied to the latter, the young Hungarian King, Louis II Jagellon, had discourteously treated the Sultan's ambassadors and on 29 August 1526 imprudently confronted his immense army on the plains at Mohacs on the Danube. The king was drowned during the rout of his armies and left Süleyman in direct confrontation with the two Habsburg rulers: the Emperor Charles V and his brother Ferdinand, Archduke of Austria, who was elected king of Hungary.

To put an end to Ferdinand's claims to a country which the Sultan considered to have been conquered by him, Süleyman attempted, in October 1529, the siege of Vienna, which he was forced to abandon before the onset of winter. For the same reason he encamped his armies at Graz in Styria (now Austria) during the "German campaign" in 1532. In the meantime Süleyman had recognised the election of the Hungarian magnate Janos Zápolya as King of Hungary, and the Hungarian grandee thus became yet another dependant of Sultan Süleyman and the Ottoman Empire.

Zápolya died in 1540 and Ferdinand continued to sue for what he perceived to be his rights; Süleyman resolved to annex central Hungary, which he then established as a province of the Empire; Transylvania became a vassal state under the pliant rule of the infant son of Zápolya. The remainder of the old kingdom, that is, the north and the west, stayed in the hands of the Habsburgs. This partition was ratified in the truce of 1547 which stipulated that Ferdinand would pay an annual tribute of 300,000 Hungarian ducats in recognition of the Sultan's rights over that part of the kingdom held by him. After the resumption of hostilities the agreement was renewed on the same basis by another truce in 1562.

Hungary and Transylvania were the principal gambles in Süleyman's European campaigns, but in 1538 the Sultan also personally intervened in Moldavia against another intractable vassal, the *Voivode* (protector) Petru Raresh. Süleyman occupied the country and its capital Succeva then retired having installed a new *voivode*. He could be well satisfied with his territorial gains, for with the annexation of Boudjak, the south of Bessarabia, he completed the establishment of the Ottoman Empire in the steppelands to the north of the Black Sea.

But the confrontation between the Ottoman Empire and the Habsburgs was not confined to Cen-

cat. no. 18

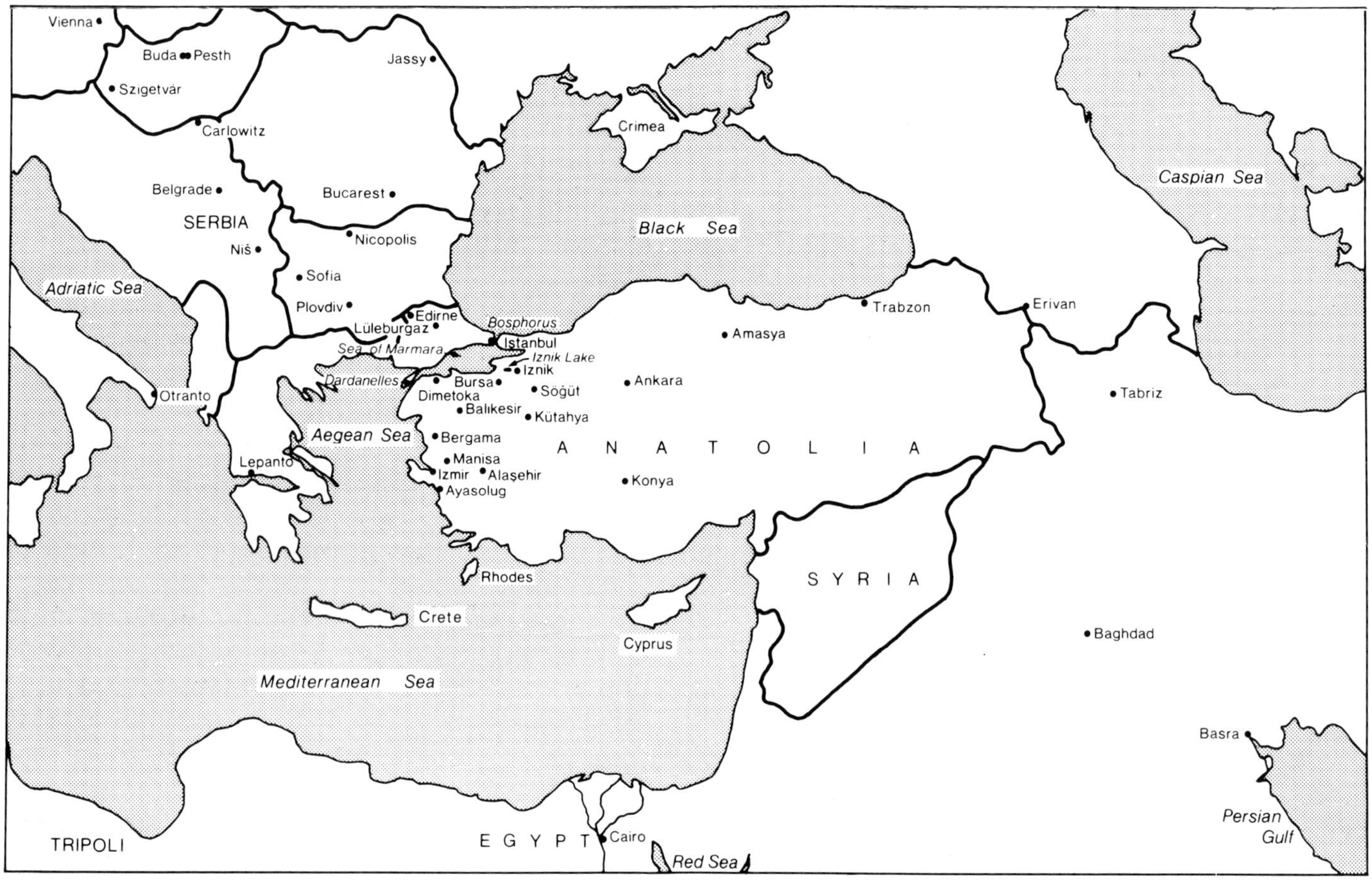

tral Europe. Through possessions in Spain and Italy, Charles V had command over several naval squadrons in the Mediterranean, which were reinforced by the fleets of his allies in the Balkans. In particular there was the illustrious Genovese captain, Andrea Doria, who, in 1528, left the service of the King of France to join forces with Charles: Süleyman had much to fear from these naval powers. Charles V had his eyes set on Muslim territories in north-west Africa, the Mağrib, which he sought to preserve from the "infidels"; furthermore, he could strike where the Ottoman Empire was most vulnerable and intervene in the eastern Mediterranean. In fact, in September 1532, at the head of a Genovese fleet accompanied by the squadrons of the Pope, Malta and Sicily, Doria secured Coron on the southern coast of the Peloponnese peninsula and was thus able to establish a Spanish garrison on Ottoman soil. The Turks did not recover Coron until April 1534 after a long and laborious siege.

Süleyman reacted to the challenge by a large-scale expansion of his naval power. He was fortunate in having an abundant supply of the necessary materials, in particular timber, a competent labour force and well located ports. The lack of experienced captains was his only problem. These he recruited among Islamic corsairs from whom the Mediterranean held few secrets, with the most famous of his sea-faring recruits being Hayreddin, known as Barbarossa (Red Beard), an old "sea-dog" who had held sway over Algiers. In 1533 he joined the Sultan's forces and was given the title of *beylerbeq* (military chief) of Algiers, which thus became a province of the Ottoman Empire, and he became virtual head, the admiral, of the fleet. Barbarossa proved to be a remarkable organiser as well as as an unequalled navigator, supervising the naval shipyards at Galata before leading the Sultan's galleys into sundry excursions of pillage and victory.

In August 1534, eight months after joining forces with the Sultan, he seized Tunis which had for long been coveted by Charles V, who admittedly had his revenge when in July the following year he was able to re-establish a prince of a local dynasty as ruler and set up a Spanish garrison at la Goulette. However, this Habsburg success did not alter the thrust of Ottoman expansion and on 28 September 1538 at Preveza, on Greece's Ionian coast, Hayreddin gained a decisive naval victory over the united fleets of Charles V, the Pope and Venice, the last having shortly before made the unwise decision to end its neutrality towards the Turks. It might be said that Barbarossa had benefited in the conflict by the relatively passive attitude adopted by his rival Andrea Doria, but it was still a resounding victory. Soon after the defeat, Venice abandoned her possessions in the Peloponnese and the Aegean Islands; but, more importantly, these events heralded an era of Ottoman supremacy in the Mediterranean region that was to assist Barbarossa and, after his death in 1546, his successors.

In 1551 another corsair, Turgut Reis, whom the Europeans called "Dragut", seized Tripoli, thereby furthering the pattern of Ottoman domination in north-west Africa; that domination, however, was not completed until after the death of Süleyman through the recapture of Tunis in 1574. Morocco always remained beyond the Ottoman grasp. In 1560 another Ottoman naval chief, Piyale Paşa, underlined Turkish superiority by driving the Christian forces from the small Island of Djerba (in reality a peninsula) off the Tunisian coast.

But such constant success could not last. In the summer of 1565, Piyale Paşa and "Dragut", accompanied by an immense armada, failed to take Malta. It was an ominous sign that ultimately heralded the disaster of the Battle of Lepanto in 1571.

Even so, the outcome (of the battle of Malta) was uncertain: the Ottoman fleet, although severely battered, was not destroyed. The titanic struggle between Charles V and Süleyman had one other significant consequence: the somewhat paradoxical alliance between France and the Ottoman Empire. Formed at the instigation of Francis I and his mother, Louise of Savoy, in 1525, after the defeat at Pavoe and the subsequent capture of Francis I in Madrid by Charles V, it was an alliance that was to survive until the death of Francis in 1547, despite his fluctuating attitudes towards the Ottomans. Then it was renewed by Henry II with some enthusiasm, only to be abandoned again in 1559 after the peace of Cateau-Cambresis and the wars of religion.

The liaison between the successors of Saint-Louis and the Padişah revealed a new concept in Renaissance Europe, a new sense of political realism that was more akin to the theory and spirit of the Florentine, Machiavelli. This unnatural alliance engendered much ill-feeling among a public of traditional values. Princes who were usually adversaries were united against the common foe with Charles V threatening the Kingdom of Valois and placing further claims on a number of its regions including Picardy, Bourgoyne, Dauphine and Provence. He furthermore continued to oppose French claims in Italy, Milan, Genoa and Naples.

Meanwhile, Süleyman merely saw Charles V as King of Spain, and no more, certainly not as any kind of universal monarch, and thus continued his confrontation with the Habsburgs in both Hungary and the Mediterranean. We can see that these fluctuating fortunes and power struggles were combining to lead Süleyman into an alliance with France and her allies, including the protestant princes of Prussian Germany. On the ground, this Franco-Ottoman alliance could undertake well co-ordinated military operations on two fronts; at sea, there was direct collaboration between the modest French fleets and the huge Ottoman armadas which gave the Sultan virtual control over the Mediterranean and access to ports and supplies.

Barbarossa became the advocate and most decisive player in this alliance. Between 1537 and 1559 he led eight major joint Franco-Ottoman naval campaigns, of which the most famous was in 1544–45 when the fleets under Barbarossa and the Duke d'Enghien undertook the siege of Nice, then a possession of Savoy. It was only a partial success and after it Barbarossa spent the winter at Toulon. Emptied of its women and children, this provincial town was transformed for several months into a small Istanbul, much to the indignation of the Christians. However, the difficulties and misunderstandings that inevitably arose out of this alliance largely negated its potential; the only lasting consequence of this initial stage in Franco-Ottoman relations were the Capitulations of 1536, which granted certain rights to the King's subjects who resided in the Ottoman empire and provided the French with many commercial benefits. But even this was still something of a promise, for it was only ratified by Selim II in 1569.

The long and complex conflict with the Habsburgs was not the only challenge facing Süleyman. On the eastern front he had to confront another adversary whose fearful power combined political and religious energy. The Shah of Persia, Shah Tahmasp, eldest son of the founder of the Safavid Dynasty, Shah Ismā'īl, was a descendant of the ancient and important Azerbaijani family which claimed descent from 'Alī, cousin and son-in-law of the Prophet. They were, therefore, fellow believers but clearly influenced by the Shī'ī branch of Islam (which appeared in the first century of Islam).

Since the middle of the fifteenth century, this doctrine of the so-called "red-heads" (*Kizilbaş*, who wore a red baton as part of their head-dress) had spread among the Turks of Anatolia, where it became a kind of symbol of these nomadic peoples' opposition to Ottoman power. Thus, as with his predecessors, Bayazid II and Selim I (the latter having resolved nothing in beating the "reprobate Shah"), Süleyman was confronted, early in his reign, with Turcoman revolts in Cilicia, Karaman and in the Taurus mountains.

However, Süleyman again had an ally, the Uzbek Khan of Central Asia. Together they fought the Shah, who in turn was in contact with Charles V. His first campaign against the Safavids lasted from June 1534 to January 1536. It took the Sultan's armies following in the footsteps of his principal general, the Grand Vizier Ibrahim Paşa, from the east of Anatolia to Azerbaijan and to Tabriz, which he occupied. Then, from the mountains in the west of Iran, he advanced to Baghdad before commencing a second march on Tabriz. The laborious perambulations of the army in difficult terrain and appalling climates brought terrible deprivations upon the troops, which were made even worse by the "scorched earth" tactics of the Shah, who thereby managed to avoid a direct confrontation. The conquest of Azerbaijan and even of the Iranian plateau of which Ibrahim Paşa had dreamed was left in suspense. On the other hand the costly campaign did allow Süleyman to consolidate his borders in the eastern region of Asia Minor through the establishment of the province of Erzurum (in eastern Turkey) and to add to his empire the only large and historical Islamic metropolis that he had lacked: Baghdad, which he also took from the Kizilbaş.

The other two campaigns led by Süleyman against the Shah, in 1548–49 and 1554, clearly illustrated the logistical problems he faced with increasingly long supply lines through thoroughly inhospitable territory. For want of destroying an enemy who was forever avoiding a confrontation, or of planning new and spectacular territorial expansions in the east, Süleyman chose to reinforce the protective wall between the two empires. Finally, he concluded the peace treaty of Amasya with the Shah, in which he abandoned his claims to Tabriz, Erivan and Nakhichevan but was recognised in his claims to territories in Iraq, the "Oriental" areas of Anatolia, western Armenia and Kurdistan.

In the east, as in the west, it was necessary to pursue the war on land and sea. The conquests of Selim in the Middle East, consolidated by Süleyman after his repression in the years 1520–25 of the Mamluk uprisings, brought the Ottomans to the Red Sea. In the same way the seizure of Iraq followed and later, in 1546, the occupation of Basra which gave them the shores of the Persian Gulf. In both cases the Ottoman concern was to control the traditional trade routes, just when the Portuguese were attempting to divert traffic from these routes to a new ocean trading link they were establishing.

In 1537 the Governor of Egypt, Süleyman Paşa, built a fleet at Suez with which he seized Aden in 1538; then, having reached the Gujarat coast after crossing the Oman Sea, he attempted in vain to remove the Portuguese from Bandar Diu on the Gulf of Cambay. Nevertheless, on his return journey he was able to reinforce Süleyman's hold on Yemen before returning to Egypt. In 1551 the Suez fleet, this time under the command of the navigator, geographer and painter, Pīrī Reis, embarked on a new undertaking to destroy the Portuguese outposts of Muscat and Oman, a foray that ended in disaster.

Three years later another famous Ottoman captain, Seyyid 'Alī Re'is, set off from Basra to confront the Portuguese but he too was defeated, this time by a storm, which left him stranded with the remnants of his fleet at Surat on the Indian coast. These repeated efforts, which were to continue long after Süleyman's reign, failed to defeat the Portuguese; the latter also failed in their attempts to wrest the traditional Muslim control of the spice trade and its routes, which remained in the protection of the Ottomans as they retained their hold over the Gulf and the Red Sea.

We can see that towards the middle of the sixteenth century the frontiers of Süleyman's Ottoman Empire had been stabilised. The Empire had reached its zenith and little was to change until towards the end of the seventeenth century, when the gradual process of erosion of the Ottoman Empire began. But in the mid sixteenth century, Sultan Süleyman was head of one of the largest and most extensive Empires known. It extended over three continents, was washed by the waters of four oceans, embraced some 22 million subjects, an enormous number in those days, and had as its capital Istanbul, with its population of 500,000. As this population was made up of various ethnic groups, the three monotheistic religions came into close contact under the Muslim rule. But the great strength and unity of the Empire did not stem solely from its vast size, diversity and richness; the generally prevailing conditions of order, prosperity and government, that were remarkably if not wholly pervasive and effective, grew from the political and social institutions inherited by Süleyman and which he subsequently perfected. There were few if any of the feudal holdings, local autonomies or local privileges, with all the attendant petty squabbles, of the kind that

cat. no. 49

his great rival Charles V administered. As well Charles was also constantly short of money to pay to his mercenaries.

Sultan Süleyman ruled over a strongly centralised state through a uniform provincial government structure. The levels and collection of taxes were controlled by government edicts, with a substantial part of the revenues finding their way into the Sultan's own considerable treasury.

Thus Süleyman was able to maintain a large permanent army composed of infantry: the celebrated Turkish footguard of *janissary*, cavalry and artillery units. These palace troops were the best trained and best equipped and certainly enjoyed the favours of the Sultan. They, however, represented only the elite of the Ottoman forces; the Sultan had at his disposal a provincial cavalry of some 10,000 horsemen known as *sipahi* (who were rewarded for their services with endowments of land or *timar*), to which he could always add a whole string of mixed units from both Christian and Muslim sources according to need. The members of the elite standing army, like senior officials in the government, were closest to the Sultan and were carefully selected principally from Christian families in Anatolia and the Balkans. After being separated from their families, they were raised as Moslems and trained in the Sultan's own schools. Such methods assured the Sultan of the most able and competent staff but, at the same time, the "*esprit de corps*" that such a closed system engendered particularly among the infantry, also created potentially dangerous factions within the ranks.

Master of his destiny, Süleyman nevertheless did not allow himself to be seen in the image of his father, the "grim" sultan. On the contrary, he sought to become a paradigm of good government, embracing political thought and Islamic ethic; his subjects recognised these qualities in Süleyman in calling him *Kānūnī*, the Legislator. He governed according to the law and ensured due right and justice throughout the Empire, giving as much regard to Muslims as to Christians, Jews and his other subjects.

However, his religious initiatives included a merciless repression of Kizilbaş, Safavid supporters, and other heretics. Europeans, in spite of their prejudices, were not insensitive to the spirit of nobility that determined Süleyman's principles and aspirations, nor could they but admire his incomparable power.

The ruler's sense of religion, and of devotion to his responsibilities, co-existed with an artistic sensitivity and a certain taste for display and ostentation without which "the Legislator" could not have been known also as "the Magnificent". His reign was certainly the peak of Ottoman power and achievement. A cultivated man, fluent in several languages, Süleyman was also a poet under the pen-name *Muḥibbī*, "the affectionate one", and a devotee of the art of the goldsmith and the jeweller, in which he could pursue his love for precious stones. In the broader view he played a direct role in the flowering of culture and the arts in his reign, a tireless patron particularly through philanthropic institutions and his direct association with the creative minds of the day. His example was surely an inspiration to members of his family and the Court, all of which reinforced the role of the state. The arts followed the traditional patterns of Islamic achievement in wood carving, metalwork, goldsmithing, ceramics, weaving and silk production and of course architecture; in literature, composition and poetry continued to be the major forms.

Indeed, all the creative arts flourished in the vigorous spirit of the age. In addition, attention to craft and skilful execution, from jewellery to metalwork to silk-weaving, brought a new and exquisite sense of achievement in techniques to the material arts in Süleyman's reign. Among the creative masters of the time whose names are renowned and who were, as with the masters of the Renaissance, men with strong personalities and wide-ranging talents, are the architect Sinan, the historian Kemalpaşazade, the compiler and bibliographer Taskopruluzade, the poets Baki and Fuzulī, the draughtsmen and painters Şahkulu, Ḳaramemī, Nīgārī and 'Osmān.

There can be no denying the historical reality of a "Süleyman century", just as there was, according to Voltaire, a "Louis XIV century". Süleyman faced the inevitable problem as, with the passing of the years, his fortunes wavered, disenchantment set in and the brilliant hero of yesterday inevitably slid into old age. From about 1552, when Süleyman's laborious and energy-sapping campaigns brought only limited gains to the Empire, there were murmurings among the troops that perhaps their *padişah*, who was by then approaching 60 years of age, could no longer lead them to victory. The promising and attractive elder son of Süleyman, Mustafa, was rapidly becoming a favoured figure among the increasing number of malcontents.

The issue was a serious threat to Süleyman, but the potential usurper found in the Sultan's consort, Hürrem Sultan, the most resolute adversary. Of Ruthenian (a Central European region now a province of Czechoslovakia) origins, Hürrem Sultan had developed such a hold over Süleyman that in 1534, quite

YATAGAN, *detail*, cat. no. 51

exceptionally in the Osmani house, he made her his legitimate wife. Indeed, legend has it that she cast a spell over her Sultan and certainly no other single individual had such influence over him since the death of his childhood friend Ibrahim, whom he had appointed his grand vizier but had executed, in 1536, upon realising the extent of the latter's ambitions.

Mustafa was the son of one of the Sultan's previous concubines and Hürrem was determined that the successor would be one of her own progeny — a scheme in which she was greatly assisted by the powerful grand vizier, Rüstem Paşa. Mustafa was finally assassinated in the name of the state in 1553. His death was shortly to be followed by that of Şehzade Cihangir, the youngest of Süleyman and Hürrem's sons and a frail, sensitive youth who, it is said, died of grief soon after hearing the news.

Süleyman's domestic misfortunes accumulated when, after the death of his beloved wife in 1558, his two surviving sons, Bayazid and Selim, became engaged in a ruthless battle with each other. Defeated by his brother in 1559, Bayazid took refuge with the Safavid Shah only to be executed with his family upon his return. Thus Süleyman had but one remaining heir, Selim, who was renowned for his drunkenness. These trials, to which soon was added his ignominious defeat during the siege of Malta, were ignored by the ageing Süleyman, seemingly insensitive to everything as he sought refuge in austerity and religion. Perhaps the seventy-year-old man was searching for a worthy end when in 1566, with the death of Ferdinand of Habsburg, circumstances offered new possibilities. Ferdinand was succeeded by Maximilian II and there was a renewal of hostilities between the Ottoman and Habsburg Empires; Süleyman once again led his armies into battle and marched towards Hungary.

His body crippled with gout, Süleyman was quite unable to ride a horse and forced to travel the long and bumpy road by carriage. He finally died in his tent on 6 September 1566, just as the Hungarian fortress of Szigetvár, which he had had under siege for a month, was about to fall into his hands. His remains were brought back to Istanbul and placed in the mausoleum, designed by Sinan, which lay in the shadow of his majestic mosque, the Süleymaniye. Through his heroic death he redeemed the final sad years of his reign, which nevertheless signalled the beginnings of the decline of the Ottoman Empire. And yet nothing could dilute the monumental image and achievement of the man who was the very incarnation of the peak of Ottoman power.

GILLES VEINSTEIN

cat. no. 59

Süleyman the Lawgiver

The Sultan, direct descendant of 'Osmān, founder of the Ottoman dynasty, was head-of-state and holder of all powers, his absolute power being only limited by his submission to the precepts of Islamic law and the guidelines of a sort of Imperial ideology. He governed through his *divan*. This counsel, supreme organ of the state, was presided over by the grand vizier, who was "absolute representative" of the monarch. He appointed several other viziers, who were at the same time dignitaries entrusted with major responsibilities as well as advisers. These included a high chancellor, the *nişancī*, and two finance inspectors, the *defterdar*: the first for the European side of the Empire, known as Rumeli; the second for the Asian side, Anatolia. The juridico-religious body of the *'ilmiye* was represented at the *divan* by two great judges or "judges of the army" Kadī'asker who held, respectively, Rumeli and Anatolia within their jurisdiction. But, in Süleyman's time, a legal expert from outside the *divan*, the *müfti* of Istanbul, became the real *Seyhülislam*, head of the whole rigidly structured system of the *'ilmiye*. The main political decisions were submitted to him and he, in turn, provided a written opinion on them (*fetvā*).

If the Sultan did not personally take a seat at the council of his *divan*, the great questions discussed in it were submitted to him for examination.

The central authority was supported by a bureaucracy whose powers continued to grow and whose organisation evolved further during Süleyman's reign. The secretaries (*Kātib*) of the Chancellery and their apprentices (*Şakird*), under the supervision of the "head secretary" (*Reisülküttab*), drew up the innumerable *fermans*, "imperial letters", treaties and other official acts, more or less elaborate and ornate according to their purpose. Onto these *Tuğrakes* the sovereign's monogram was affixed (*tuğra*), thereby validating them. A particular section was devoted to financial documents, under the direction of the *defterdar*. The latter was also the chief of various offices (*Kalem*) in which specialised agents kept books of expenditures and returns for the different parts of the Empire. A "superintendent of records" (*defter eminī*) maintained the voluminous archives of the central administration.

In the provinces, authority was divided between three divisions of agents, all equally dependent on the central administration: the provincial governors (*beylerbeq* and *sancakbeq*) were responsible for law and order and military matters; the *defterdar* occupied positions which related to the allocation of military pay (*timar*) and were required to know about matters relating to revenue and supply. At the same time overseers (*emin*) kept meticulous watch over the different sources of public income. The task of local administration was especially that of the *kadī*, who were simultaneously judges and lawyers in their areas of responsibility. These *'ilmiye* preserved in their documents, *sicill*, written records of a great variety of activities.

Other more autonomous regions of Europe and Asia, which were attached to the Empire by a simple tie of vassalage mixed with a few obligations, retained their own specific political and administrative institutions.

G.V.

The Catalogue

All measurements are in centimetres, height by width by depth (where applicable). When a work is dated according to the Islamic lunar calendar, this date is included in the entry, e.g., *Ramaḍān* 965/July 1558.

1 TUĞRA OF SÜLEYMAN *frontispiece*

Turkey, after 1535
Gold and opaque paint on thick prepared paper; 158.0 x 240.0

Istanbul, Library of the Topkapı Sarayı Müzesi, G.X. 1400
Treasury of the Topkapı Palace

The *tuğra*, the imperial monogram of the Ottoman sultan, was made up of the principal letters of his name and was inscribed at the top of the decrees issued by the Imperial Council (*Dīvān-i Humāyūn*).

Inscribing the *tuğra* was the task of a High Chancellor (*nişanci*) of the *dīvān*. From the sixteenth century onwards, the *tuğra* on important documents were illuminated. They added a great artistic value to the archival documents issued by the Ottoman bureaucracy. Until the eighteenth century the *tuğra* was used mainly on *ferman* documents, on stamps, coins and the seals used to control the issuing of money.

This unusually large *tuğra* of Süleyman is a beautiful example of the art of illumination. The letters are dark blue, outlined in gold. The *sere*, letters forming the name of the sultan, are decorated with tulips, flowering trees, carnations, hyacinths, buds, roses and *rūmī* motifs in various colours, all on a blue background.

The *tuğ* — three long strokes — is also illuminated, on a background of gold or the natural colour of the paper, with flowers, flowering trees, medallions of leaves enclosing interlacing *ḫaṭāyī* motifs, Chinese clouds and various *rūmī* decorations. The *beyze*, or large loops to the left of the name, are decorated by fine spiralling stems bearing *ḫaṭāyī* flowers which interlace to form an increasingly dense design.

The illumination of this *tuğra*, one of the masterpieces of the palace workshops, was executed by Ḳaramemī and his students. In the Topkapı Palace collection are other *tuğra* of similar size, most richly illuminated, belonging to Selim II, Murad III, Aḥmed I and Murad IV. The *tuğra* of Selim II measures five by three metres and was executed by the *nişanci* of the time, Aḥmed Feridun. That of Aḥmed I is signed by the calligrapher Ḥasan Paşa who for a short time was also vizier of the Imperial Council (*Dīvān-i Humāyūn*)[1].

The large *tuğra* were executed in the sixteenth and seventeenth centuries by the *nişanci*; it would appear therefore that this *tuğra* of Süleyman was executed by Celālzāde Musṭafā Paşa, better known as "Ḳoça (Great) Nişanci". He occupied the position from 1534 to 1557, when he resigned at an advanced age. In 1566, he was asked to resume the position but died shortly after.

Because of their size, the *tuğra* of Süleyman and others dating from the sixteenth and seventeenth centuries were hung from the wall. However, because it was only from the beginning of the sixteenth century that the Ottomans began to hang drawings, pictures, engravings and large manuscripts on the walls, it is still difficult to identify the reason for the size of these *tuğra*. It was not until the beginning of the eighteenth century in the reign of Sultan Aḥmed III, a gifted calligrapher, that the *tuğra* became a calligraphic work.[2]

The *tuğra* executed by Sultan Aḥmed III have been gathered in an album. They were also carved into the marble on each side of the door leading into the sultan's private apartments (*Hasoda*). From this time onwards, the *tuğra* of the sultan was often incorporated into decoration, on the interiors and exteriors of buildings and beside the notices about the construction or restoration of edifices. The large *tuğra* on paper from the sixteenth and seventeenth centuries must have served a specific function, being hung in the Imperial Council, where affairs of state were discussed, the empire was governed and the justice and power of the sultan were symbolised by the shape of this domed room: the *Kubbealti* (*Dīvān-i Humāyūn*).

The *tuğra* of Süleyman and his successors were present in the room of the *Divan* for two possible reasons: first, to serve as examples for the *nişanci* charged with inscribing the *tuğra* on the decrees; second, as a symbol of the sultan if he was not present.

1 *Only the* tuğra *of Sultan Aḥmed I have been edited: Istanbul, 1983, E193; Istanbul, 1987, first pages*
2 *See Atil, E., 1980, ill. 125; Istanbul, 1983, E314*

Photograph Jacqueline Hyde F.Ç.

2 PORTRAIT OF SULTAN SÜLEYMAN

Ḳiyāfetü'l-Insānīye fī şemā'ilü'l-'Osmānīye *ill. page 14*

Turkey, c.1579–80
Opaque colours and gold on prepared paper; page 34.0 x 20.2

Istanbul, Library of the Topkapı Sarayı Müzesi, H.1563 f. 61r°
Topkapı Palace collection

According to a *muhallefat* inscription dated 1034/1625?, the work belonged at one stage to the Ağa Darüssaade el hacc Mustafā.

The *Ḳiyāfetü'l-Insānīye fī şemā'ilü'l-'Osmānīye*, completed in 1579[1], was written by Seyyid Loḳmān ibn Husayn al-'Asurī el-Huseyni el'Urmani, palace historiographer, during the reigns of Selim II and Murad III. The calligrapher and the date of this copy are not specified. The work consists of 77 pages, each with 11 lines inscribed in *ta'līk*. The frontispiece is illuminated and the frames (*cedvil*) are gilded. The book includes 12 portraits of Ottoman rulers, from 'Osmān Gazi to Murad III.

The binding, with flap, of claret colour is decorated with oval medallions of the *ṣāz* style.

On page 1r°, the seal of Sultan Selim's Treasury, and on page 2r°, the seal of Sultan Aḥmed III's Treasury, dated 1115/1703, show that the work was kept in the Treasury for a long time.

In his foreword, Seyyid Loḳmān praises

Sultan Murad III, the Grand Vizier Sokollu Meḥmed Paşa and the historian Hoca Sadeddīn, then explains the conditions of the production of his book. He wanted the books that he was writing as historiographer of the Ottoman court to be illustrated with portraits of the sultans. However, there were no available examples. Seyyid Loḳmān recounts that, with the collaboration of the best painter of the palace, Master ʻOsmān, he went searching for portraits. As he wanted these to be realistic portraits, much research was necessary and it was realised that some portraits of the sultans might be found in the possession of foreigners.

Seyyid Loḳmān explains that he and Sokollu Meḥmed Paşa were able to obtain some of these paintings. This story is corroborated by various documents: in one of these, sent by the council of Venice to its agent in Istanbul (Balyo) on 16 January 1579, we read that "the portraits of the Sultan are ready as well as Sokollu's other requests . . ."[2]. On a letter sent on 20 September 1578 to the council of Venice by its Istanbul representative we can see that Sokollu, on the orders of Murad III, commissioned in Italy a series of portraits of Ottoman sultans[3].

The portraits mentioned in this document have not survived. We can consider as certain, however, the connection between these paintings and those mentioned by Seyyid Loḳmān. Furthermore, he writes that the portraits were compared with the illustrations which had been prepared for Murad III and that they commenced work on the illustrations for this book only after they had made sure that the portraits were realistic. Loḳmān also specified that for the costumes and the particularities of each sultan they obtained information from histories, particularly from that by Hoca Sadeddīn.

Seyyid Loḳmān ends his foreword, which makes up the first section of this book, with a discussion of physiognomy and its use in understanding individuals through their physical traits. In the second section of the book called *terhip* (gilding), we are told about the life of the sultans, the important events during their reign as well as the particularities of their appearance; there we find the 12 portraits of sultans painted by Nakkaş Osmān. In the chapter concerning Süleyman, Seyyid Loḳmān describes at length the character and innovations of this sultan, and sums up his physical traits as follows:

A beautiful round face, frowning brows, azure blue eyes, a ram's nose, an imposing and majestic build like a gracious lion, with a luxuriant beard, a long neck and a good height; a handsome man with a wide chest and flat shoulders, long fingers, strong feet and arms; a fearless, faultless and glorious ruler.

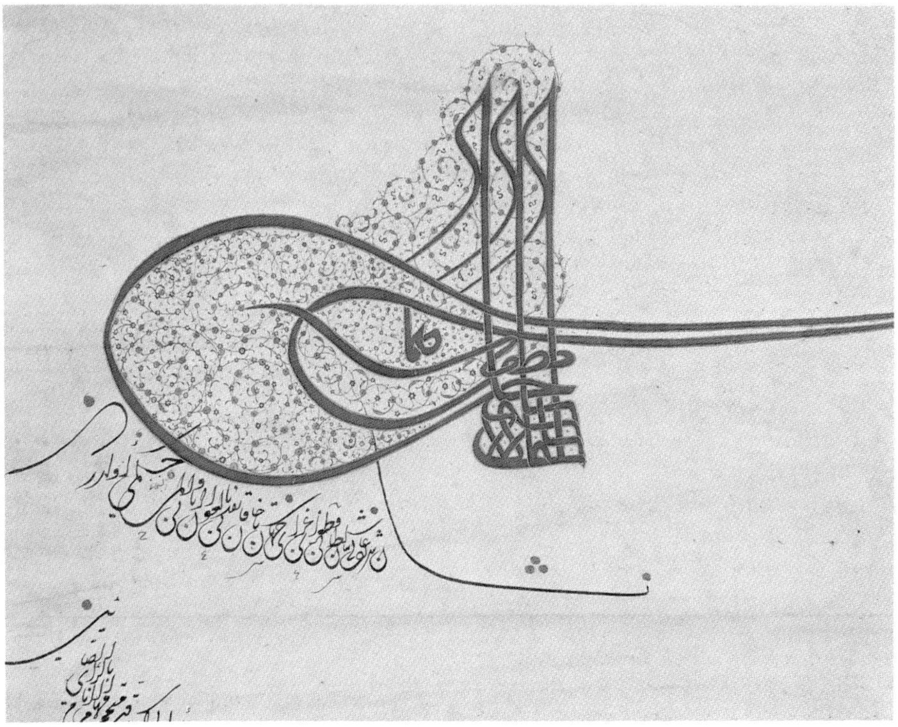

3 *detail*

As to his attire, it is said that Süleyman wore his turban on a *müceweze*, and a ceremonial kaftan, short and elegant, as was appropriate for rulers, and decorated with the rare materials and embroideries which, at the time, were widely used. In the portrait illustrating this description, the sultan is represented sitting down, as in the other sultans' portraits. His legs are folded with one knee raised. His dark-red *müceweze* and his white muslin turban are decorated with extremely fine embroideries. His dark-blue under-kaftan is embroidered with gold and his ceremonial kaftan is lined with white fur. The embroidery has *ḫaṭāyī* motifs, set out in medallions, a popular decoration of the time.

1 *In the copy kept at the National Library of the University of Istanbul (T6087), the date given is 987. This copy and the one kept in the Topkapı Palace's library were illustrated between 1579 and 1580 by Nakkaş Osmān*
2 *Reyhanli, 1983, pp. 59–60; 1987, p. 459*
3 *Reyhanli, 1987, pp. 458–60*

Bibl:. Karatay, no. 711; Stchoukine, I., 1966, p. 69; Atasoy, N., 1972; Atasoy, N., Çağman, F., 1974, pp. 38–39; Çağman, F., Tanindi, Z., 1979, no. 151; Çağman, F., 1980, p. 226; Çağman, F., Tanindi, Z., 1986, pl. 156; Renda, G., 1987, pl. 28; Reyhanli, 1987, pp. 456–60, fig. 12

Photograph Jacqueline Hyde F.Ç.

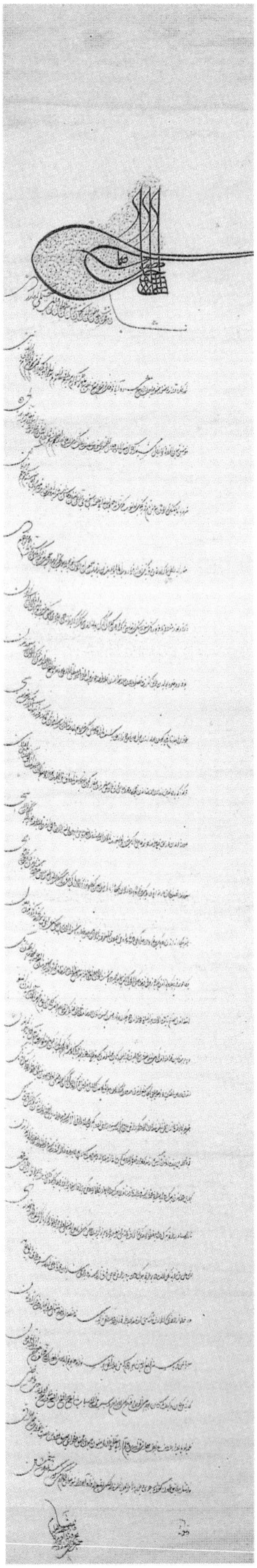

3 SINIRNĀME OF THE SULTAN SÜLEYMAN

Turkey, Edirne, Şevvāl 953/December 1546
Gold and cobalt blue on paper, black ink sprinkled with gold (rig); 27 lines of Turkish text in dīvānī; 245.0 x 41.0

Istanbul, Türk ve Islam Eserleri Müzesi, 2401
Transferred from the Ministry of Vakf

Among the most important documents in the fields of diplomacy, laws and economic history bequeathed by the Ottoman Empire are the imperial decrees known as *fermans*. The quality of their *dīvānī* script and the elegance of the superbly illuminated *tuğra* give these works great artistic value.

The term *ferman*, meaning an order or edict, is of Iranian origin and dated originally from the Il-Khānid period. In the Ottoman world a *ferman* in its strictest meaning is a decree on any topic, issued in the name of the sultan, from the deliberations of the *Dīvān-i Humāyūn* (state council). It carries the *tuğra* rather than the seal or the signature used on official documents from other chancelleries.

Fermans relate to civil and military administration, relations with foreign rulers, or address a particular person who is mentioned by name. They are distinct from the *berāt*, which announce the implementation of an imperial decision such as the appointment of a high official or the concession of a property.

The *berāt* takes a different name according to the terms of the decree. The document presented here is a *sinirnāme*, a decree defining the limits of previously granted ownership. The text specifies the borders of the village of Subasi in the district of Hayrabolu in eastern Thrace. This village had been granted to the Grand Vizier Rustem Paşa.

The *tuğra* of Sultan Süleyman is executed in cobalt blue outlined with gold. The outside *beyze* is decorated with fine blue stems embellished with tiny blue and golden flowers which twist in continuous spirals of varied dimensions. The upper section of the inside *beyze* is adorned with the same motifs on a smaller scale. In the lower section, the stems with elongated fine leaves form a scroll of overlapping circles.

On the *tuğ*, spiral motifs, differing slightly from those on the outside *beyze*, spread out to form a large triangle which encloses the spikes and spills over onto the right. These tangent spiral motifs which decorate many *tuğra* were adopted by Ottoman potters for the adornment of a very beautiful series of ceramics in the years 1530–40.

The *dīvānī* style, derived from the *ta'līk* style, is a supple and elegant calligraphy which characterises the *fermans*. Arranged in a slight diagonal, the letters draw from parallel lines at the beginning and then horizontal, at first curving upwards and gradually becoming larger. The dynamism of this composition is emphasised by the rhythmic character of the curving elongation of the letters, above and particularly below the line. The text is usually written in black ink, often powdered with *rig* gold (gold mixed with sand used to dry the ink) or adorned with minute particles of gold leaf, known as *zerefşan*. Gold ink is also used.

Photograph Jacqueline Hyde

T.B.

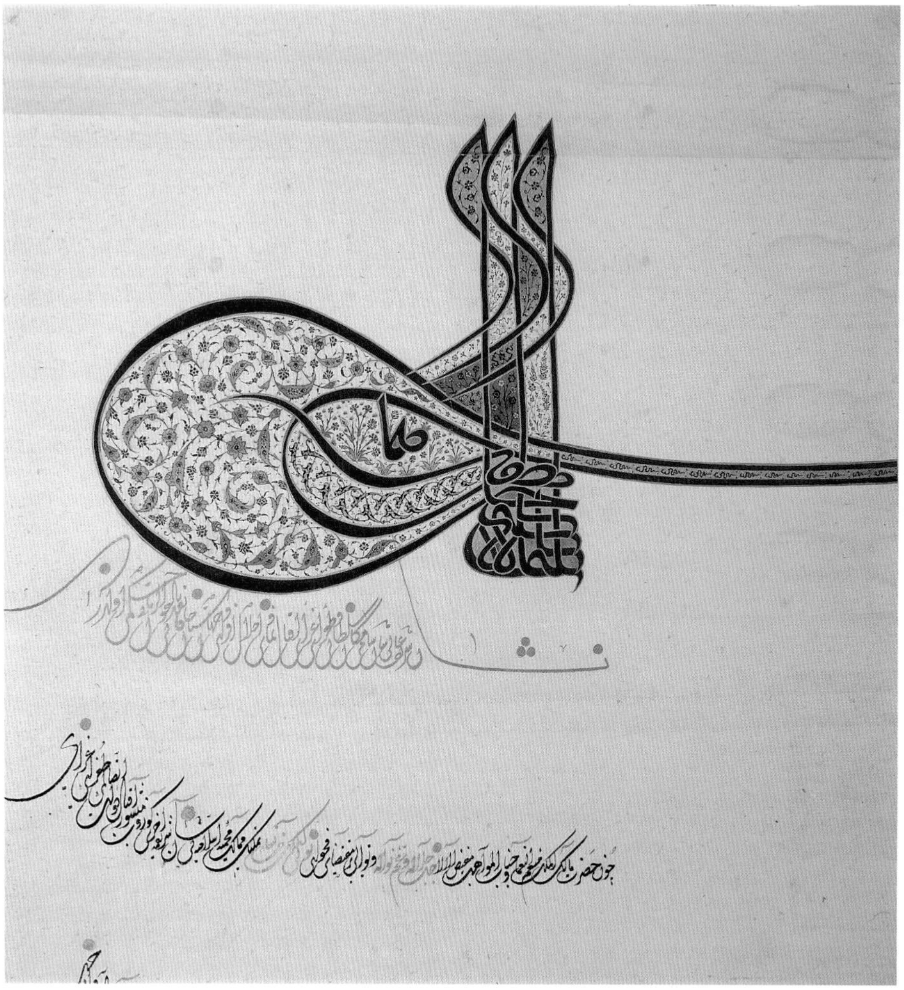

detail

4 MÜLKNĀME OF THE SULTAN SÜLEYMAN

Turkey, 21 Rebiülahir *959/16 April 1552*
Gold and colours on paper, black and gold ink; 13 lines of Turkish text in dīvānī*; 168.0 x 41.0*

Istanbul, Topkapı Sarayı Müzesi, E 7816/2
Palace archives collection

The most beautiful examples of Süleyman's *tuğra* decorate a group of 11 *mülknāme* which appeared between 1550 and 1555. These *mülknāme* (property deeds granting free ownership) related to the donations made by Süleyman to Hürrem Sultan in order to provide for the maintenance of his religious institutions. The text mentions the gifts of land and the revenues of villages located in the *sancak* of Trablus (Tripoli, Lebanon).

The *tuğra* is traced in cobalt blue outlined with gold, which is also applied to the background of the *sere*, on the triangular cut at the base of the *tuğ* and on the three semi-circular cuts which alternate between the vertical strokes.

Black and gold *rūmī* motifs stretch out on the lower section of the inside *beyze*, emphasising the line of the *kol* from which spring, in the top section, six small bunches of blue, red and yellow carnations, tulips and *ḫaṭāyī* flowers, proudly upright.

Elongated bunches, from which bloom foliated scrolls and a flower flanked by cloud banks, decorate the golden sections of the *tuğ*, while other sections are ornamented with blue flowers, red carnations and clouds.

The harmoniously placed decoration accentuates the dynamic lines of the *tuğra*, emphasising the verticality of the *tuğ* and the large circular movement of the *beyze*. Their internal elements — *rūmī* motifs, elongated and curved *sāz* leaves, and *ḫaṭāyī* flowers mixed with more naturalistic blooms — are characteristic of the style of this period.

Photograph Jacqueline Hyde

T.B.

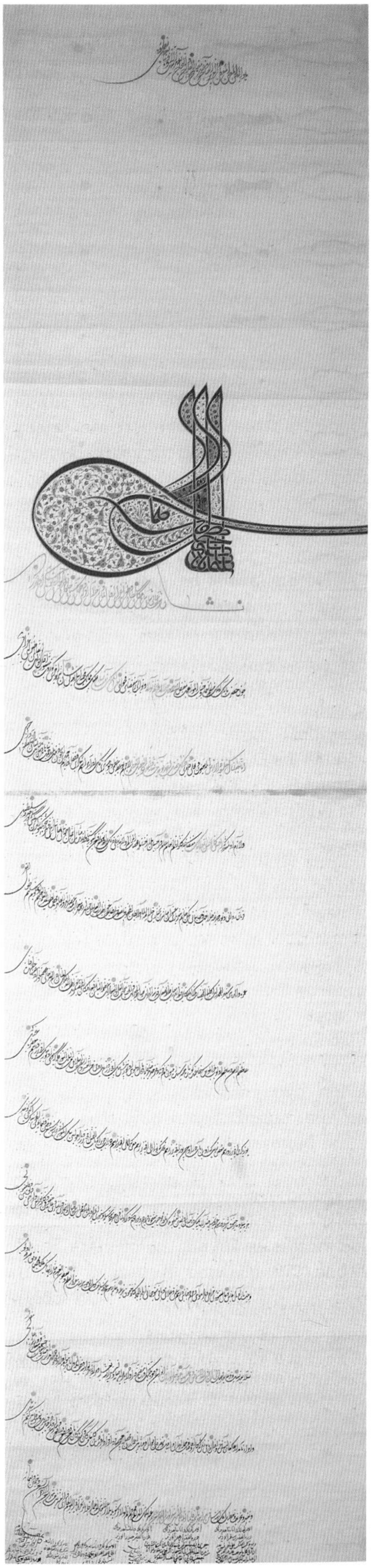

4

5 MÜLKNĀME OF THE SULTAN SÜLEYMAN

Turkey, Istanbul, first ten days of Ramaḍān *965/17–26 June 1558*
Gold and colours on paper
10 lines of Turkish text in dīvānī, gold and black inks sprinkled with gold; 172.0 x 47.0

Istanbul, Türk ve Islam Eserleri Müzesi, 2316
Transferred from the Ministry of Vakf in May 1915

By means of this *mülknāme*, Süleyman granted to his daughter, the Princess Mihrimah, the free ownership of three estates in the *sançak* of Koçaeli, another near Gebze called Tekfur Cayiri and two others in Uskudar. High-ranking dignitaries witnessed the document: Abūkebir 'Alī Paşa and Meḥmed Paşa, viziers; Hamid b Meḥmed and Meḥmed Abdūl vahhab *Kazasker*, from Rumelia and Anatolia; the *nişanci*, Meḥmed b Ramazan; and three members of the imperial Treasury, Meḥmed b Abdī, Ibrahim b Musa and Kasim.

The *tuğra* is traced in cobalt blue outlined with gold. The letters of the *sere* stand out on a pale pink background and, as on the *mülknāme* of 1552 (cf., no. 4), four sections of the *tuğ* are covered in gold.

On the outer *beyze* two scrolls, one gold, the other dark blue, spotted with red and adorned with leaves and flowers, intertwine their gradually enlarging spirals, beginning from the *sere* and covering the entire field. Small bunches of blue and red carnations with golden leaves are arranged in a frieze on the lower section of the inner *beyze*; the upper part the field covered with gold arabesques is scattered with blue clouds.

Some clouds, like red ribbons, flutter across the gold sections of the *tuğ*. The other sections are decorated by gold scrolls with blue flowers and clouds of the same colour.

Photograph Jacqueline Hyde

T.B.

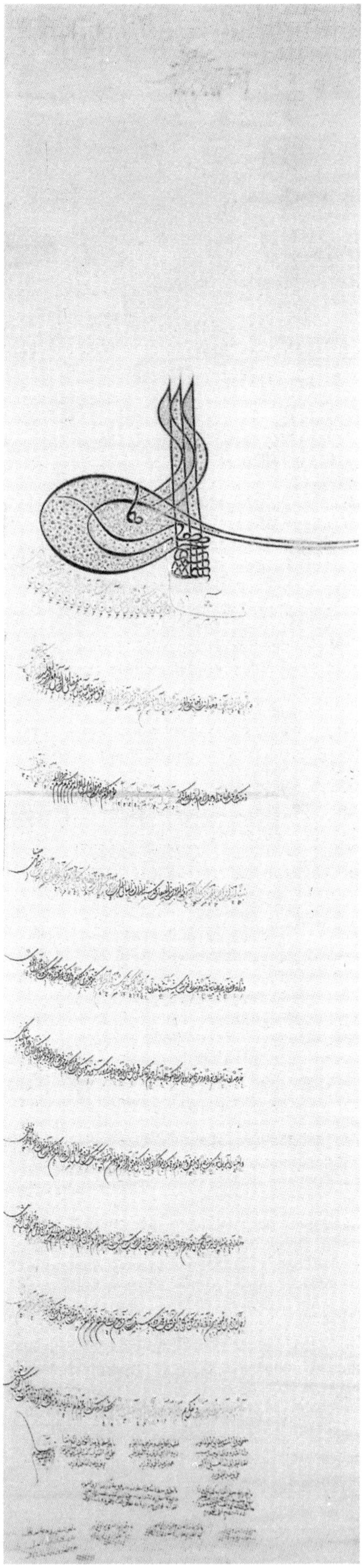

5

Süleyman, Shadow of God on Earth

In 1258, after the conquest of Baghdad by the Mongols, the successor of the last 'Abbāssid *caliph* fled to Mamluk Egypt and the centre of the caliphate was thereby transferred from Baghdad to Cairo. Al-Musṭansīr, the new *caliph*, and his successors no longer had any political power, but they retained their title "Guide of the Community", and Mamluk Sultans and Islamic sovereigns would come to them to confirm their investitures.

Selim I, having conquered Egypt in 1517, inherited from the Mamluks the succession of the 'Abbāssid *caliphs*. The Sherif of Mecca and the people of Jeddah swore allegiance to him. Süleyman, in turn, took Jerusalem, then Baghdad, then Karbela and Nejef. All the holy places of Islam were from then on under his effective authority and he ordered the Prophet's relics to be taken to Istanbul. He was the protector of the *Ḥajj*, the annual pilgrimage, and of the routes to Mecca and Medina; he had notably spread Islam's territory at the expense of the "infidels" and the wording of his title shows the extent of his religious power: "Shadow of God over the Lands . . . Sultan and Padiçah . . . of Holy Mecca and Revered Medina, of Jerusalem, of Jeddah . . . Lord, refuge of the Caliphate . . ." It is obvious that the Ottoman sultans should have pretended to the title of *caliph*.

Süleyman was a religious man. Although he liked to surround himself with luxury and splendour, to receive and give sumptuous presents, and he valued precious objects such as porcelain from China[1], he also had quite simple tastes as his kaftans show (compare nos 27 and 28). Towards the end of his life, he was even inclined towards asceticism: for instance, he only used clay dishes.[2]

He was conscious of the pivotal role vested in the sovereign in the religious field; he assumed this role, and European prints of the period show him making his way to the mosque for the congregational prayer.[3]

Süleyman particularly favoured religious architecture and the *Vakf*[4], such as in the *Vakfiye* of Hürrem Sultan (Roxelana) of 1557. On this he confirmed to the *ḥadith* (tradition of the Prophets): "The only thing that remains of man after his death is the good work he accomplished . . . giving a *Vakf* is a good work . . ."

He had some of the Holy sites in Jerusalem restored; the Dome of the Rock owes him its outer ceramic revetment where a tomato-red colour, then recently discovered by the Iznik ceramists, is associated with a deep blue. In Istanbul he completed a mosque started by his father, Selim I (1522), and with the help of his outstanding architect, Sinan, he had the Şehzade Mosque (1548) built for his son, Şehzade Mehmed, who had died prematurely in 1542. Then he built the grandiose complex of the Süleymaniye. His example was followed by his close relatives and those in his entourage, especially the women. Architectural patronage by women developed spectacularly in the sixteenth century and the constructions were not simple district mosques but far-reaching pious and charitable foundations.

They comprised a great variety of buildings, mosques, *medrese*, hospices, living quarters, soup kitchens, bakeries, caravanserai, and the beneficiaries were expected to pray for their benefactresses.

The first foundation of this kind was that of Hafsa Sultan (Süleyman's mother) in Istanbul. Hürrem Sultan had several built: one in Aksaray by Sinan in 1539, with a mosque, a hospital, a *medrese* where medicine was chiefly taught, and hospices, intended for the use of women of all faiths and all origins; in Jerusalem in the al-Sitt district (*Vakfiye* of 1557); a mosque in Ankara and an *imaret* (hospice) in Medina.

Mihrimah, Süleyman and Roxelana's daughter, had two great mosques coupled with *medrese* built in Usküdar (1548) and Istanbul (1550). In 1561 she also had a mosque erected, in the name of her husband, Rüstem Paşa, with walls covered in ceramic panels.

Architectural patronage by these women was encouraged by Süleyman's extreme generosity; he provided his close relatives with *mülknāme*, gifts of full ownership which provided the income necessary to underwrite the construction and the maintenance of these charitable foundations.

Selim II, in turn, had a mosque erected in Edirne in 1575, undoubtedly Sinan's masterpiece. The latter also built a little mosque, a model of that style, for Sokollu Mehmed Paşa, the grand vizier of that sovereign and an enormous mosque for Selim II's grand admiral, Piyale Paşa. The last examples of this great religious architectural tradition, which later disappeared, is Sultan Aḥmed's Blue Mosque, built by a disciple of Sinan at the beginning of the seventeenth century. Huge copper chandeliers arranged on either side of the *miḥrāb*, ceramic lamps (compare nos 18, 19 and 20), and prayer rugs with multiple niches (*saf*) decorated these mosques. From the numerous mausoleums, generally built within the precincts of mosques, come the very beautiful Koran stands and chests in various forms (compare no. 31). This woodwork, richly decorated with ivory, mother-of-pearl and tortoise-shell, had a religious function and was given special care, which explains why it is so well preserved.[5]

Other objects were also placed in the mausolea: turban ornaments, belts, embroidered handkerchiefs, (arranged on the cenotaphs, as can still be seen today) and, above all, Korans.(6)

Süleyman particularly encouraged the great sixteenth century calligraphers, the most famous of whom was Aḥmed al-Ḳaraḥiṣārī, who adopted and developed the style of Yāqūt al-Musta'ṣimī, a renowned thirteenth century calligrapher. He excelled in the six styles of writing and was a master of the *celi* (monumental script). He designed the inscriptions for the Süleymāniye mosque.

The magnificent illuminations of these Korans are witness to the timelessness of certain motifs used in Bayazid's time (1481–1512) and the appearance of new themes, influenced by Timurid and Safavid art and created by the imperial *nakkaşhane*. The illuminated pages of the Koran, where the calligraphy was provided by Aḥmed al-Ḳaraḥiṣārī by 1546–47 (compare no. 9) for Süleyman, are highly revealing about this.

T.B.

1 *He had Sinan build him a* çinahane *to shelter his porcelain collection. Pope, J. A., 1952, pp. 10–18*
2 *Clot, A., 1983, p. 103*
3 *British Museum, P&D 1866, 7–14, 55, ill. in London, 1985, p. 8*
4 *A licence of mortmain for religious and charitable institutions*
5 *Some of these pieces go slightly beyond the historic limits of this exhibition but were included because the earlier pieces were too fragile to be moved*
6 *One mausoleum may contain several cenotaphs*

6 KORAN

Istanbul, 905/1499
Opaque painting, ink and gold on sized paper; page 33.5 x 22.5; frame 21.7 x 13.3

Istanbul, Topkapı Sarayı Müzesi Library, EH 71, f. 2vr°
Topkapı Palace collection, library of the Hasoda

The binding with flap in brown leather is original, enhanced with an embossed ornamentation: *rūmī* motifs, a medallion with *ḫaṭāyī* motifs, large corner-pieces and borders. On the cover edge a verse from the Koran (LVI-77-80) is written in relief in a *sülüs* calligraphy. The inside covers are in olive green adorned with borders, quarter-medallions and medallions with *ḫaṭāyī* motifs.

The work contains 351 pages. It comprises the entire Koran (f. 2v°–343r°), as well as the prayers indicating the end (*hatīm*), and the *fa'l-i kuran* (f. 344v°–351r°). Apart from the *fa'l-i kuran* which is written in *ta'līk* calligraphy, the manuscript is written in vocalized *naskhī*, with 12 lines per page.

The punctuation rosettes and the *cedvel* are gilded. The pages at the start (f. 1v°–2r°) and at the end (f. 343v°–344r°) of the Koran are highly illuminated. The opening verses of all the *sūra* as well as the rosettes of the reading rules are also illuminated.

According to the colophon, the copyist is Hamdallāh, known as al-Şeyḫ, and the date is 14 *safar* 905 (f. 343r°).

This is, therefore, one of the Korans copied under the reign of Bayazid II by the most famous calligrapher of the time, Şeyḫ Hamdallah, who created a style of writing. The Korans written in his hand are some of the best examples of the art of the book during the Ottoman period, for their illuminations and binding as well as their calligraphy.

The pages exhibited give the text of the *Fātiḥa*, the first *sūra*, and the beginning of *al-Baqara*, the second *sūra*. On this frontispiece each page bears three lines of writing on a finely chequered gilded background enhanced with small blue flowers and leaves.

The illuminated panels of the frame reflect the classical Ottoman style which developed and flourished during this period: the spacious setting of the decorative elements, the stylisation of the *ḫaṭāyī* flowers, and the use of *rūmī* motifs and small flower-buds on fine entwined stems. The choice and distribution of colours also reflect the taste of the period; the various hues of gold and dark blue balance each other by defining certain areas of more intense colours.

Bibl.: Kataray, F. E., 1962–69, no. 799; Arseven, C., fig. 657

Photograph Jacqueline Hyde

F.Ç.

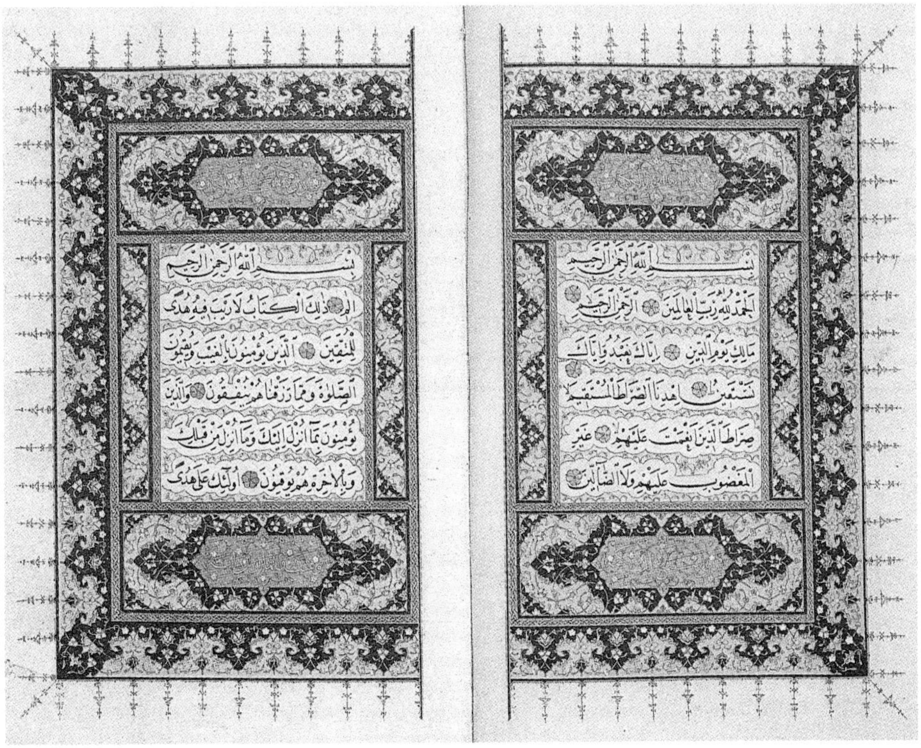

6

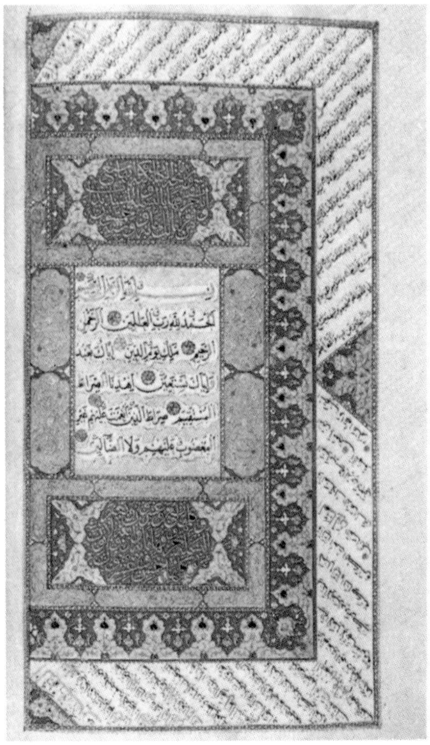

7 *right hand page*

7 KORAN

Turkey, c. 1530–40
Ink, gouache and gold on beige-coloured sized paper; page 30.8 x 14.2; text 18.5 x 9.9; frame 24.9 x 13.0

Istanbul Topkapı Sarayı Müzesi EH 60
Library of the Hasoda (private apartments)

This work, consisting of a complete Koran and an essay on the science of psalmodized reading of the Koran, *tecvid 'ilmi*, has been executed with great care. The binding with flap is original.

The boards bear an oval medallion with pendants and quarter medallions embossed in high relief, gilded and decorated with Chinese clouds and *ṣāz* style flowers and leaves. On the border the same motifs are used in a different pattern.

On the restored brown leather *sertab* (edge-cover) a verse from the Koran is inscribed in a small cartouche (Koran LVI 77). The back of the binding has also been restored. The inside covers in light brown leather are adorned with oval medallions with pendants decorated with *ḫaṭāyī* flowers and Chinese clouds embossed on a gold ground. The manuscript consists of 348 pages. Part of the text and the rosettes indicating the end of verses are gilded, as well as the beginning of each *sūra*, written in *sülüs*. Each page bears 15 lines of text in *naskhī*. Commentaries concerning the *sūra*, the verses and the way to read the Koran are written in black, blue, light green and dark red, diagonal in the margins.

On the first page (f. 12) on the gilded ground of a circular medallion, finely illuminated and divided into eight parts, verses from the Koran (LVI-77-80), reminders of the obligation to purify oneself before touching the Koran, are written in white *sülüs* script.

The frontispieces, containing the first *sūra* and the beginning of the second, are entirely illuminated. The spaces between lines are decorated in red ink and finely filigreed. This style is specific to the Ottoman Korans of the fifteenth century and comes from an ancient tradition of the Islamic world.

On every page, in illuminated rectangular cartouches on both sides of the text, multi-lobed medallions contain the name of each *sūra*, the place where they have been revealed, and the number of verses, words and letters, written in gilded *sülüs* on a night-blue ground.

The blue and the golds balance each other in the illuminations of these frontispieces. Other colours such as red, pink, white, turquoise green, yellow and black are used. The motifs used, *ḫaṭāyī* flowers and *rūmī* scrolls, as well as their placement, reflect classical Ottoman taste.

At the end of the Koran (f. 301V°) is found a long discourse (*risālī*) on the science of psalmody of the Koran and on the art of reading it, *Kirrat ve Tecvid* (f. 302r°-348v°).

The first page of the essay (f. 302r°) is illuminated and decorated with a round medallion containing a verse from the Koran (VI-115) in gilded letters on a dark blue ground. The text, written by a calligrapher of the Koran, contains 23 lines per page, in *naskhī*.

This scientific essay, which gives an explanation of the composition of the Koran, its writing and development, the characteristics of the letters, the explanation of difficult words and the way to read the explanations, is concluded with information on the writer and on the calligrapher (f. 348r°-v°): the principal author of this essay glories in the name Hayr ad-Dīn Abū 'l-Hayr Muḥammed b. al-Şayḫ al-Mukri al-Muhaddis Şams ad-Dīn abū 'Abd-Allāh Muḥammed b Mūsa Ibn Umran.

The calligrapher of the work, Muṣṭafā b 'Abd-Allāh, declared having copied this Koran and the essay at the time of Süleyman for Salman Ağa from the Old Palace.

This high-ranking official directed the construction of the *'imaret* (hospice) of Hürrem Sultan in Medina. Edicts concerning this undertaking are still kept.[1]

Salman Ağa died in 965/1557.[2] Although this copy is not dated, we can be sure that because of its binding and illumination it cannot be later than 1540.

1 *Altindag, 1985, nos 99–100*
2 *A document dated 965/1557 from the archives of the Topkapı Palace concerning the muhallefat of Salman Ağa (no. E2625)*

Bibl.: Karatay, 1962–65, no. 805

Photograph Jacqueline Hyde F.Ç.

8

8 KORAN

Turkey, 933/1526–27
Gold, opaque colours and black ink on prepared paper of light cream colour; page 26.8 x 17.0; frame 11.7 x 7.6

Istanbul, Türk ve Islam Eserleri Müzesi, no. 400, f. 1v°–2r°
Transferred from the mausoleums of the Süleymāniye in 1914

The black leather binding, with flap, is decorated with medallions and embossed corner-pieces in *ṣāz* style. The border repeats the same designs. On the edge-cover, Koran verses are in *sülüs* script in relief. The inside covers are claret-coloured and embossed with medallions and corner-pieces adorned with intertwined stems, flowers and Chinese clouds. The back of the binding has been restored.

The work consists of 445 pages of 11 lines each in vocalised *naskhī* script. Beyond the *cedvel*, the edges of the sheets are lined with thick paper in the *vassale* technique.

According to the gilded inscription (in *sülüs* script underlined in black) of the colophon (f. 444v°–445r°), the calligraphy of the work was done by Aḥmed al-Ḳaraḥiṣārī, *min talāmīdh* (student of) Sayyid Asadullāh al-Kirmānī in 933/1526–27. At the end of the manuscript (f. 455v°) an inscription notes that it had been offered by Sultan Selim to the Mausoleum of the Prince Meḥmed.

The frames and the rosettes are gilded. The small panel of the first page (1r°), the frontispiece and the beginning of the *sūra* as well as the *aser* and the *ḥizb* roses are illuminated. On the exhibited pages (1.v°–2r°) are the *sūra Fātiḥa* and the *al-Baqara*. These pages bear six lines of writing and the spaces between the lines, delineated in gold and ink, are painted in light pink and decorated with small leaves.

The illuminations which surround the text of the frontispiece, and the other illuminations in this work, have been done at a later date, probably in the time of Selim II (1566–74), when the manuscript was given to the Mausoleum of the Prince Meḥmed.

The partially degraded state of the illuminations, the quality of the gilding and of the navy-blue, red and blue tones on the small motifs, as well as the style of brush-work (far from perfect), all suggest the work of a painter who was imitating the illumination of the period of Süleyman. The composition of the illuminated border imitates the calligraphy of the frontispiece of the Koran of Ḳaramemī, which was produced in 953/1546–47 by Aḥmed al-Ḳaraḥiṣārī, the most famous Ottoman calligrapher of the Süleyman period.

Photograph Jacqueline Hyde F.Ç.

9 KORAN

Calligraphy by Aḥmed Ḳaraḥiṣārī

Turkey, 953/1546–47
Opaque pigments and gold on prepared paper; page 28.7 x 11.7; frame 16.0 x 95.0

Istanbul, Library of the Topkapı Sarayı Müzesi, YY 999, f. 1v°–2r°
From the Treasury of the Topkapı Palace; the colophon bears the seal of Sultan Aḥmed I, 1012/1603

This work comprises 239 pages of 15 lines, each written in vocalised *naskhī* in black ink. The frame and *durak* (points marking the end of each verse) are gilded. The *serlevha* and the beginnings of the *sūra* are illuminated, as are the rosettes in the margins. The titles are inscribed in white *sülüs* script. The seventeenth century binding preserved in the Palace Treasury[1] is set with gold and precious stones. The name of the calligrapher, Aḥmed Ḳaraḥiṣārī, *min talāmīdh* (the student of) Sayyid Asadallāh al-Kirmānī, and the date of the manuscript's completion (953/1546–47) are inscribed on the colophon (f 236v°). The *serlevha*, executed by the most famous calligrapher of Süleyman's time, is entirely illuminated. On the page containing the *Fātiḥa* and the beginning of the *Sūra al-Baqara*, the first and last lines are inscribed in *sülüs*; the five lines separating these are written in black ink in *naskhī* script. In the predominantly navy-blue and gold decoration of the frontispiece are various classic Ottoman illuminations: *rūmī* motifs, Chinese clouds and fine interlacing stems with small flowers.

In the panels framing the text are shrubs with branches scattered with pink and blue flowers standing out against a black background. This typically Ottoman design is characteristic of Ḳaramemī, a celebrated artist of Süleyman's time.

The outer border of the illumination is surrounded by a serrated edge recalling *ṣāz* leaves and is extended by a series of fine floral needle-shaped motifs in navy blue.

These flowered stems can be seen on the panels of other illuminated frontispieces: the *Süleymannāme*[2] of 'Ārifi dating from 1558; the copy of the *Dīvān-i Muḥibbī* dated 973/1566 comprising the poems of Süleyman. This work is now based in the Library of the University of Istanbul (T.5467)[3] and bears the signature of Ḳaramemī.

1 Istanbul, 1983, E 269; Washington, 1987, no. 9B
2 Atil, E., 1986, pp. 88–89; Demiriz, Y., 1980; Demiriz, Y., 1986, fig. 208; Washington, 1987, no. 26

Bibl.: Demiriz, Y., 1978, p. 53; Atil, E., 1980, ill. 91; Rome, 1980 (facsimile); Demiriz, Y., 1980. fig. 13; Demiriz, Y., 1986, fig. 126, p. 194; Atil, E., 1986, fig. 35

Photograph Jacqueline Hyde F.Ç.

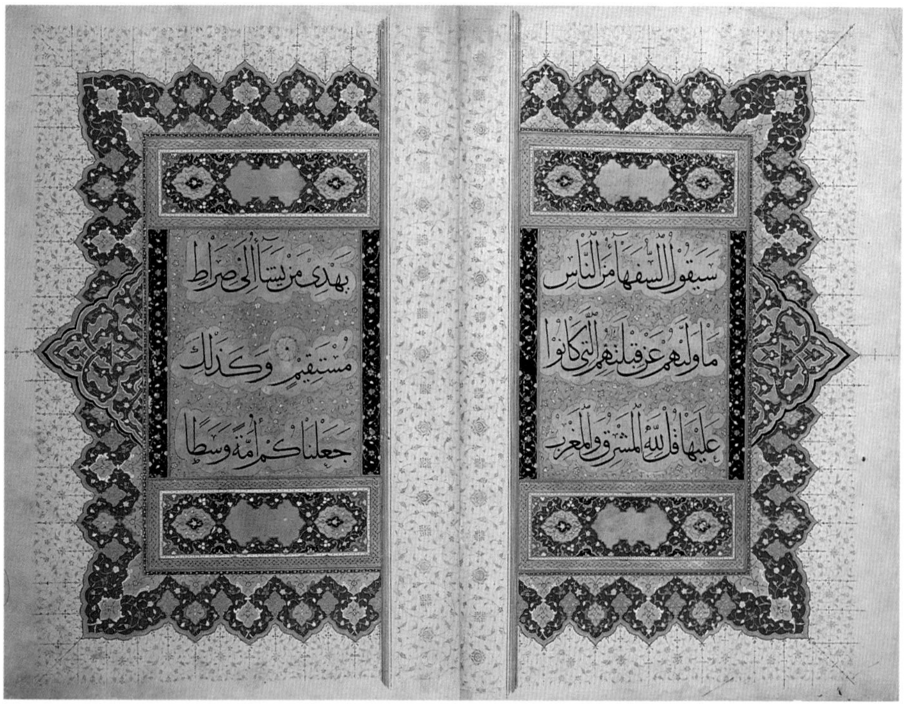

10

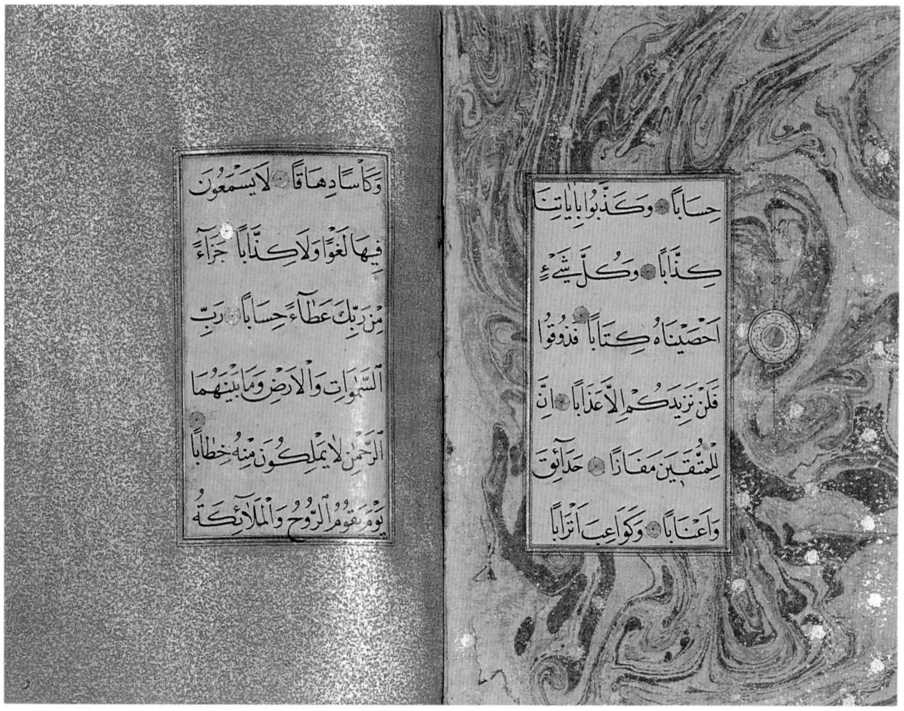

11

10 FASCICLE OF THE KORAN

681/1282–83 (calligraphy)
Turkey, Istanbul, middle of the sixteenth century (illumination and binding)
Ink, opaque colour and gold on sized paper; page 33.8 x 23.0; text 21.0 x 12.5

Istanbul, Topkapı Sarayı Müzesi, E.H. 227, f.1v°–2r°
Topkapı Palace collection, Library of the Hasoda

This manuscript, which is the second part of a Koran, includes the *sūra* al-Baqara (verses 142 to 252) and consists of 50 pages; on the colophon of the original the name of Yāqūt al-Mustaʿṣīmī as well as the date 681/1282–83 are written in *rik'a*. The calligraphy used in the text is a *muḥaqqaq*. The pages of the *serlevha* contain three lines, the others five.

The work, dating from the thirteenth century, was affected by humidity. It was restored, illuminated and bound in the workshop of the Palace in Istanbul towards the middle of the sixteenth century. The outside of the binding with flap is in brown leather. The medallion and the four corner-pieces of the boards are embossed, gilded and adorned with *ṣāz* style motifs. The inside covers bear a medallion and corner-pieces in the Safavid style (filigreed).

In order to hide the humidity stains on the pages, the spaces between the lines have been gilded and decorated with fine entwined stems bearing *ḫaṭāyī* flowers. Furthermore, all the pages have been lined using the *vassal* technique, with sheets of cream colour. All the spaces between the lines of the text have been decorated with gold and other colours and all the margins have been framed with fine gold floral designs. The exhibited pages are entirely illuminated. This type of illumination, where gold and dark blue are dominant, is related to contemporary Safavid illuminations.

Bibl.: Karatay, F. E., 1962–69, no. 99; Tanindi, Z., 1986, p. 149; Alpaslan, 1985, p. 38

Photograph Jacqueline Hyde F.Ç.

11 FASCICLE OF THE KORAN

Turkey, c.1540
Gouache and gold on sized and painted paper; page 21.2 x 14.3; text 11.0 x 6.0

Istanbul, Topkapı Sarayı Müzesi, EH 266, f. 4v°r°
Topkapı Palace collection, originating from the library of the Hasoda

This manuscript is the thirtieth part of a Koran called the *Amme* fascicle. It starts with the Fātiḥa (first *sūra* of the Koran) and also contains *sūra* LXXVIII and CXIV.

The leather binding and flap are original. The faces are in brown leather. The medallion with pendants, and the embossed and gilded quarter medallions, are decorated with Chinese clouds and entwined stems bearing small flowers. The inside covers are in dark red leather, adorned with medallions representing the same motifs on a gold ground.

The manuscript, which contains 50 pages of six lines each, is written in vocalized *naskhī*. The rosettes marking verse-stops are gilded. The beginning of each *sūra* is illuminated. The margins are decorated using the technique called *vassal* (the lining of paper with other sheets of different colours). In this case sheets of *ebrī* (marbled) paper with blue dominant, and other sheets in light brown, dark grey, turquoise, light pink, light cream, cinnamon and blue, have been used. Furthermore, they are delicately powdered with gold, *zerefşan*. The top part of the *serlevha*, the frontispiece of the work, (f. 1r°) is illuminated with leaves in *ṣāz* style, Chinese clouds and classical motifs, harmoniously treated in tones of blue and gold.

On the same page, the spaces between lines are very finely decorated with Chinese clouds and flowering stems, in black ink with two tones of gold. The chromatic range of the illumination at the beginning of the *sūra* of the page on show is very subtle. In the title cartouche, the medallion where the title of the *sūra* is usually written has been left empty. In the margins the roses of *ḥizb* and *ʿaşar* are illuminated. Other works executed under the reign of Süleyman around 1540 feature the same type of decorated margins.[1]

1 *For instance the Kirk Hadīth (40 traditions) copy with margins of the same size is decorated in the same way: that is, by use of the* vassal *technique on coloured and* ebrī *sheets. This copy is made on cut-out paper (Washington, 1987, no. 18a–b). The other work also produced on cut-out paper is the copy dated from 945/1539–40 of the work of ʿĀrifī, called Gūv-i Çavgān (cf., Çağman, F. and Tanindi, Z., 1986, no. 140; Washington, 1987, no. 30).*

Bibl.: Karatay, F. E., 1962–69, no. 939

Photograph Jacqueline Hyde F.Ç.

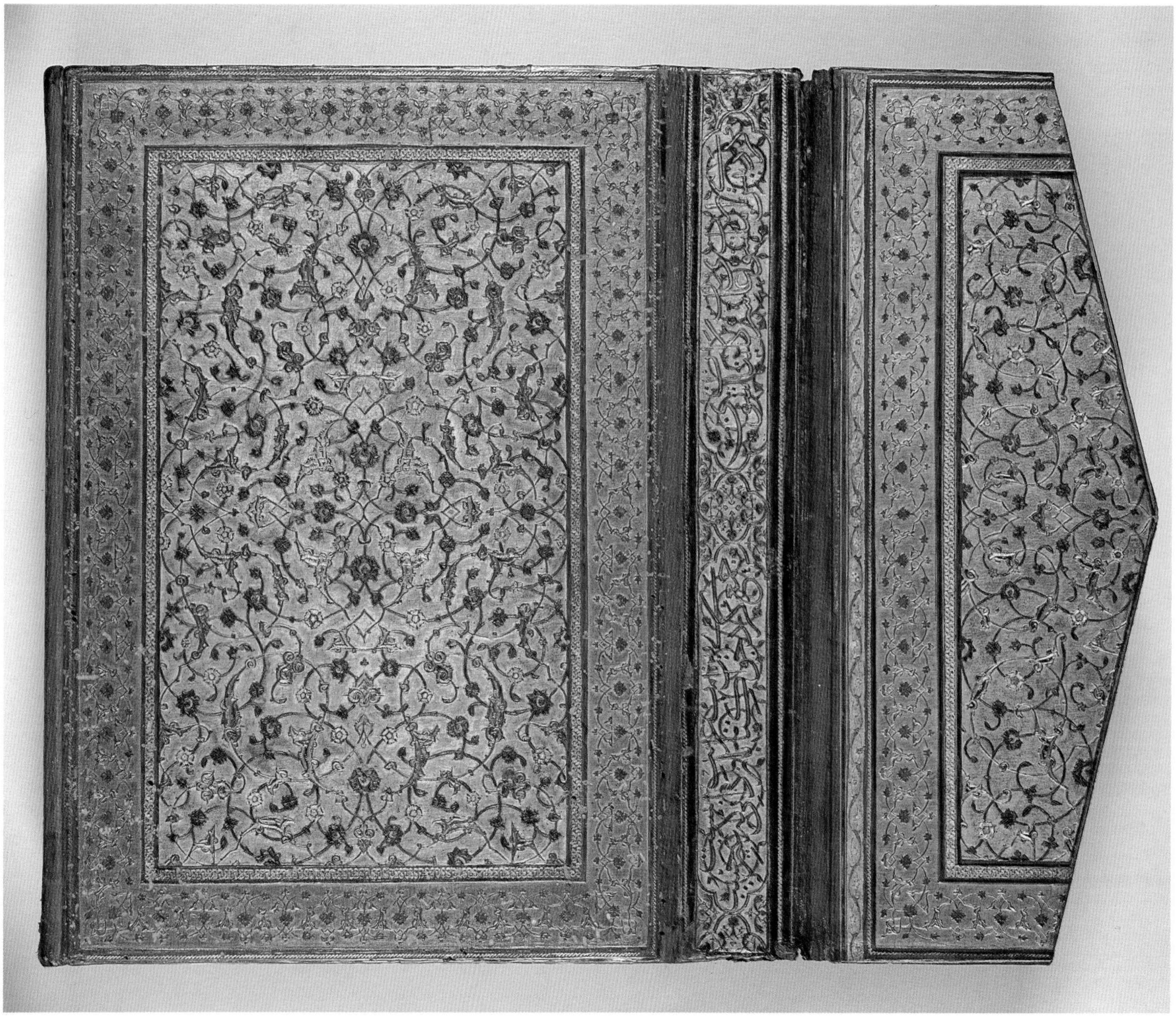

12 KORAN BINDING

Turkey, Istanbul, 921/1519
Morocco leather, gold and silver; 32.6 x 23.5

Istanbul, Library of the Topkapı Sarayı Müzesi, A21
Topkapı Palace collection; from the library of Enderūn, established by Aḥmed III

This book of Persian commentaries by Kemaleddīn Ḥusayn b 'Alī al-Kāshifī, written in 899/1493–94, is known as the *Muahīb-i'alīyā* or *Tafsīr-i Ḥusaynī*. This example, according to the *colophon* (f. 408r°), was copied in Ramaḍān 925 (15 September 1519) by 'Rafī 'al-Dīn FadlAllāh al-Tabrīzī in Kanstantiniye (Constantinople).

The work comprises 300 pages inscribed in *ta'līk*, with 28 lines per page. The *cedvel* and the beginnings of the *sūra* are illuminated. The *serlevha* is gilt in the classical Ottoman style (f. 1v°). The artistic interest of this binding lies in the leather cover's originality. The flap and the two boards are a hazelnut colour. The centres of the two panels are embossed in relief and covered in a network of fine stems decorated with *ḫaṭāyī* flowers. Superimposed over these is a layer of large *rūmī* motifs. In the centre of the panel symmetrically opposed *rūmī* motifs form a lozenge-shaped medallion.

The golden background of the panel is of the most exceptional workmanship. Some of the leaves of the *ḫaṭāyī* motifs and the interiors of the *rūmī* motifs are silver-plated; the flowers have yellow centres and white leaves. Remaining traces of colour indicate that red and blue were used to outline the *rūmī* motifs.

The panel is separated from the outer border by a lacework band. The border also bears a design of *ḫaṭāyī* flowers and *rūmī* motifs. As with the stems and the background, this border is gilded; the *ḫaṭāyī* flowers and their stems are in the natural colour of the leather.

In order to achieve a different shade of gold between these motifs, the background of the panels and the borders have been pricked with a needle identical to that used to give a varying lustre to jewellery. A religious text is written in Persian on the spine.

The inside covers are decorated with a filigree engraving, a technique frequently encountered in Turcoman and Timurid manuscripts of the fifteenth century. The panel of the inner cover, which is the same size as the panel on the outer cover, is engraved in claret-coloured leather. Fine interlacing stems, stylized flowers and *rūmī* motifs in the Timurid tradition make up a geometric network disposed across a gold, blue, aqua and light green background. The border, in dark blue on claret-coloured leather, is decorated with *ḫaṭāyī* flowers, stems, leaves and gilt Chinese clouds.

This binding is undoubtedly the work of

a court binder influenced by the art of Herat and by artists from Tabriz who came to Istanbul around 1514; it may be the work of Alaeddin, the chief binder of the period.

The remarkable technique used for the ornamentation of the entire surface of the outer boards of this binding is very similar to that on a *Manṭiq al-Ṭayr* of 'Attār dating from 921/1515. The decoration of this work demonstrates the influence of the Timurid artists of Istanbul Palace. However, the binding has lost a lot of its original character through successive attempts at restoration.

1 *Çağman, F., 1978, figs 18–19; Atil, E., pl. 17; Çağman, F., 1980., pl. 160; Istanbul, 1983, E55*

Bibl.: Karatay, F. E., no. 5

Photograph Jacqueline Hyde F.Ç.

13 SŪRA OF THE KORAN

Baghdad?, 706/1306–07 (calligraphy)
Istanbul, mid sixteenth century (illumination and binding)
Black ink, opaque colours and gold on prepared paper; 32.2 x 25.0

Istanbul, Topkapı Sarayı Müzesi, EH 222, f. v°–2r°
From the Library of the Hasoda

This collection contains five *sūra* in calligraphy by Arghūn al-Kāmilī (706/1306–07; I, VI, XVIII, XXXIV, XXXV). It was restored, illuminated and bound towards the middle of the sixteenth century in the imperial Palace workshops.

The black leather binding with flap is a remarkable example of the art of this period. At the centre and in the corners are an embossed medallion and spandrels which, as with the border, are gilded. The inside covers are in claret-coloured leather with a central medallion in filigree leather.

This work contains 102 dark-beige coloured pages, each bearing five lines in *sülüs* calligraphy. The illumination of the *serlevha*, the gilding of the frames and of the rosettes at the end of the verses were executed in the Palace workshops. At folio 102r°, the name Arghūn and the date are written in *rik'ā* style at the bottom of the page.

On the exhibited pages the *Basmala* and the first *sūra*, the *Fātiḥa*, are written in gold *muḥaqqaq* script which has also been used for the notes concerning the *sūra* (two lines at the top and bottom of the page). The background is a navy-blue colour adorned with a *rūmī* design.

The *Basmala* is framed by a navy-blue fillet decorated with intertwined gold leaves and stems scattered with numerous *ḫaṭāyī* flowers of various colours.

On the page of the *sūra*, the rosettes are in the shape of *ḫaṭāyī* flowers. Between the lines *ḫaṭāyī* flowers bloom on leafy stems

amid navy-blue clouds. The spaces between the flowers and the leaves are finely hatched in gold.

At the time of Süleyman the Magnificent great importance was attached to the works of the famous calligraphers of the past and many of them were restored and illuminated[1].

The illumination of these pages was probably done by the head of the *nakkaşhane*, Ḳaramemī, who was very famous at this time[2].

1 *Tanındı, Z., 1986, pp. 148–49. According to her, the binding should be attributed to Meḥmed Çelebi and the illumination to Ḳaramemī*

Bibl.: Karatay, F. E., 1962–69, no. 135; Tanındı, Z., 1986, figs 12–13

Photograph Jacqueline Hyde F.Ç.

14 BINDING OF KORAN

Turkey, c. 1530–40
Gold and opaque colours, lacquer varnish; 19.2 x 14.7

Istanbul Topkapı Sarayı Müzesi Library, EH 77
Topkapı Palace collection, library of the Hasoda

This Koran, written in the thirteenth century by the famous calligrapher, Yāqūt al-Musta'ṣīmī, was restored, illuminated and bound in the *nakkaşhane* of the imperial palace at the time of Sultan Süleyman the Magnificent.

The inside, outside and flap of the binding are adorned with a gold decoration on a lacquered background. The back and the edge-cover are in black leather. In the middle of each of the faces is displayed a large oval medallion, covered in fine interwoven stems and flowers mixed with *rūmī* ornamentation and Chinese clouds. Around the medallion, stems culminating in clusters of very small flowers unfurl in a symmetrical scheme surrounded by knotted cloud bands. A slightly smaller medallion adorns the centre of the inside cover; quarter medallions decorate the corners. The centres of these medallions are scattered with small *rūmī* motifs, swamped among bushy stems. They are surrounded by a large gold border filled with black Chinese clouds knotted in large loops. The treatment of the background around the medallion is different from that of the outside covers: narrow entwined stems and flowers form a fine network with Chinese clouds and *rūmī* motifs on stems describing large curves superimposed in a general geometrical pattern. The various types of *rūmī* motifs, the bunches of flowers, the various ways of treating the Chinese clouds and the decorative composition of this lacquered Koran binding accurately embody the style of the imperial workshops between 1515 and 1540.

The gold border which frames the inside and outside covers indicates an old restoration.

After 1515 and in particular during the first 20 years of the reign of Sultan Süleyman the Magnificent, the imperial workshops produced many bindings with motifs and decoration deriving from the style developed at Herat at the end of the fifteenth century.[1] They show the influence of the artists of the Herat workshop who were installed at Tabriz and brought to Istanbul by Selim I after his victory over the Safavid Shah in 1514.

1 Known in 1984

Bibl.: Karatay, F.E., 1962–69, no. 106

Photograph Jacqueline Hyde F.Ç.

15 KORAN BINDING

Turkey, 1570–71
Gold, jade set with gold, rubies and emeralds; leather; plaques diam. (max) 4.8; clasp 2.4 x 1.2

Istanbul Topkapı Sarayı Müzesi, 2/2896
Treasury of the Topkapı Palace

This binding seems to be the only such example which can be given a definite date; it protects a Koran (not included in the exhibition) copied in 1570–71 by the calligrapher Ibn Halūl Muḥammed Ẓāhir. It comprises two pale-green jade plaques inlaid with gold, joined by a gold hinge made of fine gold threads and beads, and a rectangular clasp fitted with a pin clasp, of which the corresponding half is missing.

The same decoration is used on both plaques: around a large central flower made of a table-cut emerald winds a network of stems delineated by a thin incised band, set in relief and bearing 16 flowers and small elongated leaves with their tips bent, arranged in two concentric circles. The 12 rubies and four emeralds are in gold-lobed mounts, finely engraved to resemble small leaves. Three flowers (a ruby between two emeralds) and four leaves ornament the clasp.

The two plaques and the hinge are lined with light chestnut-coloured leather (which has turned brown), decorated with an embossed gilt design of a central multi-lobed mandorla enclosing arabesques.

The clasp is lined in gold leaf with a different style of finely engraved floral design featuring a cypress framed by tulips.

Photograph Jacqueline Hyde M.B.T.

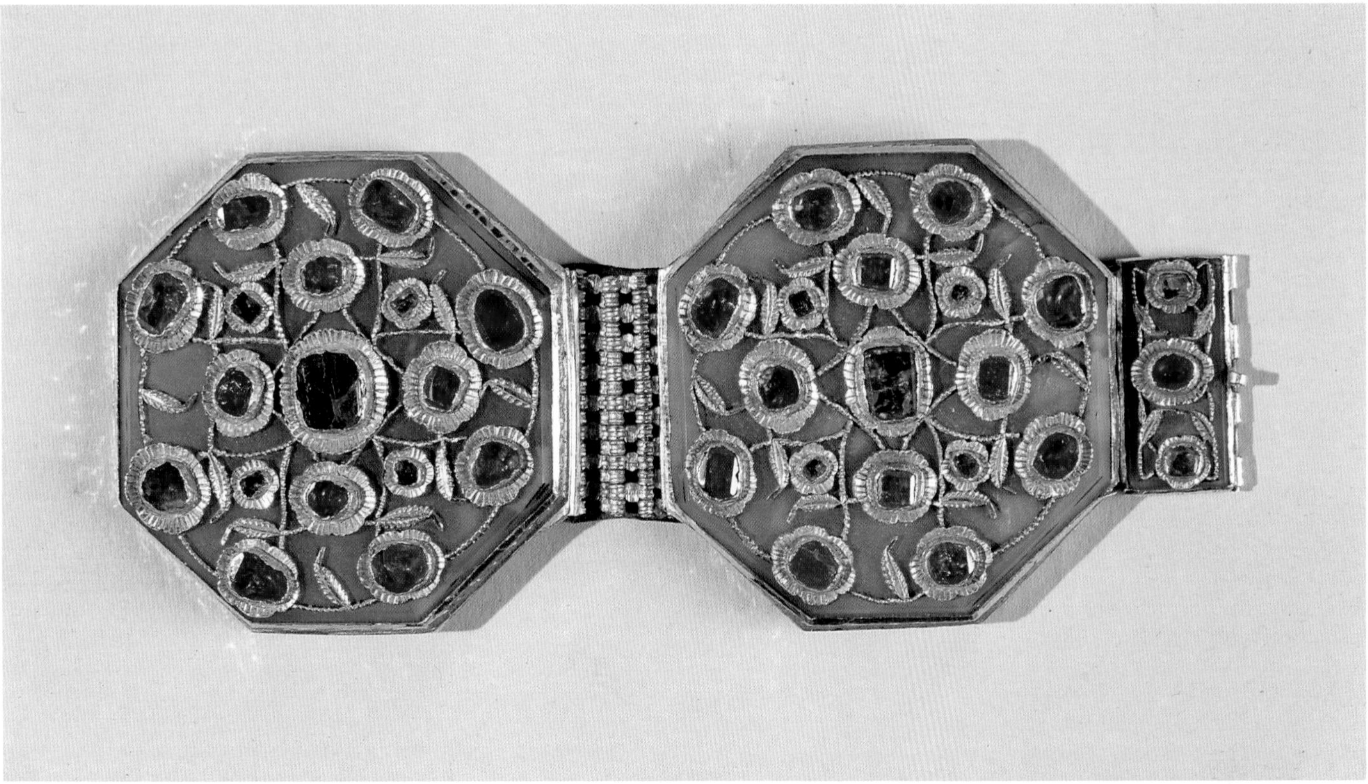

15

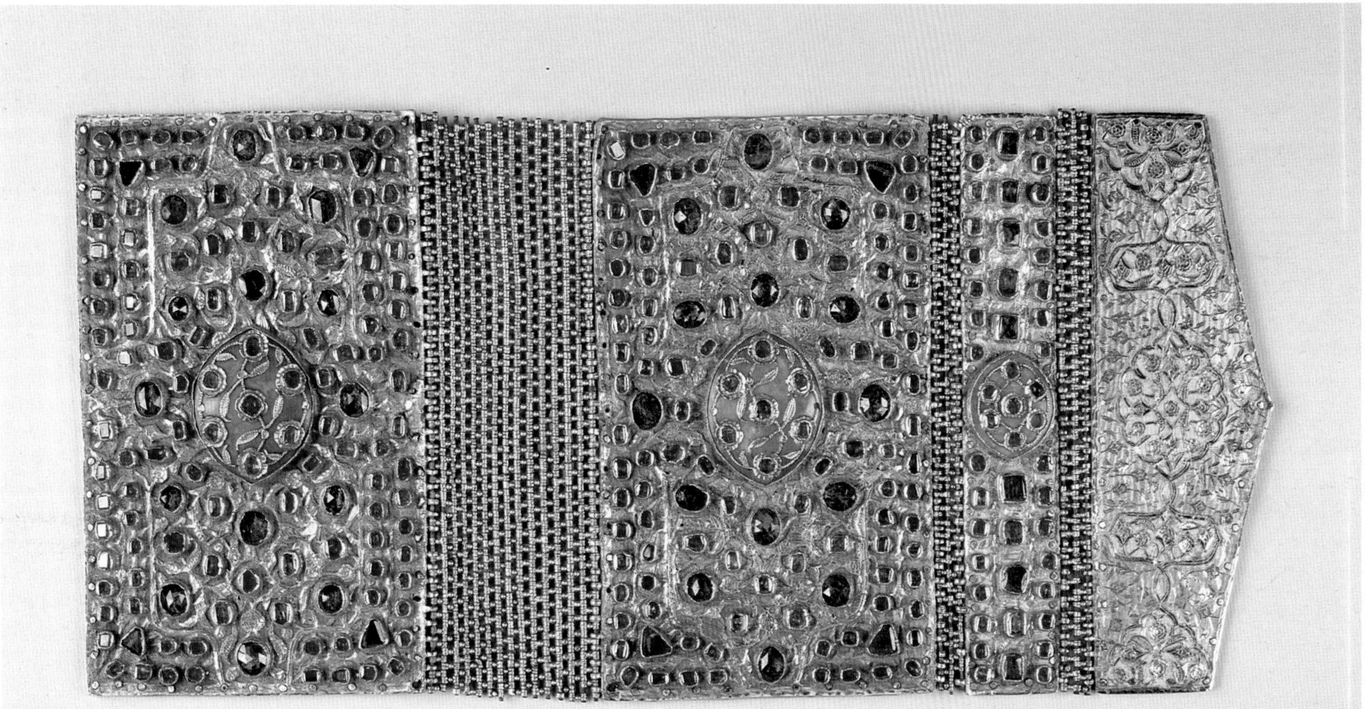

16

16 KORAN BINDING *ill. page 41*

Turkey, second half of the sixteenth century
Repoussé and chased gold, engraved jade (nephrite), inlaid with rubies and emeralds; 12.8 x 27.0

Istanbul, Library of the Topkapı Sarayı Müzesi, 2/2086
From the Treasury of the Topkapı Palace
The binding from an undated Koran, transcribed by the calligrapher Abdül-Raḥman

This binding consists of four gold plates attached by hinges of uneven width (the same type as those of no. 15). The two boards are worked on two levels with a large lobed rectangle applied in relief over most of the surface. Like the edge-cover, the boards are adorned with a chased decoration of leaves and flowers, as well as a grey jade oval medallion on which unfurl stems with thinly ribbed leaves and flowers composed of rubies set in bezels on finely striated gold collars. Rubies and emeralds (the larger ones faceted) set in bezels frame these jade plaques.

The flap displays fine arabesques alternatively linking lobed polygons and oblong medallions, inside which unfurl finely engraved and guilloche leaves and flowers.

A fine open-work gold sheet also adorned with medallions displaying finely engraved and serrated flower patterns covers the reverse side.

Photograph Jacqueline Hyde M.B.T.

17 BINDING

Turkey, sixteenth century
Jade inlaid with gold and ruby, cut and engraved gold; 11.5 x 7.5

Istanbul, Topkapı Sarayı Müzesi, 2/2095

This binding is made of pale-green jade. the two plaques are bound by a wide articulated gold chain composed of beads and threads twisted around perpendicular pins; a narrower chain, in the same style, binds the flap to the plaques below.

On each plaque the decoration is the same, evoking motifs found on leather bindings: a multi-lobed central medallion, enclosed by another with pendants, and corner-quadrants. A garland fills the space between the corner-quadrants and the medallion, echoing its shape.

All this decoration is defined by a finely grooved thin gold thread set in relief in the jade, and punctuated by small curling engraved leaves and flowers around rubies set in multi-lobed, gold-engraved collars. The flap is decorated with a gold arabesque of vines and supple, double-pointed florets, set flush in the jade in contrast to the treatment of the boards. The inside is entirely decorated in pierced gold leaf, forming a network of elongated, supple and engraved leaves.

Photograph Jacqueline Hyde M.B.T.

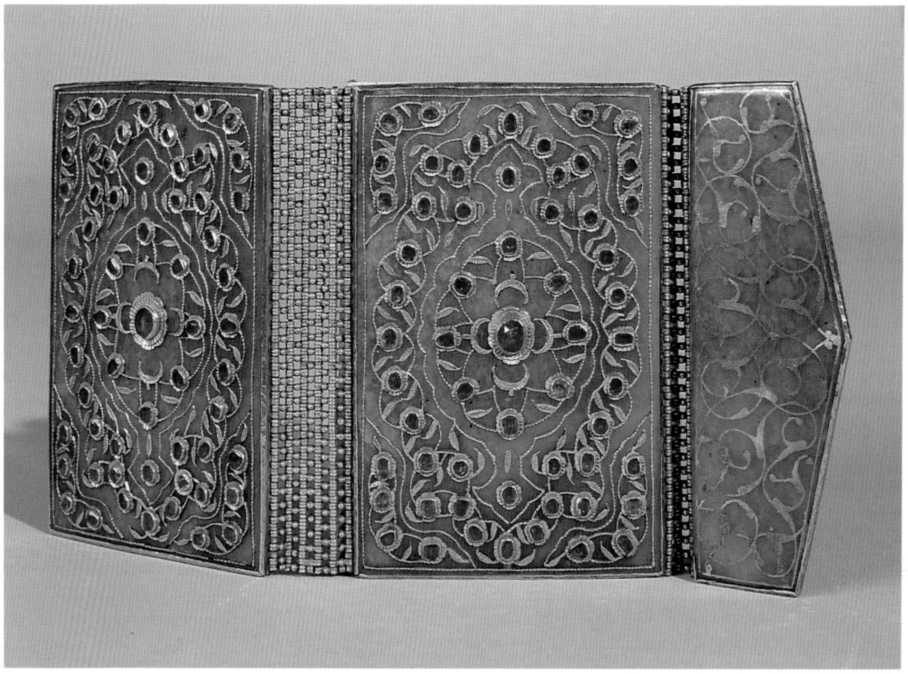

17

18 MOSQUE LAMP WITH ARABESQUE AND KNOT DESIGN *ill. page 17*

Turkey, Isnik, c.1512
Fritware with underglaze design on slip-painted ground; 27.6; l. base 10.6; diam. mouth 18.2

Istanbul, Arkeoloji Müzesi Çinili Köşk, 41/2
Transferred from the Sokollu Mehmed Paşa Mosque, 1885

This mosque lamp, with three small handles, slightly pear-shaped body on a low foot and a tall flaring neck, reproduces the classical form of the glass mosque lamps with enamelled and gilded design, produced in Egypt and Syria at the beginning of the fourteenth century. It is part of a group of 10 pieces of similar size, shape and design, painted in two hues of cobalt blue on a brilliant white background and probably contemporaneous. Some come from the mausoleum of Bayazid II, who died in 1512; this lamp was found in the mosque of Vizier Sokollu Mehmed Paşa.

The design comprises, on the body, three horizontal rectangular cartouches with the ends scalloped into concave festoons, and on the neck, three multi-lobed circular cartouches extended vertically by ribbons adorned with knots. All bear an inscription reserved on a blue background, finely speckled with a darker shade of blue. The inscriptions on the body all repeat the names "Allāh, Muḥammed, 'Alī"; those of the neck repeat pious invocations to 'Alī in *kufic* letters. The motifs of the design which surround them are typical of the repertory of the early sixteenth century: on the neck, three large knotted cloud scrolls and three other clouds arranged like lappets around the rim; on the body, an arabesque of stems with single or bifurcated leaves with incurved tips, small cruciate flowers, star-shaped medallions and cloud motifs crowning the top of the handles. Tiny dots cover the white background. A double line separates the upper part of the body from the lower zone which is decorated with a scroll of flowers and palmettes, and, as is usual in defining the separate sections, twisted bands encircle the base of the neck and foot; a patterned band decorates the handles. Traces of gold can be seen on the band circling the neck and around the handles.

There is a design on the base of this lamp: the entwined petals of a rose form a star radiating towards the foot ring. A design on the base is found on other lamps[1]. This particular feature may be explained by the fact that the bottom of these ceramic lamps was visible as they were hung in the mosques; they seem to have had only a decorative purpose as their lighting capacity is doubtful. However, the shape of glass lamps adapted for ceramics by the potters of Isnik remained in favour during most of the sixteenth century. Important variations in size can be noted (from 22 to 49 centimetres in height) but the variations in shape were limited to subtle differences in the width of the neck or body or in the height of the pedestal foot. Later examples of Ottoman lamps in metal[1] are also known.

1 cf. Raby, J., Allan, J., 1982, pl. 29

Bibl.: Ettinghausen, R., 1966, p. 190; Tuncay, H., 1978, fig. 21; Soustiel, J., 1985, fig. 349; Atasoy, N. and Raby, J., 1989, fig. 91

Photograph Jacqueline Hyde G.J.

19 MOSQUE LAMP WITH ARABESQUE DECORATION

Turkey, Iznik, c.1515
Fritware with painted decoration over slip under a lead glaze; 33.2 x 25.0

Paris, Musée du Louvre, Islamic section, 5547
Acquired 1902

Most of the decoration on this classical mosque lamp is treated in reserve in a style similar to that found on the first pieces in the *rūmī-ḫaṭāyī* style. We can, however, see the stylistic evolution of early sixteenth century blue and white Iznik ceramics: the cobalt blue of the ground is less intense, the scrolling network of half-palmettes and flowers is less dense and large areas of white appear. Here, the white areas take the shape of rectangular cartouches with arched ends placed on the body and around the rim. Those on the body enclose a panel of writing in reserve. Decorating the middle of each side of the cartouche is a knot, a motif of ancient origin in Eastern Islamic art but which was used on Iznik ceramics at this time. One of the cartouches gives the names of Muḥammad, 'Alī and the first two *caliphs*; the other two contain prayers.

The three curved handles, adorned with strips of scales, are reminiscent of the dragon-shaped handles on the metal and hard-stone pitchers of the Timurid era.

Under the base, a network of star-shaped polygons forms a circle around a central orifice.

Bibl.: Migeon, G., 1922, no. 207, pl. 39; Kuhnel, E., 1925, dif. 88; Atasoy, N. and Raby, J., 1989, no. 80

Photograph Jacqueline Hyde M.C.

20 MOSQUE LAMP WITH FLORAL DESIGN

Turkey, Isnik, c. 1572
Fritware with painted design over slip under a lead glaze; 47.0; l. base 17.0; diam. mouth 29.0

Istanbul, Arkeolojī Müzesi Çinili Kösk, 41/16
Transferred from the Sokollu Mehmed Paşa Mosque, 1885

This tall, imposing lamp was made in two parts with a ridge marking the junction of the neck and the body.

Geometrical and floral bands structure the design which is painted in red, white, turquoise and black on a brushed cobalt blue ground. The declaration of the Faith is displayed in large white cursive letters on the neck: "There is no god but God and Muḥammad is the Prophet of God". An error in calculating the spacing of the words resulted in one of the words being written above the others. A few white roses with green centres and jagged leaves are interspersed among the strokes of the letters.

The body bears large floral motifs and three hemispherical bosses between the handles. These bosses, decorated with a fine greenish black scroll around a small central rose of red-and-white trimmed blue petals, on a turquoise ground and with traces of gilding, are framed with a band (made of a series of white trefoils with red centres) identical to the one around the neck. Large composite flowers, borne by thin stems which terminate in long white sprays with small red flowers, are placed under the handles and the bosses. The base of this piece is pierced and decorated with a floral motif.

This lamp and another very similar one[1] come from the mosque of Vizier Sokollu Mehmed Paşa, built in 1571–72. Some details of its design, such as the band of trefoils, are typical of production during the years 1570–80.

1 *Atasoy, N. and Raby, J., 1989, fig. 713*

Bibl.: Arseven, C. E., 1952, fig. 442; Ettinghausen, R., 1966, p. 193; Tuncay, H., 1978, fig. 8; Tuncay, H., 1980, fig. 11

Photograph Jacqueline Hyde G.J.

21 TYMPANUM

Turkey, Iznik, 1573
Fritware with painted decoration on slip under a lead glaze; 70.0 x 136.0

Paris, Musée du Louvre, Islamic section; 7509
From the Mosque of Piÿale Paşa in Istanbul
Gift of G. Bapst, 1889

Of the 16 tiles which make up this tympanum, eight have an irregular shape in order to fit the arch of the lunette. On the wide cobalt-blue border, two long serrated *ṣāz* leaves on each side of a blooming rose form an "S" motif which, when repeated, develops into a foliated scroll highlighted with red. The central composition, on a white background, is divided by stylized knotted cloud bands which form a long serpentine red ribbon looping around a blooming lotus. Thin stems, bearing leaves, buds and *ḫaṭāyī* flowers, emerge from the central motif to form spiral scrolls intertwining dynamically. The technical quality and the treatment of the different elements, especially the clouds, are reminiscent of the panels on the mausoleum of Selim II.

The decoration of these panels must have been done from a stencil because there are about a dozen identical tympana, preserved in different museums[1], all almost the same size. It is thought that they come from a building erected by Piÿale Paşa, but doubt remains as to whether this was a palace or a mosque. Piÿale Paşa, grand-admiral and favourite of Selim II, married his daughter, Hace Geuheri Mülük Sultan. In 1573, he had a large mosque built by Sinan (or by another architect: expert opinions differ on this point) near the quarter of Mershane which included the sailors' barracks and the grand-admiral's pavilion. The beautiful *mihrab* retains almost all its ceramic tiles but the tympana of the 16 windows have disappeared, replaced by painted decorations. Following an earthquake in 1890[2] the mosque was roughly restored. Some of the tympana may have then been dismantled because the first examples appeared on the art market at this time[3]. Furthermore, in 1909, a letter from the Ministry of Vakf addressed to the Ministry of Public Instruction mentions ceramic tiles stolen from the mosque of Piÿale Paşa. In a file then established, the missing pieces were valued at 500 *kurus*. It seems, therefore, that these different tympana come from the mosque.

1 *Paris, Musée du Louvre, inv. 7508 and 7509; Musée des Arts Décoratifs inv. 5991; Boston, Museum of Fine Arts, inv. 06.2437; London, Victoria and Albert Museum; Cologne, Kunstgewerbemuseum, inv. NE 810; Berlin-Bergamon, Islamisches Museum; Lisbon, Fundaçào Calouste Gulbenkian, inv. 1798 A and B; Hamburg, Hamburgisches Museum für Völkerkunde, inv. 1901; Vienna and Kuwait*
2 *Goodwin, G., 1971, p. 279*
3 *Tympana of the Musée du Louvre acquired in 1889 and those of the Musée des Arts Décoratifs acquired in 1890*

Bibl.: Migeon, G., 1922, no. 237, pl. 42; Öz, T., 1957, p. 31; cf. Düsseldorf, 1973, p. 234; London, 1976, p. 270; Frankfurt-on-Main, 1985, vol. II, no. 270

Photograph Jacqueline Hyde T.B.

22 LEDGER OF THE BUILDING SITE OF THE SÜLEYMANIYE MOSQUE NO. 21

not illustrated

Week of 9–16 June 1554
34.5 x 12.0

Istanbul, Archives of the Topkapı Sarayı Müzesi
D. 43/21, f. 1v°-2r° in index

The first stone of Sultan Süleyman the Magnificent's mosque was laid on 13 June 1550 and the building was inaugurated on 15 October 1557. The excavation work started at least one year earlier and the whole of the complex, including the colleges, hospice, hospital, baths and shops, was not completed until the beginning of spring 1559.

For the period from 9 November 1553 to 22 April 1559 we have a detailed ledger of the building site in the form of 165 copy-books[1]. Whereas the second date is probably that of the end of the construction, the first date is that of the departure of the first superintendent, Hüsayn Çelebi. The period between 9 November and 8 December 1553, which is that of the interim superintendent, the accountant of Anatolia Muṣṭafā, is dealt with in a separate copy-book, kept in the Topkapi archives (ref. nb D. 44). A series of 164 copy-books follows concerning the role of Sinan Beğ (not to be confused with Sinan, the architect of the mosque).

The ledger shown here is the twenty-first of the series and concerns the week 9–16 June 1554. One can read in the f. 1r°: *Detailed accounts of expenses for the construction of the noble mosque of his Excellency the Sovereign guardian of this world . . . under the care of the first of the illustrious, intendant Sinan Beğ and under the pen of the unworthy Ḳalif the secretary dated the 8th* Receb *the fortunate 961.*

The following page bears at the top: "Saturday the 8th of the month of *Receb* the fortunate. Expenses. Wages of the carpenters." The list of the names of the workers follows with the details concerning each of them set out in five lines.

The remainer of the text details work, wages and the social and religious composition of the workforce.

The wealth of documentation contained in the 27 folios of this small copy-book, multiplied by the 164 copy-books kept, indicates the importance of these ledgers not only for the history of architecture, but also for the social history of the Ottoman empire.

1 Except for no. 72 which is lost

Bibl.: Barkan, Ö. L., 1979; Yerasimos, S., 1988, pp. 46–49

S.Y.

23 SILHOUETTE OF THE SÜLEYMANIYE

Al-Kāfiya (Book of Arabic grammar)

not illustrated

Turkey, Şevvāl *980/February 1573*

Black ink and gold on prepared paper; page 18.5 x 11.2; framed text 12.7 x 4.0

Istanbul Topkapi Sarayi Müzesi, YY159 f. 6v°-7r°

Acquired in 1943

This work is by Ibn Hājib (died 1249) with a commentary (the al-Fawā'id al-Dīyā'īya) by Maulānā Jāmī (died 1492). The manuscript contains 49 pages of 15 lines each, in *ta'līk* calligraphy.

The commentaries of Maulānā Jamī are inscribed in a very small script called *ğubarī,* in the margins within various motifs.

The binding in dark brown, without flap, is decorated with a medallion, four corner-pieces and a gold border. The gilding has been restored.

According to the colophon of the work, the calligrapher named 'Alī b Sinan 'Abdūl 'Azīz started this copy at the beginning of *Muḥarram* 977 (June 1569) and finished it in *Şevvāl* 980 (February 1573).

The interest of the work resides principally in the commentaries of Maulānā Jamī, written in *ğubarī* and in the various gold-outlined designs which contain them. For example, we find the Ḥaram-i Sharīf of Mecca, the Ḥaram-i Nabī of Medina, the Aqṣā Mosque of Jerusalem, some mosques of Istanbul, as well as some more traditional ornaments of the time: flowers, *ḫatāyī* and *rūmī* motifs, horses, birds, dragons, clouds, geometrical figures, boats, fortresses and the obelisks of the hippodrome. Some of the motifs are highlighted in red, blue or orange.

This work constitutes a catalogue of the decorative repertoire of the years 1550–75.

On the exhibited pages, the commentaries are framed in representations of the Süleymaniye mosque, cypresses and flowers. Tulips, rose buds, bushes and cypresses are placed in rows along the margins.

The calligraphy of the *ğubarī* type practised by the Ottoman calligraphers from the beginning of the sixteenth century is mainly used for small Korans rolled in parchment.

Bibl.: Karatay, F. E., 1969, no. 9032

F.Ç.

24 FUTŪḤ-AL-ḤARAMAYN

Turkey c.1545

Opaque paints, ink and gold on prepared paper; page 14.0 x 87.0; miniature 18.0 x 12.0

Istanbul, Topkapi Sarayi Müzesi, R 917 f° 14.r°

Palace of Topkapi collection, Library of the Pious Foundation of the Revan pavilion

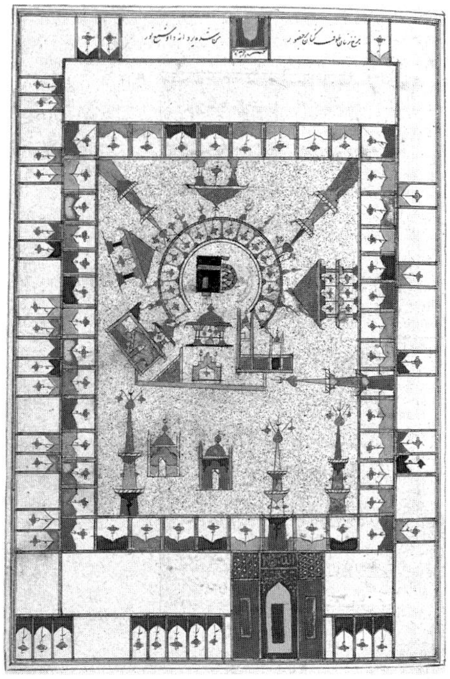

24

This work, which deals with the practices to observe during the pilgrimage and contains descriptions and explanations concerning Mecca and Medina, was written in 1506 by Muḥyī Lārī (died 1526–27) in the Persian language in the form of a *mesnevi.* It is dedicated to the Sultan of Gujārāt Muẓaffar b Maḥmūd Shafi (1511–26)[1].

At the time of Sultan Süleyman, the sacred places of Islam attracted a lot of interest at the Ottoman court, resulting in the production of manuscripts[2], similar to this one by Muḥyī Lārī, which served as guides for the pilgrimage.

This work consists of 58 pages each with 12 lines of calligraphy written in *nasta'lik* in two narrow columns. It is not dated.

The double frontispiece is illuminated with fillets of gold, black and ultramarine which enhance the *cedvel.* The binding with flap, in leather, is original. The front and back covers in light cherry colour, enhanced with gold, are adorned with embossed motifs in the *ṣāz* style. Inside the manuscript, the illustrations of the places to visit during the pilgrimage, executed with great care, are displayed and accompanied by a commentary. There are 15 illustrations which represent, in the following order: the Holy Mosque of Mecca, Mount Arafat, the pilgrimage sites around Mecca, the mosque of the Prophet in Medina (where Muḥammad is buried) and the sacred sites around this city.

The page shown (f. 14r°), the first illustration of the manuscript, displays the Holy Mosque of Mecca. The interior porticoes and the six minarets are oriented towards the centre; the exterior porticoes are turned in the opposite direction. All the elements of the courtyard of the sanctuary are represented: the Ka'ba, the Ibrāhīm makkam, the Zamzam well and the wall of Ḥatim in the shape of a moon crescent; the mausoleum reserved for the Imams of the four-rites are also shown. Lamps are suspended throughout. The buildings and the arcades are coloured yellow, light green, red and ultramarine with frequent gold highlights. The Ka'ba is shown covered with the black *kiswa.* The courtyard is lightly powdered with blue.

The design and the colours of this page resemble that of the pilgrimage certificate executed for Şehzade Mehmed.

1 The Safavid Shah Ismā'īl entrusted this work to a delegation of ambassadors sent to the sultan of Gujārāt. cf., Tanindi, Z., 1984, p. 408

2 Tanindi Z., 1984

Bibl.: Karatay, in Persian, 1961, no. 772; Tanindi, 1984

Photograph Jacqueline Hyde

F.Ç.

25 LOCK OF THE KA'BA

Turkey(?), 973/1565-66.
Silver gilt, moulded with hammered and chased decoration; 10.5 x 75.0; l. of barrel 26.5

Istanbul, Topkapı Sarayı Müzesi, 2/2274
Treasury of the Topkapı Palace

A large number of keys, locks and padlocks which were offered to the sanctuary of the Ka'ba in Mecca are kept in the Topkapi Palace. Several of these pieces were part of the treasury of the mamluk sultans which was taken as booty by Selim I during the conquest of Egypt in 1517. Most of them were presented to the sanctuary when a new sovereign ascended the throne. This practice, already recorded under the 'Abbāsids, was continued under the Ayyubids, the Mamluks and the Ottomans, dynasties which proclaimed their authority over the holy places of Islam. With the passing of time, offering a key became a symbol of suzerainty and of their role as guardians of the sacred sanctuaries.

The padlock shown here is of the classic type in silver gilt and consisting of a long cylindrical pin connected to a seven-sided barrel which contains an inner mechanism in steel for which the key has been lost. One end of this pin is circled with a ring; the other, on the right, is crowned with a cartouche in the shape of a multi-lobed stele, covered with eight lines of calligraphy of varying length separated by ribbing. The very elegant cursive graphic is chased in flat relief. The matt background is discreetly decorated with *ṣāz* leaves which interweave around and under the strokes of the letters. The text, in Arabic, refers to Sultan Süleyman:
This is the lock of the door of the House of God, the benevolent King placed by the one who hopes for His pardon on the day of the Balance (Judgment), Sultan Süleyman Ḫān, son of Sultan Selim Ḫān — let it be useful to him and let it fulfil its purpose — in the year 973/1565-66[2].

The date corresponds to the last year of the reign of the sovereign. He had previously contributed to the maintenance and embellishment of the sanctuary, particularly by the gift of a gold roof gutter[3].

1 *Sourdel-Thomine, J., 1971*
2 *Reading and translation by Janine Sourdel-Thomine*
3 *Gaudefroy-Demombynes, M., 1923, p. 40*

Bibl.: Sourdel-Thomine, J., 1971, no. 16

Photograph Jacqueline Hyde — T.B.

26 RELIQUARY CASKET *ill. opposite*

ill. opposite

Turkey, mid sixteenth century
Ebony, ivory, turquoise and rubies; pierced and chased gold; 5.5 x 9.0 x 5.5

Istanbul, Library of the Topkapı Sarayı Müzesi, 2/4736
Treasury of the Topkapı Palace

Ivory rods reinforce the edges of this small rectangular flat-lidded ebony casket. On each face, the wood panel, with its central part lightly carved out, forms a frame. An open-work gold sheet with a pattern of *rūmī* arabesques is set into this frame, with the spaces between the stems and the serrated, engraved leaves set with thin sheets of turquoise (the *fīrūzekārī* technique) which enhance the decorative pattern. Rubies mounted in gold bezels within four-petalled collars are set into the foliage scroll: two rubies on each of the larger faces of the casket and one on each of the others. The cover is attached by two hinges and has a gold pin-clasp and chain. The bottom of the box is carved in the same style as all the other sides, but is not decorated. The inside is wooden.

According to the records of the Topkapı Palace this small casket might have been used as a reliquary for hair from the beard of the Prophet Muḥammad. The pattern of *rūmī* arabesques and the choice of materials — ebony, ivory, turquoise and gold — date it to the middle of the sixteenth century.

Photograph Jacqueline Hyde — T.B.

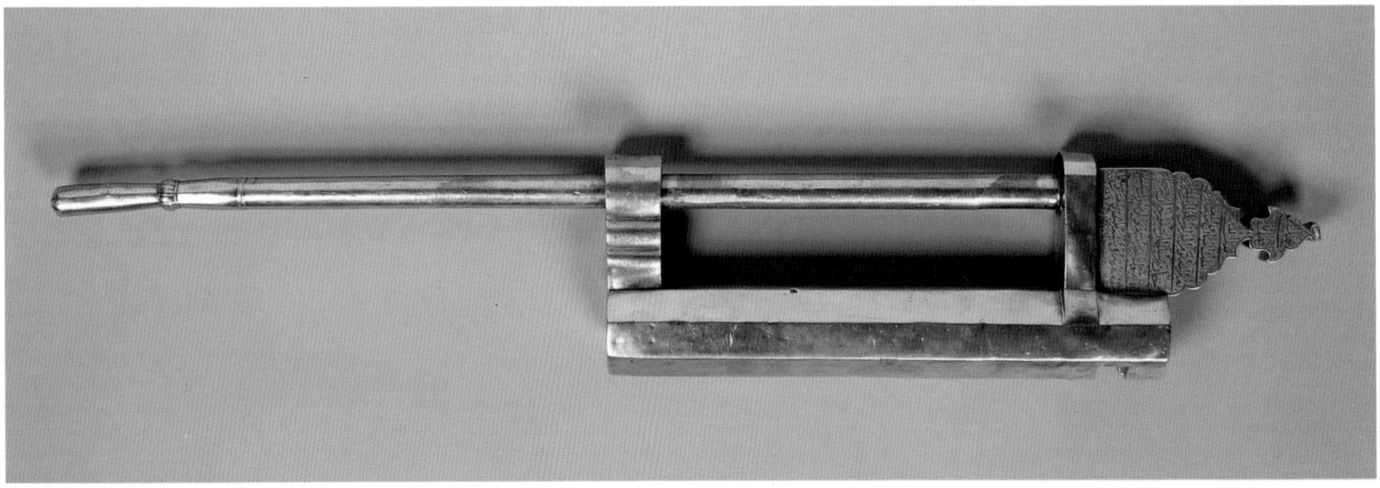

26

27 TALISMANIC SHIRT *ill. page 48*

Turkey, sixteenth century
Cotton or linen painted with pigments and gold; h. (back) 113.0; w. (max. sleeves) 127.5

Istanbul, Library of the Topkapı Sarayı Müzesi, 13/1183
Topkapı Palace collection

This short-sleeved "shirt", which is open in front, split on the sides and without a collar, is made of white cotton or linen, lined with white cotton with a four-centimetre border in grey silk. The pattern, which is entirely painted in gold and pigments, covers the whole surface of this garment. It is made of overlapping bands which follow the general shape of the garment and contains writing in various calligraphic styles, some minute, in a chromatic range with gold dominant but highlighted by blue, orange, green and pink. Dominating the central panel are blue-ground medallions with motifs traditionally used in illumination. On the back, the design is centred on a large square, surrounded by square cartouches in the corners; the bottom of the garment is decorated with illuminated designs: bands of medallions of blue clouds on a gilt scroll ground; blue and gold polygons with pink highlights, foliage scrolls and gilded clouds.

All these motifs and inscriptions are adorned with a very fine border which is a line of writing in tiny characters. Some decorative motifs or texts which look grey are also covered in fine writing. These texts are all religious or prophylatic and reproduce totally or partially various *ḥadīth* of the Prophet and *sūra* of the Koran, for instance: *sūra* XVII (*Banī Isvā-īl* — The Children of Israel); *sūra* II (*Baqara* — The Cow); the *Ayat al-Kursi* or Throne verse; *sūra* XLVIII (*Fat-ḥ* — Victory); *sūra* XXXIV (*Sabā* — The City of Sabā); L. (*Qāf*) and XL (*Mū-min* — The Believer).

The square cartouches, often tipped on their edge, reproduce magical diagrams also known from amulets and mirrors; they contain religious formulae set out in a certain way with letters whose numerical values had magical powers. The garment was worn next to the skin and was supposed to protect the owner from diverse dangers such as illness, wounding or spells. The manufacture of these special garments, which was long and exacting, was not left to chance but based on the decisions of astrologers and specialists in numerology and onomancy. Apart from the one made for Cem Sultan, son of Meḥmed II[1] and the one made for Selim II in 1565[2], the recipients of these clothes are unknown, although they are almost certainly the work of important artists from the *nakkaşhane*. Only that made for Selim II is signed.

1 Topkapı Museum, 13/1404; cf. Istanbul 1983, E 25
2 Topkapı 13/1133; cf. Washington, 1987, no. 123

Photograph Jacqueline Hyde — M.B.T.

27

28 SHORT TALISMANIC SHIRT

Turkey, sixteenth century
Cotton or linen painted with pigments and gold; 62.0 x w. (max. at shoulder) 110.0; w. (at bottom) 100.0

Istanbul, Topkapı Sarayı Müzesi, 13/1182
Topkapı Palace collection

This shirt is of a slightly different model from that of the preceding one: short, with a small collar, with added sleeves and side panels. The design is treated in dark and light blue, black, pink, green, red and orange with gold highlights. It is arranged over the whole garment in squares of different sizes laid on their edge, separated by bands of varying width. On the front, a network of flowers and *ḫaṭāyī* leaves, treated in the style of illumination, decorates the lower part.

The numbers and the writings have religious and magical significance. For instance, on the front we find the *basmala* and the name of the first four *caliphs* (in the two rectangular panels on the chest), the *sūra* I (the *Fātiḥa*), and verses from the poem *al-Burda* (the cloak of the Prophet). On the back are *sūra* XLVIII (*Fat-ḥ*, the Victory), CX (*Naṣr*, Help) and some verses praying for protection of the owner against the wind.

Photograph Jacqueline Hyde M.B.T.

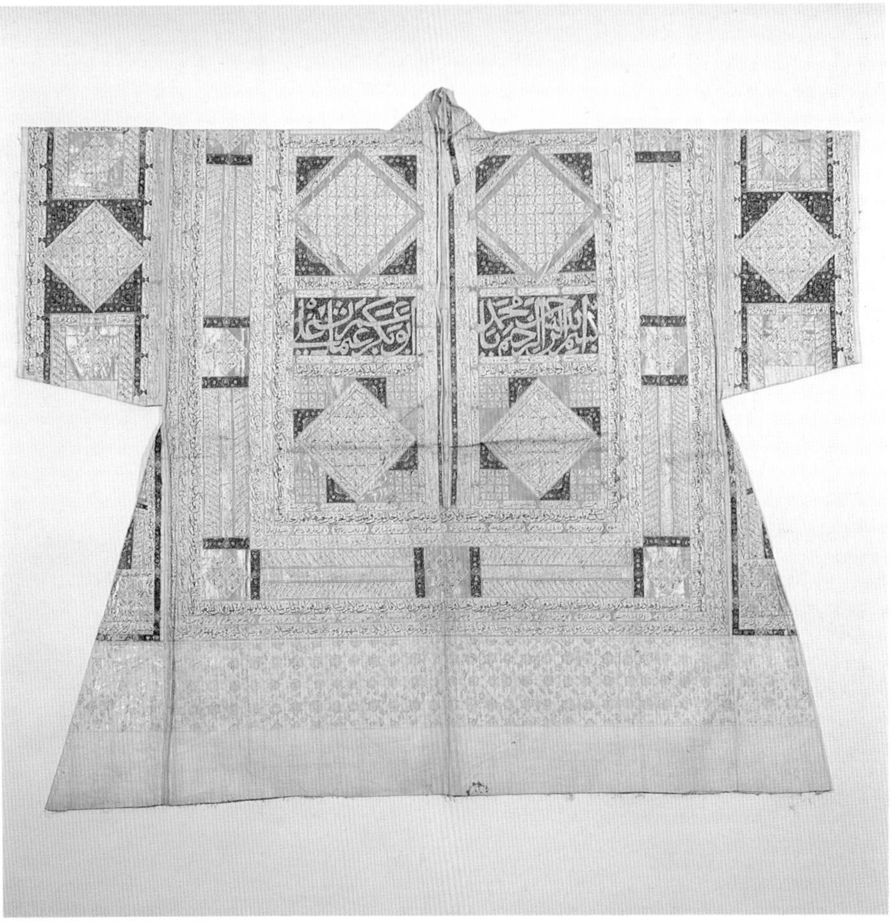

29 NICHE PATTERN CARPET *not illustrated*

Turkey, Ushak(?), second half of the sixteenth century
Wool, symmetrical knot; 157.0 x 733.0

Istanbul, Türk ve Islam Eserleri Müzesi, 774
Transferred in 1911 from the Selimiye Mosque in Edirne

Whereas Ushak medallion carpets, "Holbein" and "Lotto" carpets were exported to Europe during the sixteenth century, prayer carpets were reserved for local clients. Their decoration is borrowed from architecture. It evokes the niche of a *mihrab* decorated with the image of a hanging lamp, a reference to the verse from the Koran: "God is the Light of the heavens and the earth. The parable of His Light is as if there were a Niche and within it a Lamp . . ." (C.XXIV, 35). Some of these *sajajide*, individual prayer carpets, were decorated with only one niche, with one or several arcades; on the very large *saf* intended for religious buildings, multiple niches are set out in horizontal rows. Modern carpets based on this decoration of multiple niches are still used in Turkish mosques.

It is impossible to determine the original dimensions of this *saf*, of which only nine niches remain. What is left of the border allows one to presume that there was at least one other horizontal row. The night-blue field of the multi-lobed niche is decorated with wild-rose branches with white and red flowers. At the centre of each niche an ogival medallion seems to spring from the knot of the waving ribbon of *ṣāz* leaves; it is furnished with bouquets of carnations and tulips, and these flowers, blended with hyacinth, are found again on the corner-piece of honey-yellow background. At the top of the niche, a lamp with a decoration of *rūmī* palmettes is suspended on three chains. A branch of flowers winds around the narrow light-blue border framing the niches, and the main border, night-blue, is decorated with the "four flowers": tulips, hyacinths, carnations and wild roses.

This multi-niche carpet, together with the one described in the following entry, comes from the Mosque of Selim II (the Selimiye) in Edirne (1575) which was designed by the architect Sinan. These *saf* would have been manufactured for its inauguration.

Although some think that they are replicas of the eighteenth century, their decoration is inspired by the *nakkaşhane* of the court and is very similar to the ceramic panels of the Selimiye and to those on the mausoleum (*türbe*) of Selim II.

Bibl.: cf. Ellis, C. G., 1969, pp. 5–22

T.B.

detail

30 CARPET WITH NICHES

Turkey, Ushak(?), second half of the sixteenth century
Wool; symmetrical knot; 155.0 x 431.0

Istanbul, Türk ve Islam Eserleri Müzesi, 804
Originally from the Selimiye mosque at Edirne; transferred in 1911

This *saf*, of which only five niches remain, is very close in its composition to the preceding carpet. The only difference is in the disposition of the colours and the choice of certain motifs. Even the dimensions of the niches are the same.

The night-blue ogival medallion, encircled by a border of *ṣāz* leaves, as well as the lamp that hangs above it, are nearly identical on both carpets. On the field within the niches, here in red, blooms a supple *ṣāz* style composition in ivory tones.

At first sight the decoration seems identical in all the niches but on closer inspection minor differences appear from one to another. The blue corner-pieces are decorated with ivory-coloured arabesques, a narrow band frames the niches and on the wide night-blue border are strewn large blooming flowers in a network of red, green and ivory tones.

The decorative compositions of the two *saf* correspond in a subtle and deliberately affected harmony, as undoubtedly they were intended for the same building. The main elements of the decorative vocabulary of the second half of the sixteenth century are thus illustrated: stylised foliage, *ṣāz* style compositions and four-flowers decoration. Fragments of carpets, similar or identical, originating from the Selimiye, are kept at the Türk ve Islam Eserleri Müzesi.

Bibl.: Ellis, C. G., 1969, pp. 5–22

Photograph Jacqueline Hyde T.B.

31 KORAN BOX

Turkey, end of the sixteenth century
Carved walnut, inlaid with ivory, wood and metal, marquetry of mother-of-pearl and tortoise-shell; 158.0 x 47.0

Istanbul, Türk ve Islam Eserleri Müzesi, 6
From the Mausoleum (türbe) *of the Sultan Meḥmed III (1596–1603) in the precincts of the Ayasofya*

The top cubical section constitutes the chest of this elevated piece of furniture, capped by a hemispheric dome. This cover, provided with a lock, moves on hinges, and the base of the chest lies on a simple pedestal of four legs with decorated spandels.

In the geometrical decorations of rosettes and quarter-rosettes that cover the chest, two related decorative techniques enhance each other: the warm glowing marquetry of mother-of-pearl and tortoise-shell on the box and the dome; and the deeply perforated sculpture of the base emphasised by its graining. A wide band of ebony(?) and a galloon of inverted "Y"s, defined by inlays of wood, ivory and metal, frame all the compositions and unify the whole work. The interior of this box is divided into four rectangular compartments, arranged in a swastika around a central panel decorated by a frieze carved with inverted "Y"s.

Different traditions lie at the origin of the structural and ornamental concept of this chest. The elevated cubical form first appeared in Egypt[1]. It was adopted in the sixteenth century by Ottoman artists who added a dome to it, and it was this form that prevailed in Turkey.

The pierced sculpture used on the base panels is reminiscent of the wood sculpture of Seljuk Anatolia and was rarely used by the Ottomans, who preferred inlays and marquetry.

The use of mother-of-pearl, developed in the second half of the sixteenth century, was promoted by the establishment of a mother-of-pearl workshop at the Topkapı Palace; the technique was considered then as a branch of architecture[2]. Tortoise-shell, the deep glow of which enhances the mother-of-pearl, was only used from the end of the sixteenth century.

1 The earliest known example was made for the Mosque (1369) of Sultan Sa'ban's mother in Cairo
2 Arseven, C. E., n.d., p. 216

Photograph Jacqueline Hyde T.B.

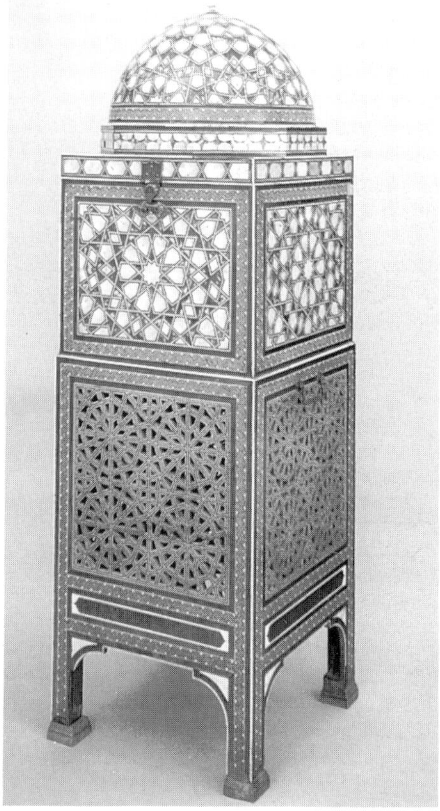

32 KORAN STAND

Turkey, end of the sixteenth century–beginning of the seventeenth century
Walnut and ebony, inlay and marquetry of ivory, mother-of-pearl, tortoise-shell and metal (tin?); h. of a panel 115.0 x 45.0
Istanbul, Türk ve Islam Eserleri Müzesi, 107
From the Mausoleum (türbe) *of Sultan Ibrahim in the Blue Mosque in Istanbul; transferred to the Museum in 1911*

This "X"-shaped Koran stand, *raḥle*, is formed by two long panels which are connected by eight hinges at a third of their height.

The lower panels are cut in an arcade shape, reminiscent of the niche of a *miḥrāb*. The upper panels of the "X" carry, on their two inner faces, the same marquetry design: a central rosace issuing from a central star, quarters of rosace in the corners, formed by a clever arrangement of inlays of wood, ivory and metal threads that also make up the galloon of hexagonal shapes bounding the compositions.

Mother-of-pearl is used for the lobes of pentagonal shapes and the tortoise-shell for the complicated geometrical forms inserted between them.

Ivory mouldings reinforce the angles of the panels and are inlaid around the edge in broken lines.

The median part of the support is decorated, on only one side, with the same design; the reverse side is plain wood. The lobed arches of the legs, cut out from a rectangle inlaid with ebony and ivory, are decorated with *çintemani* (three pearl dots arranged in a triangle) made of ivory inlaid with ebony. This motif, repeated four times, was frequently used in the sixteenth century on various materials.

The origin of this "X" form of furniture can be traced back to antiquity. It was then used as a seat and only much later was it used as a manuscript holder. The hinge joint seems to be an innovation of the Islamic world, where it is recorded from the end of the twelfth century.[1] The first examples originated from Selǰuk Anatolia, such as the *raḥle* from *türbe* of Mevlana Rūmī in Konya[2]. The decoration of such stands was essentially carved but occasionally lacquered or gilded.

The Ottomans maintained the shape of the stand but their preference for inlaid and marquetry designs undoubtedly reflected the influence of Mamluk Egypt and Syria. On an Egyptian *raḥle* of the second half of the fifteenth century, now preserved in the Louvre Museum[3], the characteristics of the Ottoman *raḥle* are clearly expressed: the use of marquetry (admittedly minute), a geometric design radiating from points of a central star, linear borders and edges inlaid with ivory in solid lines in the angles and in broken lines along the sides following a scheme often repeated on Ottoman woodwork.

1 *Illustrated in the* Kitab al-Dirayaq, *Book of the Theriac, Paris, Bibliotheque Nationale Ms. or., arabe 2964, f.32 and 34*
2 *Konya Museum, inv. 332, dated 678/1279 and inv. 333*
3 *Islamic Section, inv. 4063, illustrated in Anglade, E., 1988, no. 59*

Bibl.: cf. Kurtz, O., 1972; Anglade, E., 1988, pp. 104–05

Photograph Jacqueline Hyde T.B.

Arms, Armour and Battles

The reign of Sultan Süleyman, as with that of his predecessor, Selim I, was marked by great military campaigns; during this period the Empire reached its greatest expansion. Süleyman personally conducted more than a dozen campaigns; he was, like his predecessors, commander-in-chief of the armed forces.

It is strange, therefore, that weapons and armour which can be securely attributed to the period of his long reign, on the evidence of inscriptions, are relatively rare and some of the items presented in this exhibition may be slightly earlier or later.

Among the weapons and armour used during his reign, a small number used for formal occasions should be singled out (ceremonial weapons), but most of the pieces were used in battle (military weapons). Some of the ceremonial weapons are still kept in the Treasury of the Topkapı Palace in Istanbul and sumptuous examples can be seen in this exhibition.

Contemporary eye-witnesses speak of the high level of organisation of the Ottoman army, and manuscripts show many illustrations of the elite troops (such as cavalry) accompanying the Sultan, in uniform and with colourful banners. Their usual equipment was the sabre, the bow, the spear, the shield and sometimes the helmet. During Süleyman's reign, guns and cannon began to be more widely used.

As for hand weapons of the period, the *kiliç* type sabre was the most generally used. The *kiliç* has a single-edged curved blade with a section before the tip always ending in a sloped counter-edge; the blade may sometimes be lightened by grooves and hollow sides. The point is always an extension of the line of the blade. The hilt was often faceted and topped by a ribbed egg-shaped pommel or by an octagonal dome of metal. This type of weapon, first developed in the second half of the fifteenth century, reached its highest development during Süleyman's reign. In Süleyman's time there was another type of sword (with a straight blade) called *mec*, which had been at the peak of its glory in the preceding century and of which there is no example here.

The daggers which can be attributed to Süleyman's period seem to have been used mostly as ceremonial pieces or for presentation as gifts. Most have a double-edged straight blade with a central groove that may sometimes be pierced; some blades are slightly curved. They are often inlaid with gold, and decorated with inscriptions and floral motifs. The hilts, made of ivory, jade, mother-of-pearl or some other precious material, are generally flattened, with lobed pommels.

The helmets of this period were usually conical. They included a nose-piece, visor, ear flaps and neck-guard, sometimes a plume-holder. Most were of steel but some gilt copper ones, occasionally set off with an engraved design, were also used (this type was very common after Süleyman's period).

Shields were made of wicker organised in a concentric pattern around a central wooden part, tied together decoratively with coloured silk or cotton threads. In the middle, on the outer surface of the wooden piece, a metallic "umbo" (boss) is fixed, sometimes richly decorated with gilt damascened motifs or even set with semi-precious stones (in which case they would have been ceremonial objects). The inside part of the shield was covered in quilted velvet glued to the wicker base. Rivets affixed a handle and a leather strap. In the middle was a pad to ward off blows.

Archery was one of the Turks' favourite activities and was strongly encouraged by the sultans, including Süleyman, who practised it himself. This activity was the occasion for many competitions but the bow was also used on the battlefield and for hunting. The arrows were kept in leather or embroidered velvet quivers, often set with leather appliqué plates. The Ottoman army had used cannon in the first half of the fifteenth century and they were increasingly used during Süleyman's period. A number of cannon of this period are now kept at the Military Museum in Istanbul and can be dated by their inscription to the period of Süleyman's reign.

L.K.

1 *Various entries about weapons and armour could only be made on the basis of previous publications, often scant, or from museum index cards. This explains the somewhat general character of the texts and why not all the inscriptions could be read*

2 Kiliç *means "sabre"*

33 ARCHER'S RING

Turkey, c.1550
Ivory, inlaid with gold and precious stones; 4.5 x 3.0; internal 2.1

National Gallery of Victoria, Melbourne
Presented by Mr M. Stebbings, 1976

The archer's ring of ivory is inlaid in gold with an arabesque design and set with gold and precious stones against a subsidiary arabesque decoration in a black compound. This kind of decoration is typical of the imperial workshops in Istanbul during the sixteenth century and it is very likely that the ring was made for the sultan's personal use. (Other objects decorated in this style include nos 43, 51, 103, 104.)

Archer's rings are used to facilitate the drawing of the bow and to prevent injuries caused by the string. They have been used since antiquity and a Chinese example of the fifth century B.C. is preserved in the British Museum (Tate, *Jewellery*, 1976, p. 252, no. 426). Far Eastern rings are generally cylindrical; those used in the Islamic world are thickened and pointed at one end. They are called *jati-ah* or *khati-ah* in Arabic, *Khustuwan* in Arabo-Persian and *angushtvan* in Persian. An anonymous fifteenth century Mamluk writer states that it is better not to use a thumb ring as it detracts from accuracy, but if one is to be used then leather is the best material, especially the skin of horses and goats. He notes that other materials are also used and among these mentions silver, copper, iron, bone and horn (Faris, *Arab Archery*, 1945, pp. 123–24; for a drawing showing how such rings are used see Tate, *Jewellery*, 1976, p. 251).

Archer's rings were important in the Islamic world, as military accoutrements and ceremonial objects. This is well illustrated in miniature painting, where rulers are frequently depicted in Ottoman, Iranian and Mughal works wearing such rings (for example, the Ottoman miniature of c.1560 showing the aged Süleyman I, accompanied by two pages, one of whom carries his sabre; on his right thumb Süleyman wears an archer's ring; Atil, *Süleyman*, 1987, p. 34, fig. 10). By wearing the ring an individual proclaimed in a very subtle way that he was a military man proficient in one of the ancestral Arab and Turkish forms of hunting and fighting, and heir to a glorious and ancient tradition which went back to Abraham's son Isma'il.

The high esteem in which archery was held in the Islamic world can be traced to a very early period. The Mamluk writer Taybugha, for example, repeats a story in which Adam was pestered by birds eating his crops. He complained to God who sent Gabriel with a bow, a string and two arrows explaining that the bow represented the force of God, the string His might and the arrows the harm He could inflict (Latham, *Saracen Archery*, 1970, p. 3). This knowledge was said to have passed to Abraham to whom the Arabs trace their descent through his eldest son Isma'īl; in Arab tradition Abraham is described as having made bows for his sons Isma'īl and Isaac (Faris, *Archery*, 1945, pp. 9–10). According to the Biblical account, when Isma'īl and his mother were exiled at the insistence of Sarah, God spoke to Abraham and calmed his fears for their safety by saying that a mighty nation would descend from the boy and: "God was with the lad; and he grew, and dwelt in the wilderness, and became an archer" (Genesis 21:20).

At the time of the Prophet, the primary weapon of the Arabs was the sword, but this did not minimize the importance given to archery.

At the Battle of Uhud in 635 A.D., the Prophet shot with his bow until its lower tip broke. This bow is said to have been taken by Qatadah ibn al-Nu'man and eventually given to the *caliphs*. A fifteenth century Mamluk author reported that it was at this time kept in the Treasury with the other holy relics (it is perhaps this bow which is now in the Treasury of the Topkapı Sarayı) and that its "sweet scent is noticeable to anyone standing near the Holy Relics, since its grip is redolent with the perspiration of the Prophet's palm, and will diffuse therefrom like musk until the day of resurrection" (Faris, *Archery*, p. 9).

The Arabs at the time of the Prophet seem to have used the bow, as at Uhud, when fighting on foot. The reverse was the case with the nomads of Central Asia, who used it primarily from horseback. The Parthians, a nomadic people who became the rulers of Persia were famous for their agility with the bow. Their armoured cavalry (*cataphractarii*) inflicted several severe defeats on the Romans, and Roman poets commenting on their skill coined the term "a Parthian shot", that is a shot fired in apparent retreat (Virgil, *Georg* iii.31: "fidentemque fuga Parthum versique sagittis"; Horace, *Odes* i.19.11: "versis animosum equis Parthum"). This method of fighting was probably introduced into the Islamic world during the Umayyad period when Turkish troops were first used by the *caliphs* during the ninth century. Al-Jahiz (776–869), describing the Turks, wrote that they: "shoot at beasts, birds, hoops, men, sitting quarry, dummies and birds on the wing, and do so at full gallop to fore or to rear, to left or to right, upwards or downwards" (Latham, *Saracen Archery*, 1970, p. xxiii).

The most important symbol of authority for the Arabs was usually the sword but for the Turks and other central Asian nomads it was the bow. Evidence for this is provided by Herodotus, who relates that the Scythians were descended from the union of Heracles and a *melusine*, a maiden half-woman and half-serpent, and that on his departure the *melusine* asked Heracles how she should treat her sons. He replied by taking one of his two bows and his golden belt and saying that if any one of them could bend it he should be girded with the belt and allowed to stay, while he who failed should be sent away (Herodotus, *The Persian Wars*, 1942, bk. IV, 9–10, pp. 293–94).

This kind of tradition explains why the bow became a symbol of sovereignty and why rulers of Central Asian origin are sometimes depicted in Islamic paintings seated in state and holding a bow (e.g., in the Kitab al-Aghani of 1217 A.D., now in the Feyzullah Library, Istanbul, no. 1566, ill. in, Rice, *Aghani Miniatures*, 1953, fig. 18; and for an Ottoman painting showing a sultan in a similar fashion see Tezçan, *Bows and Arrows*, 1977, p. 24). It also explains the numerous stories about Turkish sultans who were able to draw exceptionally heavy bows or who took up one of the crafts associated with archery, such as Bayazid II (1481–1512), who made his own bows (Tezçan, *Bows and Arrows*, 1977, p. 24).

Bibl.: Atil, E., The Age of Süleyman the Magnificent, *Washington, 1987; Faris, N. A. and Elmer, R. P.,* Arab Archery, *Princeton, 1945; Herodotus,* The Persian Wars, *tr. Godolphin, F. R. B., New York, 1942; Latham, J. D.,* Saracen Archery, *London, 1970; Rice, D. S.,* "The Aghani Miniatures and Religious Painting in Islam" *in,* Burlington Magazine, *vol. 95, 1953, pp. 215–48; Sadeque, S. F.,* Baybars I of Egypt, *Lahore, 1956; Tate, H.,* Jewellery, *London, 1983; Tezçan, T.,* "Turkish Bows and Arrows" *in* Ilgi, *Istanbul, 1977*

D.A.

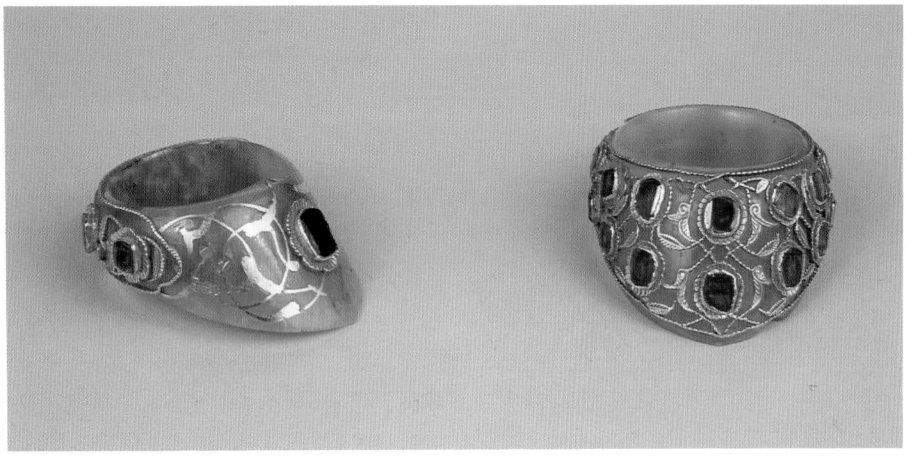

34 ARCHER'S THUMB RING

Turkey, second half of the sixteenth century
Jade inlaid with gold, rubies and an emerald; (max.) diam. 4.0; (max.) diam. (inside) 3.6

Istanbul, Topkapı Sarayı Müzesi, 2/74
Treasury of the Topkapı Palace

Narrow, notched gold wire, joined to small oval leaves, sometimes bifid, elongated or curling, and set into white jade, forms a net into which are set two rows of 18 table-cut rubies in bezels on finely engraved gold collars. An emerald, also table-cut, set in the same manner adorns the front of the ring.

Worn on the thumb of the right hand, this type of ring enabled the archer to pull the bow back more easily and forcefully, and protected against possible injuries caused by the vibrating string.

Such rings appear in many miniatures, sometimes adorning the thumb of an archer[1], sometimes suspended from the belt on a ceremonial occasion. They were equally common in the Ottoman, Iranian and Turkish empires. It seems they could also be worn as a simple ornament[2]. According to the celebrated voyager Tavernier, who made several journeys to Turkey, Iran and India in the seventeenth century, the ring could also be used to tighten the neckerchief with which disgraced courtiers were strangled to death[3].

1 *For example, the portrait of Selim II painted by Nīgārī, and preserved in the library of the Topkapı Sarayı Müzesi (inv. H 2134/3)*
2 *For example, in two portraits of the Mughal emperor Jahangir housed in the Freer Gallery of Art in Washington; one painted by Bichtir, of Jahangir seated on an hour-glass shaped throne; the other, painted by Abūl'l-Ḥasan, shows Jahangir embracing the safavid sovereign Shah 'Abbās, the latter also wearing a thumb ring*
3 *Cited by Rogers, M., London, 1988, p. 152*

Photograph Jacqueline Hyde M.B.T.

35 ARCHER'S RING

Turkey, end of the sixteenth century
Jade inlaid with gold, emerald and rubies; max. diam. 3.7

Istanbul, Topkapı Sarayı Müzesi, 2/83
From the Treasury of the Topkapı Palace

In pale green jade, the front of the ring is adorned with a flower made from a table-cut emerald, set in a bezel against a finely engraved gold-lobed collar. This jewel stands out against a background of arabesques with thin stems carrying bifurcated florets with long supple lobes, set into the jade. The back of the ring features a thin strip in finely engraved relief forming a cartouche. It is set with five table-cut rubies and mounted, as with the emerald at the front, in a bezel against a collar with delicately striated lobes. The rubies are framed by small pointed and elongated leaves, set in relief into the jade and engraved.

The play of colours and the contrast between the smooth surface of the inlaid motifs and the engraved motifs in relief give this piece a highly refined appearance.

Photograph Jacqueline Hyde M.B.T.

36 BOW-CASE

Turkey, c.1550–70
Leather, velvet embroidered with silk and gold thread; silver-gilt studs; 74.0 x 34.0

Istanbul, Topkapı Sarayı Müzesi, 1/10989
Treasury of the Topkapı Palace

The entire bow-case is made of red leather covered in dark red velvet. The front is ornamented with three multi-lobed oval medallions of *rūmī* arabesque designs and with trefoil pendants. The medallions descend in decreasing size on a vertical axis against a background strewn with the "three pearls" motif. These motifs are also used on the border. The decorative elements are embroidered in gold, with blue, green and red silk highlights. A pair of brocaded straps is attached by silver-gilt studs decorated with *ṣāz* flowers.

Bibl.: Gönül, M., pl. 22; Tezçan, H. and Delibas, S., 1986, pl. 92

Photograph Jacqueline Hyde — L.K.

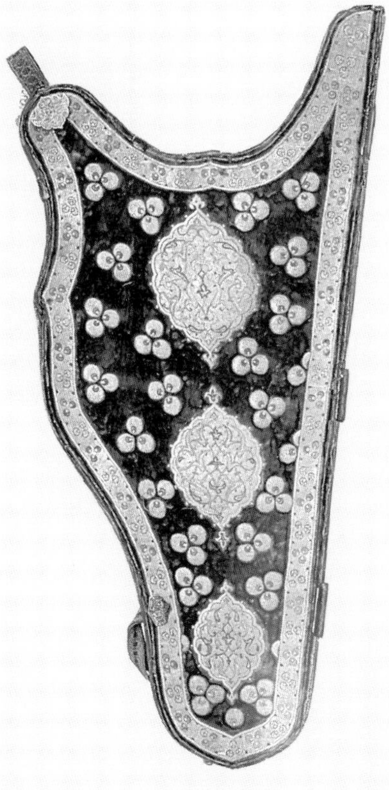

37 BOW-CASE AND QUIVER

Turkey, second half of the sixteenth century
Leather, embroidered and appliqued; bow-case 68.0 x 35.0; quiver 42.0 x 26.0

Vienna, Kunsthistorisches Museum, Waffensammlung, C5 and C5a
Registered in the collection of Schloss Ambras in the Tyrol since 1583

The ochre-coloured ground of the outside of the bow-case is edged by a dark red leather border, decorated with two superimposed scrolls in cream with touches of black and gold. One of the scrolls bears *ḫaṭāyī* flowers, buds and leaves. The other is decorated with *rūmī* leaves. The ground is also decorated with two scrolls of this type, spiralling and featuring flowers and cloud motifs. The scrolls overflow into the two central red cartouches. In the upper right-hand corner, an unadorned space is no doubt designed for a decorative clasp attaching a strap. The back of the cover has a large black leather border, surrounded by an ochre leather band. The ground is covered in dark blue satin decorated by two lobed oval sections with vertical pendants, filigreed in leather and decorated by two superimposed scrolls of *rūmī* flowers.

The outside of the quiver is ornamented in the same manner as the bow-case, but its ground is decorated with a single cartouche above which is a horizontal row of trefoils surrounded by roundels formed by the scrolls. On the right-hand side, on the upper and middle corners, the unadorned space is probably intended for the same purpose as that of the bow-cover. The back has the same decoration as the cover, with a single oval compartment flanked by cloud motifs.

The bow-cover and quiver are part of a large collection of Ottoman objects of this type, assembled by the Archduke Ferdinand at Schloss Ambras.

Bibl.: Sacken, E., 1859–62, p. 280; Grosz, A. and Thomas, B., 1936, p. 97, no. 7; Thomas, B., 1963–64, fig. 5; Beaufort, Ch. and Gamber, O., 1990, pp. 230–31 and 232–33

L.R.

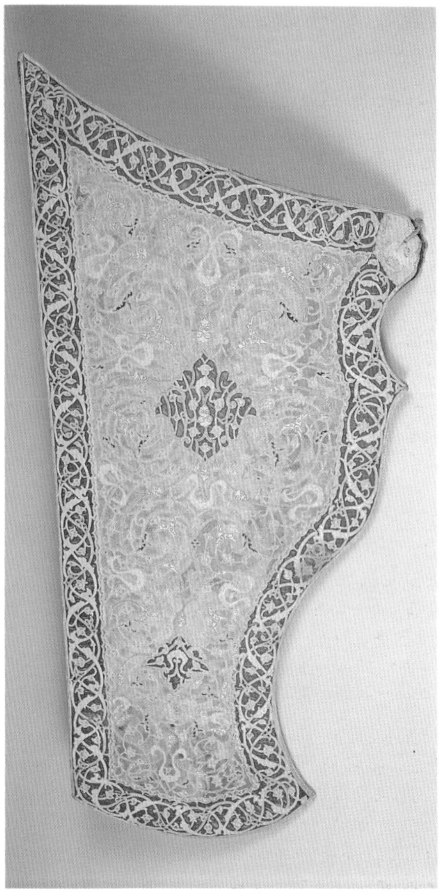

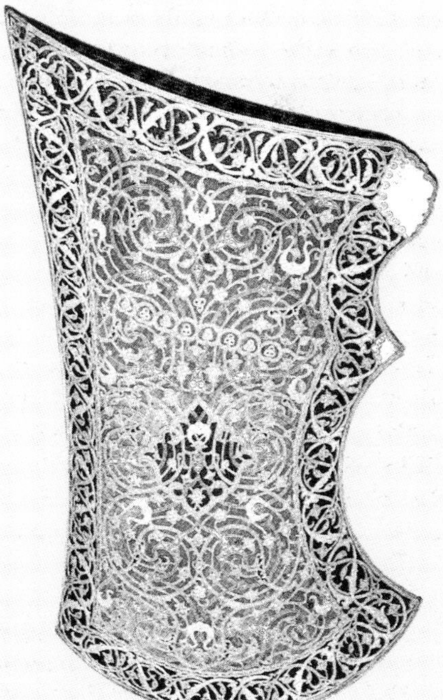

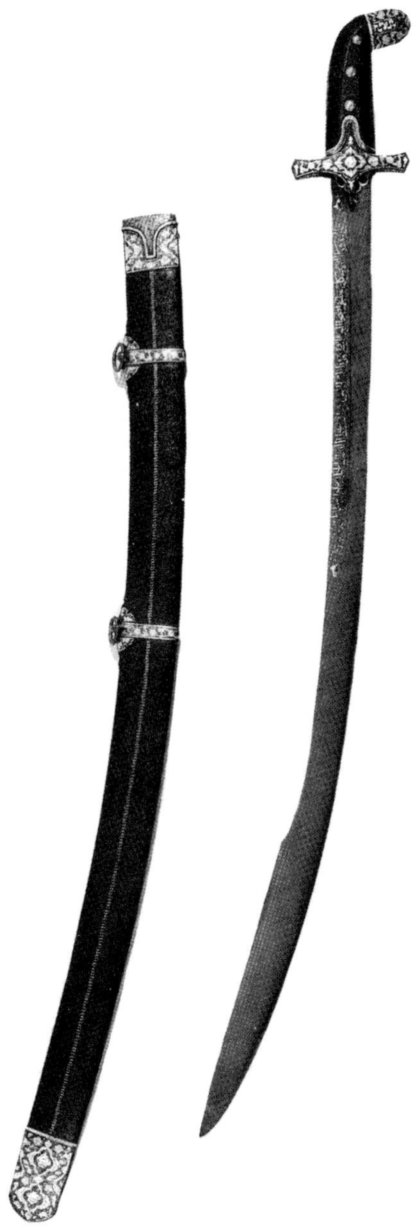

38 KILIÇ AND SCABBARD

Turkey, c.1550
Steel blade inlaid with gold; hilt covered with leather; pommel and hilt in steel inlaid with gold; scabbard covered with leather; sling mounts and chapes in steel inlaid with gold; 1. of sword 93.8; 1. of sheath 87.8

Istanbul, Topkapı Sarayı Müzesi, 1/463
Treasury of the Topkapı Palace

On this example of a *kiliç*, a characteristic Ottoman sword, each side of the steel blade bears an inscription inlaid with gold. One text is a verse from the Koran (Kor. LXV2–3); the other is a dedication to Sultan Süleyman.

The mounting consists of a straight, faceted wood hilt covered with black leather. It is attached to the tang of the blade with three studs, the rosette-shaped gold heads of which appear on the two opposite sides.

The pommel resembles a pistol grip and its faceted cap, in blackened steel, is inlaid with gold and decorated with floral scrolls and Chinese clouds delicately chiselled and slightly in relief. The decoration of the guard, short and sturdy, is very similar.

The wooden scabbard is covered with black leather; the sling mounts and chapes are embellished with gold-inlaid blackened steel in the same style as the cap of the pommel and the guard.

Photograph Jacqueline Hyde L.K.

39 SABRE WITH SCABBARD

Turkey, mid sixteenth century
Steel blade; handle in wood covered in leather; pommel and guard in silver-gilt; l. of sabre 93.5

Vienna, Kunsthistorisches Museum, Waffensammlung, A 1337
Registered in the collections of Schloss Ambras in the Tyrol since 1583. Provenance of the Turkish Room of the Archduke Ferdinand

Near the top of the blade are three hollows. The handle is fluted, with four notches for the fingers. On the end of each quillon is a grooved ball.

Bibl.: Grosz, A. and Thomas, B., 1936, p. 99; Beaufort, Ch. and Gamber, O., 1990, p. 243

L.K.

40 KILIÇ WITH SCABBARD *not illustrated*

Turkey (or Hungary?), mid sixteenth century
Steel blade; handle in wood covered with leather; pommel and guard in silver-gilt; scabbard covered in leather, with silver-gilt ornaments; l. of kiliç 96.0; l. of scabbard 86.0

Vienna, Kunsthistorisches Museum, Waffensammlung, A 1341
Registered in the collection of Schloss Ambras in the Tyrol since 1583. Provenance of the Turkish Room of the Archduke Ferdinand

The blade has no ornamentation. The mount is made up of a faceted wood hilt, a slightly-curved dome on the pommel and a cross-shaped guard, with elongated quillons each terminated by a rounded element. The pommel and the guard are partly engraved on a stippled ground; the centre of the guard is decorated with interlacing *ṣāz* leaves enclosed in a pointed oval cartouche; the quillon ends are decorated with palmette motifs.

The scabbard has a silver-gilt chape, two sling mounts and an end-piece. As with the centre of the guard, the chape and the end-piece are decorated with interlacing *ṣāz* leaves enclosed in two-pointed oval cartouches. The sling mounts are in the shape of large pointed ovals, while the chape and end-piece end in half of the same motif pointing inwards along the scabbard. These motifs are decorated with a composition, at the centre of which is a cypress flanked by two pairs of tulips and encircled by a beaded band tracing the contour of the motif; the wide outer zone contains multi-petalled roses framed by overlapping feathery leaves, each overlaid by a spray of flowers. The dorsal edge of the end-piece is stamped with the *tuğra* of Sultan Süleyman.

Bibl.: Grosz, A. and Thomas, B., 1936, p. 99, no. 21; Ex Oriente Lux, 1989; Beaufort, Ch. and Gamber, O., 1990, p. 243

L.K.

41 SABRE – KILIÇ

Turkey, 914/1509
Steel blade; handle (much later) inlaid with green-tinted ivory; 89.5; handle 12.0

Collection Rifaat Sheikh El-Ard, Riyadh

The sabre (*kiliç*) has a deeply curved double-edged blade. The right side is inlaid in gold with alternating circular and elongated cartouches containing Arabic inscriptions. Reading towards the handle the text translates as follows:

1, 2, 4, 6, 8: The names of the seven sleepers of Ephesus and their dog

3: "It is from Solomon and is (as follows) In the name of God, Most gracious, Most merciful" (Kor. XXVII, 30)

5: "Help from God and a speedy victory. So give the Glad Tidings to the Believers!" (Kor. LXI, 13) "O. Moḥammed!"

7: "God will suffice thee against them. He is the All-Hearing, the All-Knowing." (Kor. II, 137) 914/1509

The spaces between the cartouches are decorated with floral motifs set into a gold ground. One of the inscribed cartouches is ornamented in the same fashion. Further down, along the back, another Arabic inscription contains the verse of the Throne, *Āyat al-Kursī* (Kor. II, 256/255).

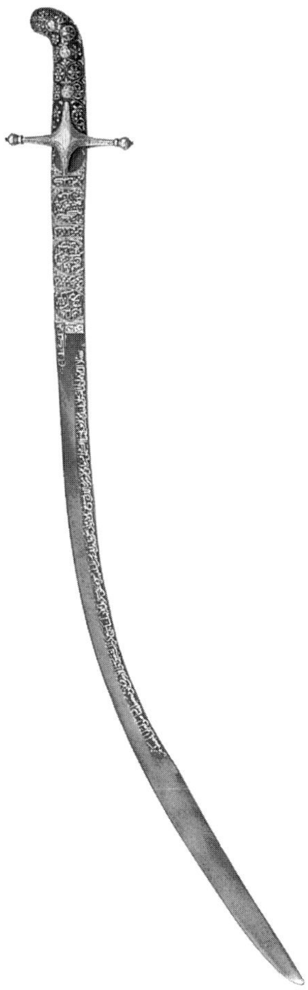

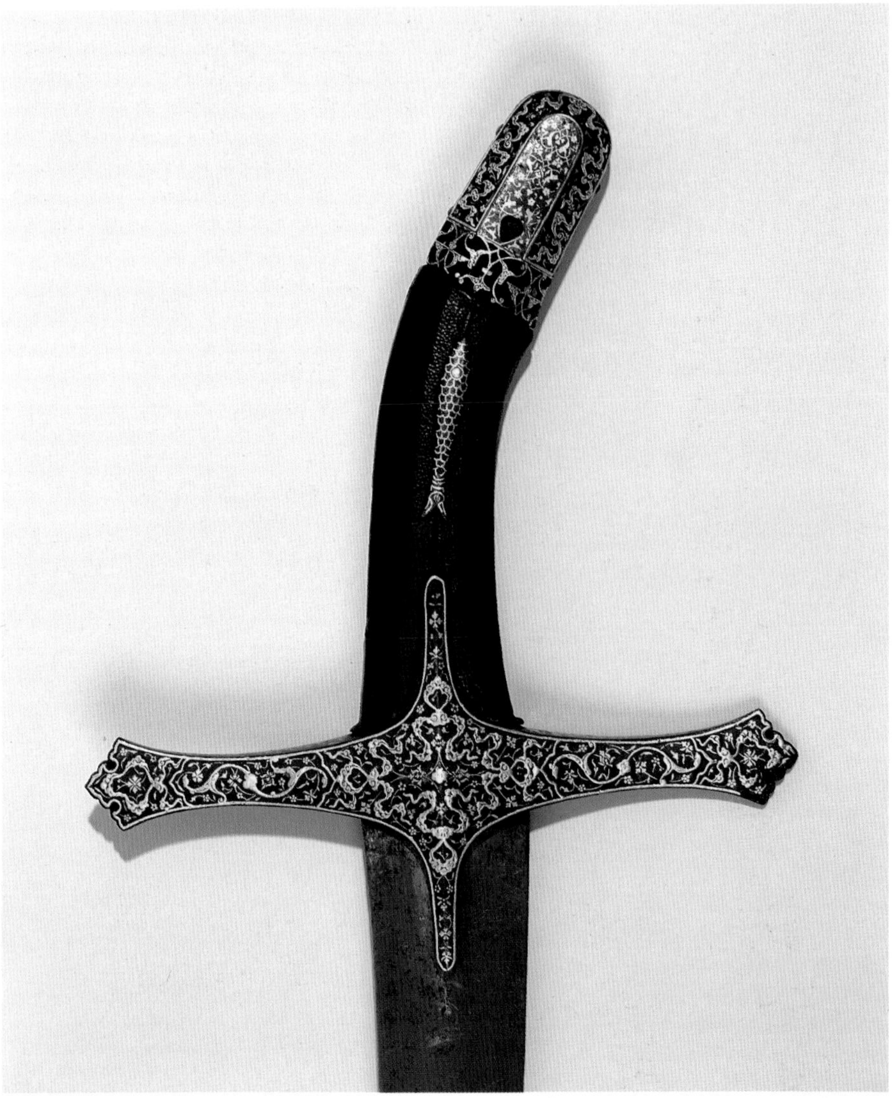

42 *detail*

The pistol-grip shaped hilt is in green-tinted ivory, inlaid with silver interlacings of rosettes and flowers. The rivet-seals are gold. The simple cross-shaped guard, in gilt copper, dates from the nineteenth century.

Bibl.: Jacob, A., 1975, pp. 48, 49 and 50; Jacob, A., 1985, colour pl. r°13 and pls n.-b. 99 and 100

L.K.

42 KILIÇ WITH SCABBARD

Turkey, c.1550
Steel blade; handle covered with leather, pommel and hilt in steel inlaid with gold and set with turquoises. Scabbard covered with leather, fitted with two sling mounts and a chape, in gold-inlaid steel; l. of sword 95.8; l. of scabbard 84.0

Istanbul, Topkapı Sarayı Müzesi, 1/294
Treasury of the Topkapı Palace

The blade of this sabre is very worn, making identification of its decoration and inscription difficult. The faceted hilt is covered with black leather and is bent slightly in the opposite direction to the curvature of the blade.

The faceted pommel and hilt are in blackened steel inlaid with gold. The quillons are elongated with the ends pointed. The cap of the pommel is decorated at its base with a border of intertwining *rūmī*; the central panel is inlaid with superimposed *rūmī* and *ḫaṭāyī* scrolls, and the flanking panels with bands of clouds in relief on a ground decorated with blossoming flowers. The band encircling the upper edge of the pommel is divided into four cartouches containing the following Persian poetic couplets, interspersed with small flowers set with rubies:

may the world be as you wish it
and the sky your friend
may the creator of the world
be your protector.

On one side of the handle is a fish inlaid with gold. The guard is adorned with floral scrolls over which are superimposed cloud bands and *rūmī* motifs in relief.

The scabbard is covered with black leather and embellished with two sling

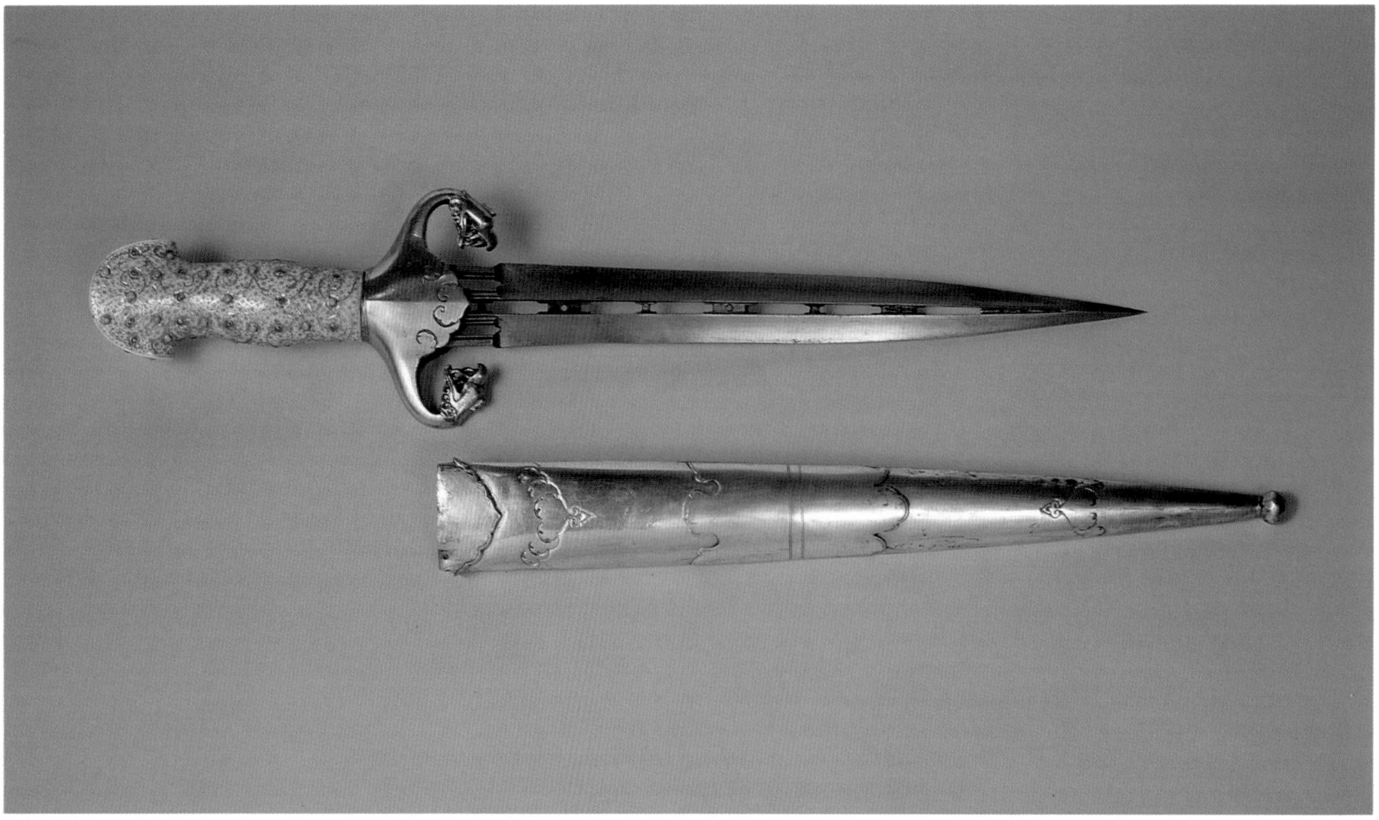

mounts and a steel chape inlaid with gold. It is the same style of decoration as found on the hilt, with the same emphasis on the contrast between the delicately inlaid floral motifs and the *rūmī* scrolls and cloud bands executed in relief. This contrasting decoration was often used on jewellery as well as arms.

Photograph Jacqueline Hyde

L.K.

43 IVORY-HANDLED DAGGER WITH SCABBARD

Turkey, second quarter of the sixteenth century
Steel blade; handle of ivory inlaid with black substance and set with rubies and turquoise; guard in silver-gilt; scabbard in silver partially gilt; l. of dagger 49.4; l. of scabbard 38.0

Vienna, Kunsthistorisches Museum, Waffensammlung, C 152 a and b
Registered in the collection of Schloss Ambras in the Tyrol since 1583

The unadorned steel blade has a central groove pierced by long vertical incisions. The silver-gilt guard was cast in two pieces, the join forming a ridge. Its lobed flange is engraved with palmettes; the two downward-curving quillons terminate in dragons' heads.

The swelling ivory handle with a rounded pommel is ornamented with fine floral interlacings inlaid with black against which are set gold floral interlacings with turquoise and rubies.

The centre of the silver-gilt scabbard is reinforced with a lobed silver band. The upper and lower sections are incised with palmette motifs ending in trefoils. The pivot on the back of the scabbard, used to attach the dagger to a belt, has a ring in the shape of a dragon's head.

Bibl.: Sacken, E., 1859–62, p. 297, no. 27; Grosz, A. and Thomas, B., 1936, p. 95, no. 7; Thomas, B., 1963–64, fig. 6

L.K.

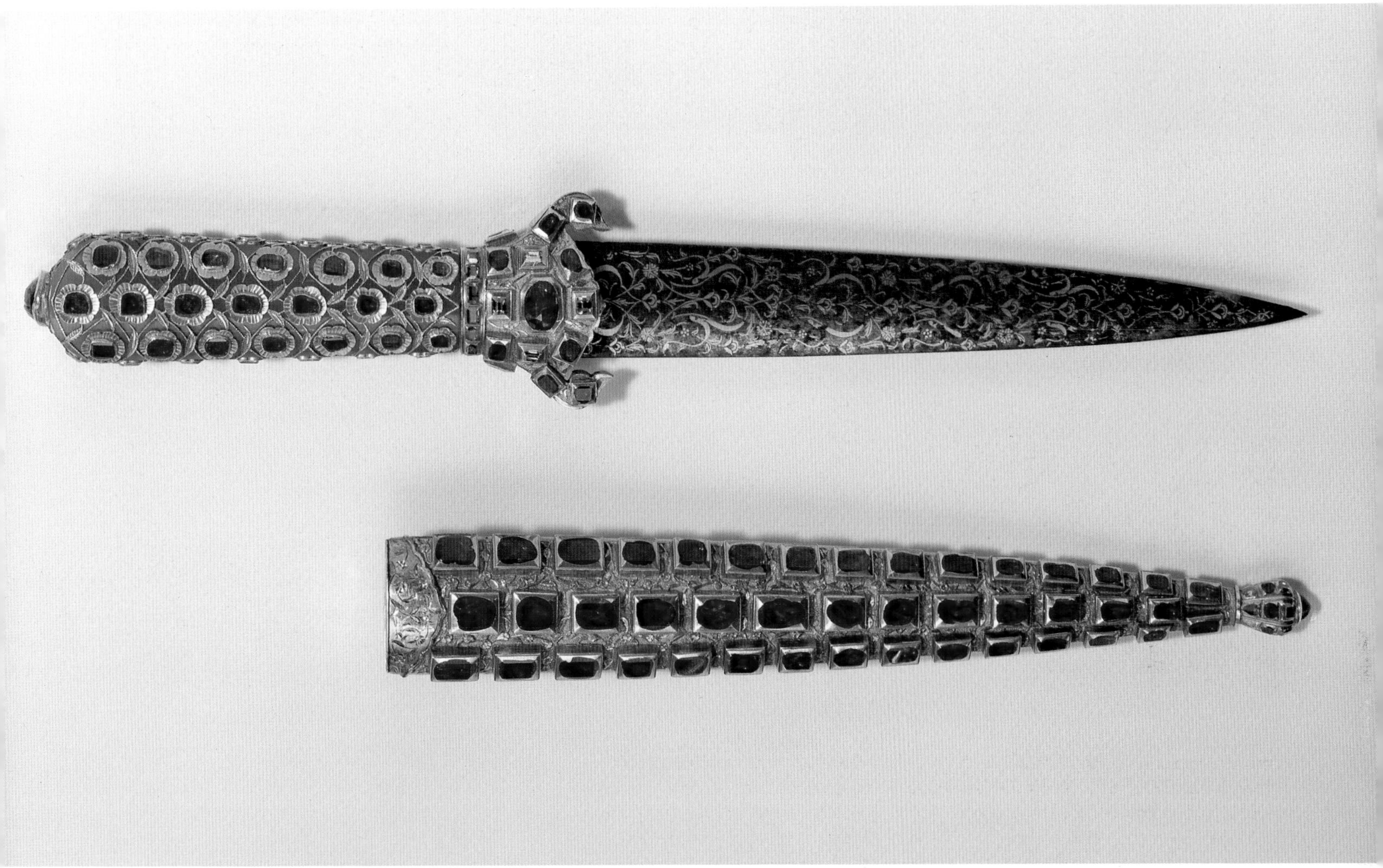

44 DAGGER WITH SCABBARD

Turkey, second half of the sixteenth century
Steel blade damascened with gold; pale celadon-coloured jade handle with gold guard; jade set with rubies in bezels and inlaid with gold wire; guard set with rubies and diamonds on an unpolished gold ground with a relief design; front and rounded end of the scabbard set with rubies and diamonds in bezels, the space between them in gold ground with a relief design; back engraved and detailed with a black compound; 33.4 x 5.5

Collection Rifaat Sheikh El-Ard, Riyadh

Both sides of the blade are ornamented with arabesques of *ṣāz* leaves and flowers, damascened with gold. The handle, rounded at the top and surmounted by a cabochon ruby, is ornamented with vertical rows of table-cut rubies set in flower-shaped bezels. The spaces between the rubies are decorated with a network of gold wire stems with *ṣāz* leaves. The quillons of the gold guard are in the shape of stylized dragon's heads. The surface of the guard is decorated with rubies; the quillons at the front also have four diamonds set in bezels. the unpolished ground is chased in relief with *ṣāz* leaves. The front of the collar is adorned by six diamonds and the back by rubies.

The tapered scabbard has a rounded end-piece crowned with a cabochon ruby, and its surface is adorned with six rubies and 12 diamonds set in bezels on an unpolished gold ground of chased motifs. The front is decorated with vertical rows of table-cut rubies set in bezels. The decoration is composed of a network of *ṣāz* flowers and leaves. The back of the scabbard has a ring to attach it to the wearer's belt and is adorned with a network of compartments containing arabesques of *ṣāz* leaves and flowers, engraved and enamelled in black. Other embossed arabesques decorate the surface between these small areas[1]. Near the opening of the scabbard is an area engraved on both sides with *ṣāz* leaves and flowers.

There is a similar dagger in the collections of the Kunsthistorisches Museum, Waffensammlung, Vienna[2]. (cat. no. 45)

1 *A similar decoration can be seen on the metal plate inside the pen box from the Topkapı Sarayı Müzesi, no. 2/22. Cf. Washington, 1987, pp. 130–31, fig. 62*

2 *Vienna, Kunsthisthorisches Museum, Waffensammlung, no. C 208. Cf. Washington, 1987, pp. 159–60, fig. 94*

L.K.

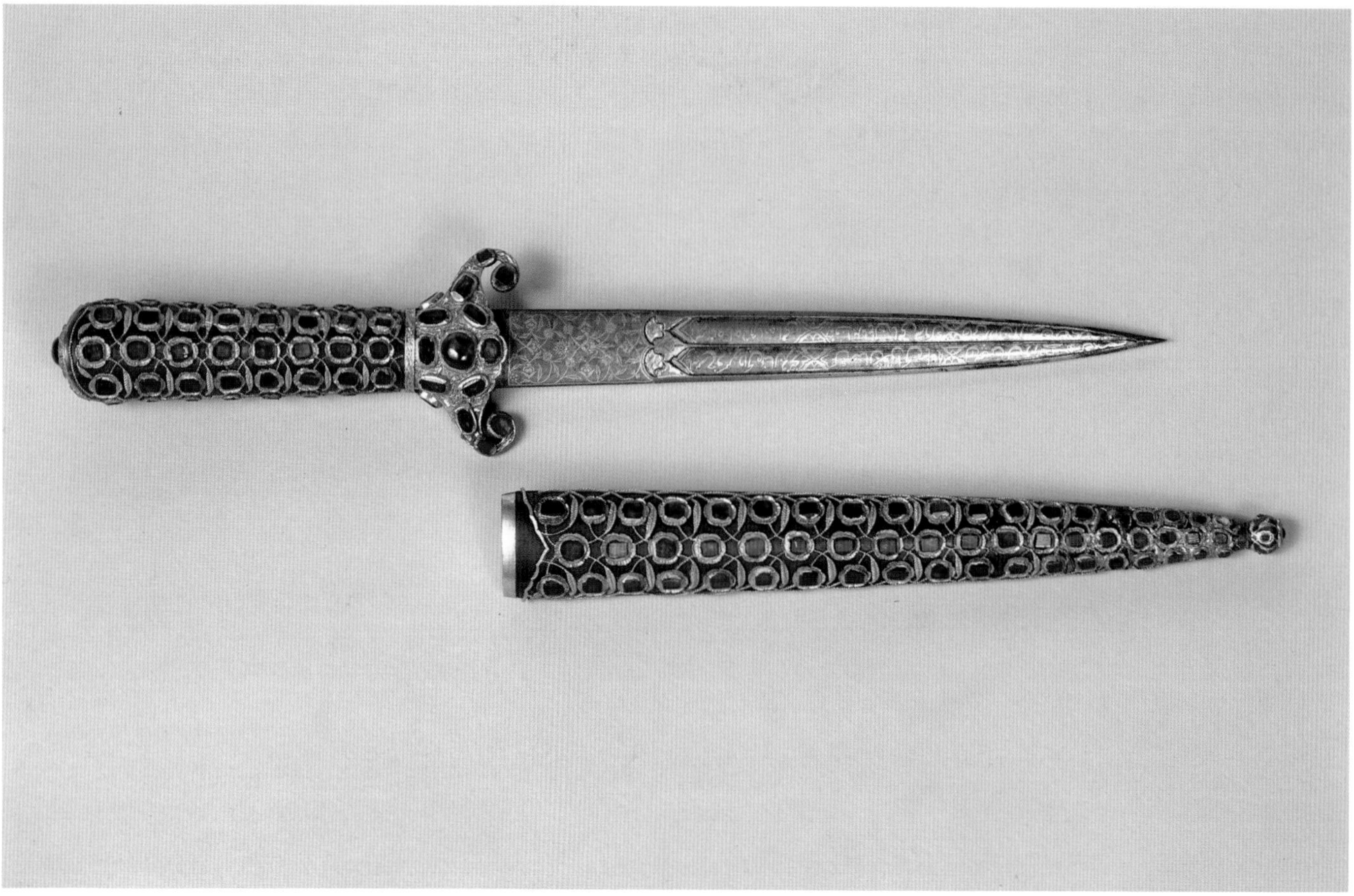

45 DAGGER WITH JADE HANDLE AND SCABBARD

Turkey, second half of the sixteenth century
Handle and scabbard in jade inlaid with gold and set with rubies; gold guard set with rubies; grooved steel blade, inlaid with gold; l. of dagger 31.6; l. of scabbard 21.6

Vienna, Kunsthistorisches Museum, Waffensammlung, C 208
Registered in the collection of Schloss Ambras in the Tyrol since 1583

The steel blade is inlaid with gold and decorated with the same motifs on both sides. The upper section is ornamented with interlacing *ṣāz* leaves and *ḫaṭāyī* flowers. The lower section, divided into two vertical convex sections each surmounted by a palmette, bears an inscription in *nasta'līk*. On one side of the blade are inscribed three Persian verses; on the other are three in Turkish.

The handle, with its curved pommel, is of jade decorated with inlaid gold interlacings of leaves and flowers with striated petals. In the centre of each flower is a ruby set in a square bezel. The tip of the pommel is decorated with a large ruby.

The gold guard has downward-curving quillons and is decorated with floral engraved interlacings and rubies set in circular bezels without collars.

The gently-tapering end of the scabbard was originally encircled by a ruby-studded ring. The point is rounded into a small sphere. The decoration is identical to that of the handle and uses the same decorative technique employed on other jade objects of the period.

Bibl.: Sacken, E., 1859–62, pp. 158–59, no. 8; Gluck, H. and Diez, E., 1925, p. 473; Grosz, A. and Thomas, B., 1936, p. 95, no. 10; Ivanov, A., 1979, fig. 67

L.K.

46 SHIELD

Turkey, second half of the sixteenth century
Wicker embroidered with silk and silver thread; steel central boss; diam. 64.0

Istanbul, Topkapı Sarayı Müzesi, 1/2571

The sides of the shield are decorated with a dense, symmetrical composition of predominantly ruby-red and gold silk embroidered tulips and carnations.

In the centre of the steel boss, which was originally damascened in gold, is a relief motif representing the sun with 10 rays. On the sides are eight rosette-shaped rivet-heads in gilt steel or iron, which secure the rivets which in turn hold a dark-red velvet pad to the inside of the shield.

The naturalistic flower design is typical of the second half of the sixteenth century.

Bibl.: Mackie, L., 1980, ill. 220; Tezcan, T., 1983, cover

Photograph Jacqueline Hyde L.K.

47 SHIELD

Turkey, end of the sixteenth century
Wicker, embroidered with silk and silver thread, central boss in steel; diam. 62.0

Istanbul, Topkapı Sarayı Müzesi, 1/2441

The ruby-red wicker base is adorned with a symmetrical composition of flowers, lotus buds and spear-shaped leaves executed in cream, blue, brown and green silk threads and silver elements. The steel boss, styled in swirling grooves, is bordered by a small inscription in cursive script containing the important and well known Throne Verse from the Koran (Koran II 256/255). Its surface was originally inlaid with gold. The padding is in red velvet.

Photograph Jacqueline Hyde L.K.

48 HELMET ATTRIBUTED TO SOKOLLU MEHMET PAŞA

Turkey, c.1560
Steel, partly inlaid with silver; silver, partly-gilt braid; 44.0; diam. 30.0

Vienna, Kunsthistorisches Museum, Waffensammlung, C 159
Registered in the collection of Schloss Ambras in the Tyrol since 1583

The almost conical, vertically-faceted helmet bowl has a faceted, acorn-shaped tip. It has a rivetted visor, movable nose-guard, flexible neck-guard attached by chain hinges and two flexible ear-guards attached by two red silk straps. The edges of the bowl, visor, ear-guards and neck-guard are reinforced with a rounded, rivetted silver-gilt band.

Part of the bowl and all the attachments are inlaid with gold. Around the apex of the helmet is a band, divided by cartouches, bearing an Arabic inscription. This band is flanked above and below by a festooned border. Another band, also bearing an Arabic inscription in cartouches, encircles the base of the helmet and is surmounted by a festoon of arabesques. The inscription at the apex is a Koranic verse: "Help from God and a speedy victory. So give the Glad Tidings to the Believers!" (Kor. LXI, 13). Around the base is inscribed the verse of the Throne (Kor. II, 256/255).

The attachments are similarly decorated with minute interlacings and several of the "Beautiful names" (*al-Asmā al-Husnā*) of God. The nose-guard, also decorated in gold, is topped by a pointed fretwork oval bearing the word "Allāh" between *rūmī* interlacings. In the centre of each ear-guard is a pointed oval stepped medallion with an arabesque on a fretwork ground. From the ear-guards hang two red and green silk chin-straps. Inside the nose-guard and ear-guards are rivetted red silk pads.

This helmet is said to have belonged to Sokollu Mehmet Paşa, Grand Vizier of Sultan Süleyman, and his successors Selim II and Murad II between 972 and 987 /1565–79.

Bibl.: Sacken, E., 1859–62, vol. II, p. 42, pl. 35; Boeheim, W., 1894, p. 25, pl. 45/1; Luchner, L., 1958, p. 68; Auer, A., 1984, no. 284; Ex Oriente Lux, 1989, p. 721, no. 769; Beaufort, Ch. and Gamber, O., 1990, pp. 210–11, fig. 126

L.K.

49 CEREMONIAL HELMET *ill. page 21*

Turkey, Istanbul, middle or end of the sixteenth century
Steel, inlaid with gold, embossed, engraved, set with rubies, turquoise and amethysts(?); 28.0 x 23.5

Istanbul, Topkapı Sarayı Müzesi, 2/1187

The swelling conical steel skull of the helmet is bell-shaped and fitted with a nose-guard, visor and neck-guard. Narrow gem-encrusted gold bands divide the decoration into sections.

At the base of the bowl, a wide band is decorated with two rows of recriprocal double palmettes, executed in two completely different techniques. One row is made up of *rūmī* motifs and *ḫaṭāyī* flowers, inlaid in gold on a blackened background. The other has applied gold plaques with *ḫaṭāyī* scrolls in relief on a ring-matted ground; alternating turquoise and rubies, set in high, petalled bezels, dominate the overall design.

The same alternating techniques and colours decorate the sides of the helmet. Pointed oval cartouches, polygons and pointed half-ovals are set with rubies and turquoise. Before being fixed to the helmet, the gold plates that comprise these cartouches have been moulded and embossed with scrolling *ḫaṭāyī*; the interstices have been blackened and ornamented with similar motifs set with symmetrically placed gems, smaller than those used on the plates.

The crown of the helmet is made up of a series of vertical panels, each decorated with two gold bands of intersecting clouds on a black background. Above these, further vertical panels are decorated with gold relief floral motifs, inlaid with gems set in lobed mounts; the tip is ornamented with a lavender-coloured stone.

The nasal, decorated with *rūmī* and *ḫaṭāyī* motifs in gold on a black ground, is topped by a large turquoise. The visor, attached with gold rivets, reflects the decoration of the sides of the bowl. The flexible neck-guard is attached by three hinges. It is decorated in a similar style, but there is innovation in the choice of motifs: two sprays of tulips, each with three flowers, are placed symmetrically on either side of a multi-lobed oval medallion which dominates the centre of the neck-guard.

The decorative techniques and motifs used are very similar to those used on the mace in the collection of the Topkapi Palace Treasury[1]. A similarly-shaped helmet, which belonged to the Grand Vizier Mehmed Sokollu Paşa and dates from around 1560, originally in the Schloss Ambras, is in the collection of the Kunsthistorisches Museum, Waffensammlung, in Vienna. (cat no. 48)

1 *cf. no. 52*

Bibl.: Öz, M., n.d., p. 58; Tezçan, T., 1975, p. 22; Közeoğlu, 1987, pl. 37

Photograph Jacqueline Hyde

L.K.

detail

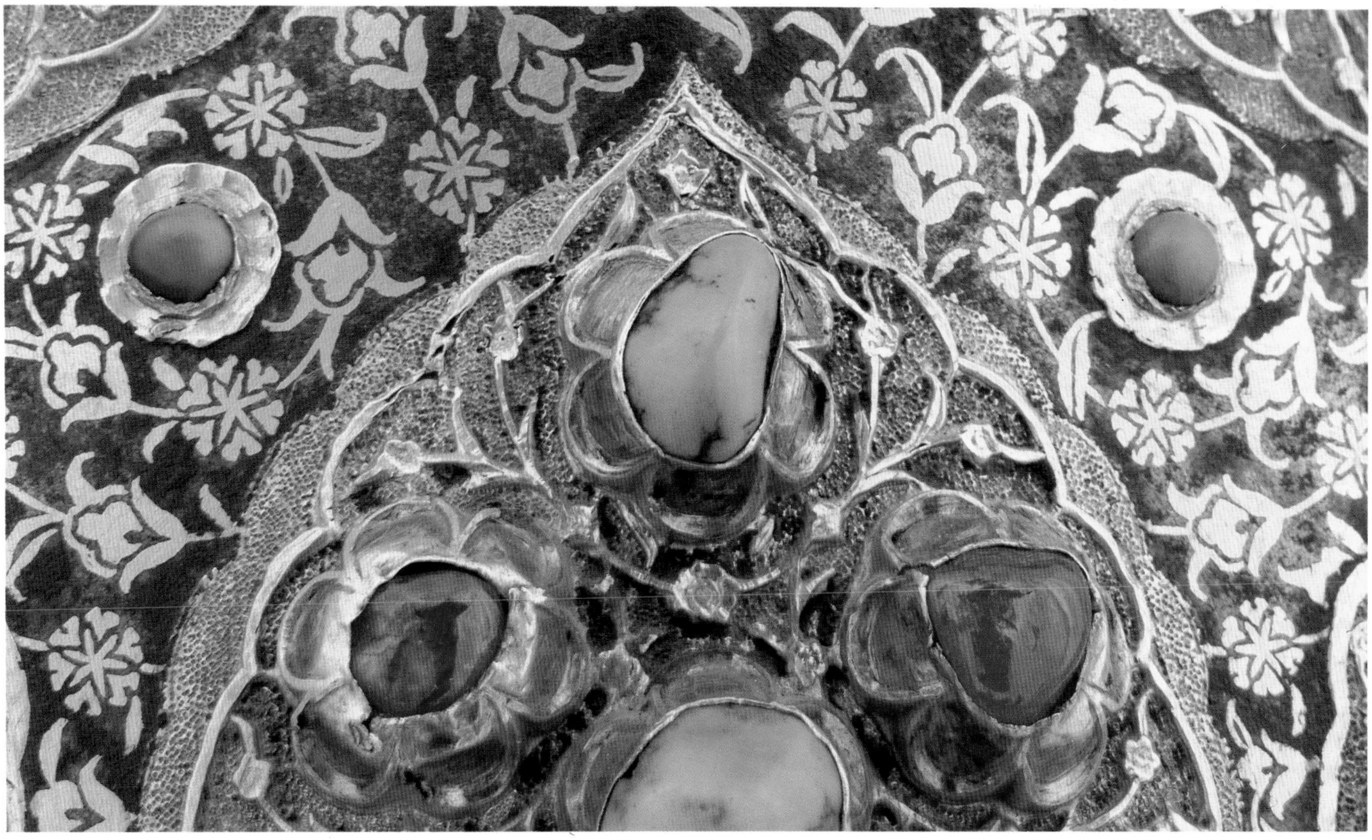

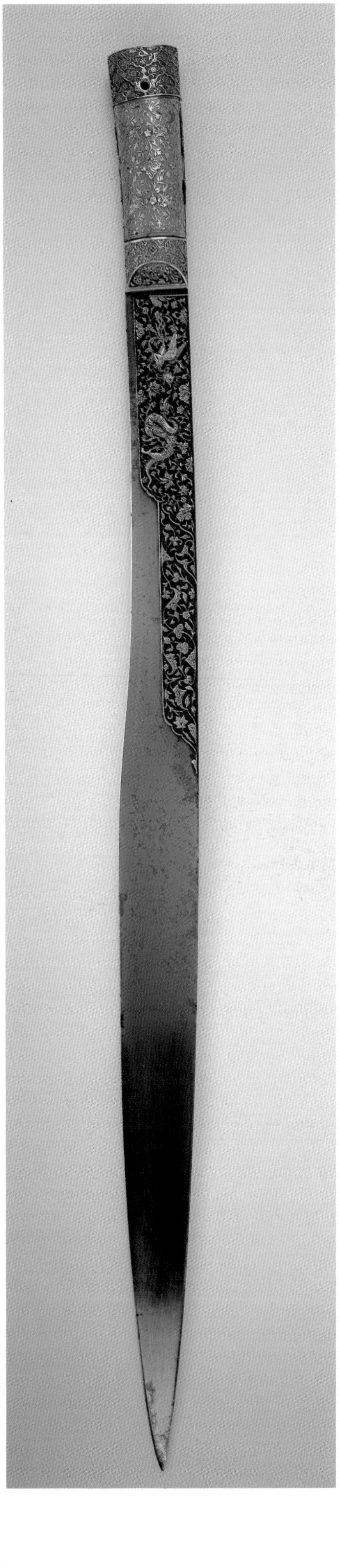

50 YATAGAN

Turkish, Court workshops of Bayazid II, c.1500–10
Total l. 81.2; l. of blade 67.8

Collection Rifaat Sheikh El-Ard, Riyadh

The hilt has a pommel cap of gold, is almost ovular in section and is chiselled and engraved on the top in high relief against a punched ground with a design of cloud bands and *rūmī* arabesque, with details of the latter in silver niello. The sides of the cap are similarly worked with interlocking *rūmī* and *ḫaṭāyī* arabesques. The grip consists of a plaque of ivory fastened to either side of the tang and framed by a shim of gold. The ivory is inlaid in gold on either side in high relief with centrally organised floral forms, the scroll-like detailing of which is carefully delineated by further engraving and chiselling, all against a subsidiary design inlaid in gold with a floral arabesque.

The shim and the ferrule are worked en-suite with the sides of the pommel cap. The long inward-curving blade is inlaid in gold on either side below the hilt with a scaled dragon and phoenix in combat amid *ḫaṭāyī* foliage, characterised by both rounded and spiky petal forms, which entwines the dragons among its tendrils.

The animals are depicted differently on either side; those on the right are worked in a far more sinuous and masterly style; on the left the dragon is formed in a single loop (the same distinction occurs on the blade from the Topkapı — compare no. 51). The fabulous beasts have been constructed in iron covered with gold and then secured by pins to the blade; the teeth of the dragon are in silver and the eyes of the animals are set with tiny rubies. The gold work on all of the animals and leaf forms is further defined by chiselling and engraving. Along the back edge of the blade are four inscriptions, each separated by a flower head.

The inscriptions comprise a diptych in Persian about the quality of the sword and a series of titles in Arabic/Persian including the name of the weapon's owner, which can be read as follows:

For the beg *of time*(?)*, breaker of armies, heavy mace, possessor of sword and standard, Aḥmed ibn harsal*(?) *Ḫān.*[1]

The identity of this individual has not been established but the titles indicate he was a renowned warrior, almost certainly from Eastern Anatolia or Iran.

Long knives or swords with inward-curving blades are often called by the Turkish word *yatagan.* Such blades were used by the ancient Greeks who called them *macheira* or *kopis* and an example of the sixth to fifth century B.C., now in the British Museum, London, shows how little

the form changed over two millennia[2]. Similar blades were also used by the Iberians in the sixth and seventh centuries A.D.[3] The type was adopted by the Turks at an early date as is shown in a Tang painting of the ninth century(?) which depicts a Turkish chieftain wearing a long knife of this form[4].

This *yatagan* and another inscribed with the name and titles of the Ottoman sultan Bayazid II (ruled 1481–1512) are the earliest surviving Islamic examples of this type of weapon. Both are of almost exactly the same proportions and both were probably made by the same smith. But while the former was decorated by an Ottoman calligrapher the latter is worked with an animal-inhabited foliate design in a style whose strength and vitality are typically Iranian and probably Timurid[5]. This style became popular at the Ottoman court during the reign of Meḥmed the Conqueror (ruled 1444–46 and 1451–81) and is often referred to as the *'Baba Nakkaş* style. Its use in a variety of media has been well documented[6] and many of the decorative features found on the blade can be compared to datable examples of the style, such as leaves turned in an almost identical manner on a mosque lamp which was made for Meḥmed II[7].

The same type and combinations of *ḫaṭāyī* foliage with rounded and spiky petals, *rūmī* decoration and cloud bands, as on the blade, occur on ceramics made during the reign of Süleyman's grandfather Bayazid I (1481–1512)[8] and it seems almost certain that the Sheikh El-Ard *yatagan* was also made at this time and must have been a creation by the master of the Imperial design atelier. This master must have been

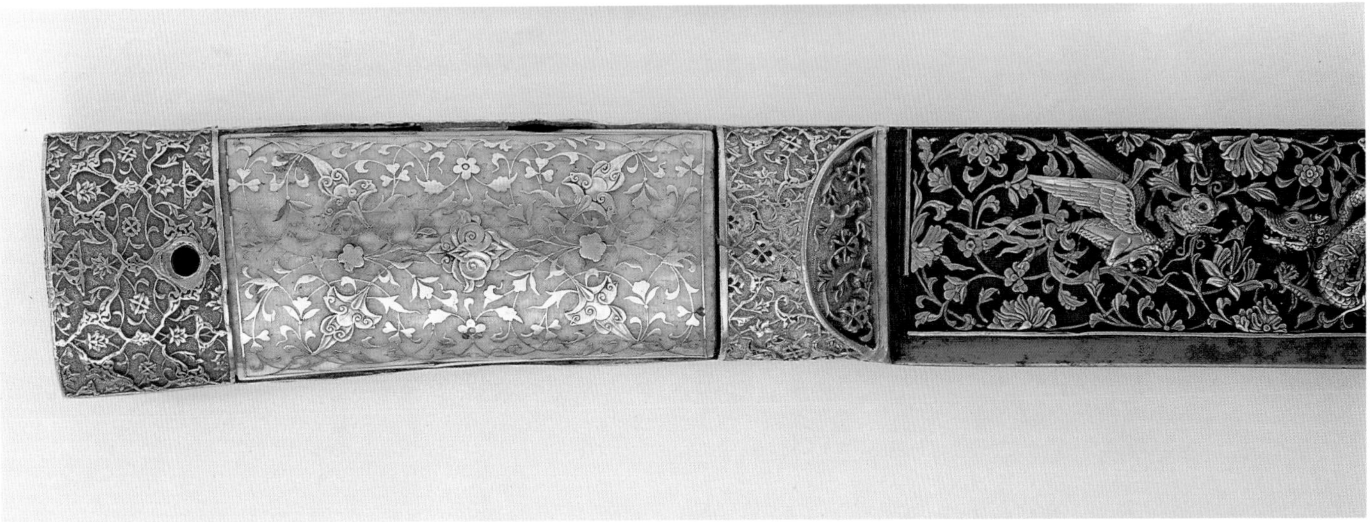

a Timurid craftsman brought to Istanbul either by Mehmed II or by Bayazid II and further research may isolate other of his works and their influence on the development of the Ottoman decorative style.

The decoration on the blade, such as the detailing of the animals and flowers is perhaps even finer than that on the extraordinary example from the Topkapı (compare no. 51) which is dated 1526–27; it is very likely that it provided the prototype for the smaller example. However, the date on the latter is not necessarily that of its manufacture but may instead have been added at the same time as the inscription in the name of Süleyman. The hilt on the Sheikh El-Ard blade is certainly earlier than the one preserved in the Topkapı. By the first quarter of the sixteenth century, Ottoman sword hilts were constructed with rounded pommels (such as on the Topkapı *yatagan*; also compare nos 38 and 39). The Sheikh El-Ard *yatagan*, however, has a hilt in the style commonly found on Ottoman swords and sabres of the fifteenth century (numerous dated examples are illustrated in Alexander and Kalus, *Catalogue of the Swords in the Topkapı Sarayı*, in press).

The style of the decoration and the shape of the hilt suggest, therefore, that this object be dated to the early years of the sixteenth century and certainly before 1526.

In contrast to the Topkapı *yatagan*, this example lacks a dedicatory inscription along its length but it is inscribed in a fine hand along the back edge. These inscriptions probably indicate that the weapon was made as a presentation piece to honour a victorious warrior. The presentation of swords as gifts to loyal and successful soldiers was a normal practice at the Ottoman court and is recorded in Ottoman chronicles and by Europeans such as the seventeenth century French traveller Tavernier. Apparently such gifts generally were returned to the imperial Treasury at the death of the recipient. In the present case the *yatagan* must then have left the Treasury, for according to family tradition it was given early in this century to an American diplomat by the last Ottoman sultan.

1 *The provisional reading of the inscription is by Ludvik Kalus*
2 *Gamber,* Waffe, *1978, fig. 295b*
3 *See, for example, Sandars,* Iberians, *1912, pp. 231–58*
4 *Ettinghausen,* Chinese Representations
5 *Cf., for example, a similar design on a Timurid dagger blade in the Wallace Collection, London, dated 1487, Ill. in Meikian-Chirvani,* Four Pieces, *1976*
6 *Atasoy and Raby,* Iznik, *London, 1989, esp. pls. 59–66*
7 *Atasoy and Raby,* Iznik, *1989, pl. 66a*
8 *Raby,* Iznik, *1989, ch. X, pls. 81–85*

Bibl.: Ettinghausen, R., "Chinese Representations of Central Asian Turks"; Gamber, O., Waffe and Rustung Eurasiens, *Brunswick, 1978; Melikian-Chirvani, A. S., "Four Pieces of Islamic Metalwork" in* Art and Archaeological Research Papers, *London, 1976; Sandars, H., "The Weapons of the Iberians" in* Archaeologia, *vol. 64, 1912, pp. 231–58*

D.A.

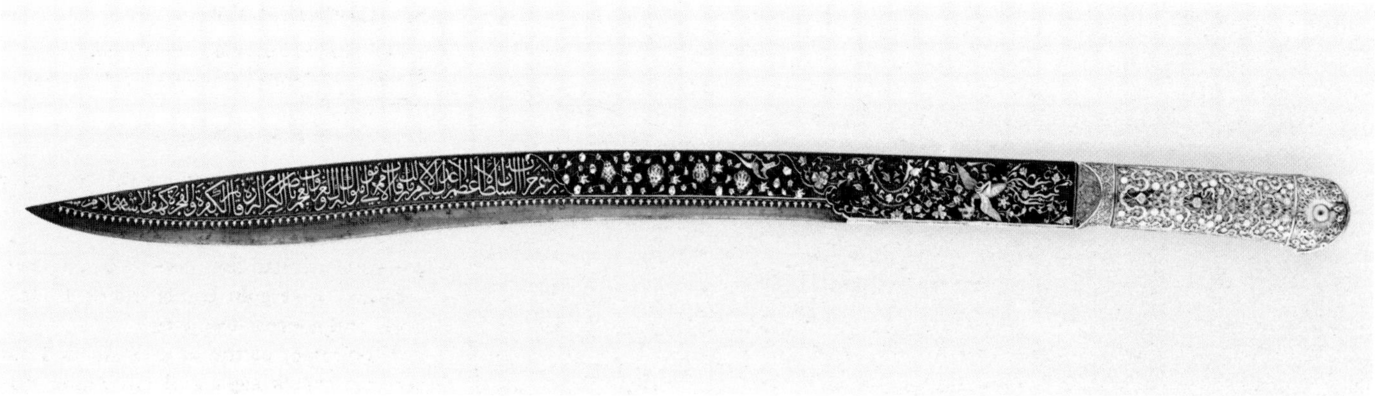

51 YATAGAN, MADE IN THE NAME OF SÜLEYMAN

see also page 23

Turkey, Istanbul, 933/1526–27
Steel blade inlaid with gold, decorated in relief with partially gilded cast steel or iron elements, set with rubies; ivory hilt inlaid with gold and a black material, set with rubies and turquoise; gold guard; l. 66.0

Istanbul, Topkapı Sarayı Müzesi, 2/3776
Treasury of the Topkapı Palace

The slightly curving one-edged blade has a prominent tip and is ornamented similarly on both sides in three distinct parts. The lowest part contains the following Arabic inscription, executed in cursive writing and set in gold. It begins on the left side and continues on the right:
For the Treasury of the very great, the very just, the very honourable Sultan, Sovereign of the nations, master of the kings of the Turks, Arabs and non-Arabs, he who destroys the infidel and the impious, asylum of Islam and Muslims, reflection of God on earth, Abū-l-Ghāzi, sultan son of the sultan, Sultan Süleyman, son of Selim Ḫān, son of Bayazid Ḫān — may he be victorious and his power eternal! — in the year 933/1526–1527.

The decoration of the central section, inlaid with gold, is composed on the left side with an animated scroll with large lion heads and smaller heads of dragons, monkeys, bears and other animals; on the right, the scroll is decorated with *ḫaṭāyī* and *rūmī* motifs. Near the handle a phoenix and a fire-breathing dragon confront each other, against luxuriant and mysterious *ṣāz* vegetation executed in finely engraved relief against a black ground, as on the serpentine body of the dragon. The phoenix and the dragon were cast separately in steel or iron, set with rubies for eyes and fixed to the blade by pins. The scene is reversed on the other side to allow for the inscription and the differences in detail indicate that each was worked separately.

On the spine of the blade is a Persian poetic text, in *nasta'līk*, and the craftsman's signature: "The work of Aḥmed Tekelü".

According to Karabacek, the second part of this name was connected with the Turkish *Teke* tribe, a member of the confederation of the Kizilbaş, established at the beginning of the sixteenth century near Meshed in Iran. This artisan was probably one of the Tabriz artisans taken to Istanbul by Selim in 1514, although his name does not appear in any existing register.

The ivory hilt is ornamented in three layers: first it is engraved with a dense network of floral scrolls, inlaid with a black substance; over this background unfurls a gold arabesque of *ṣāz* leaves and *ḫaṭāyī* flowers; the top layer consists of gold relief cloud bands that create large intertwining and looping volutes.

The slightly rounded pommel, originally set with a gem, is decorated with scrolling flowers inlaid in black, surmounted with gold scrolling *ṣāz* leaves decorated by flowers set with rubies. The gold guard is embossed with *ṣāz* motifs.

The range of materials and diverse techniques combined in a vigorous yet extremely fine ornamentation make this *yatagan* a beautiful example of the art of goldsmithing during the time of Süleyman.

Bibl.: Van Berchem, M., 1912, p. 20, no. XII; Karabacek, J. von., 1913, pp. 29–33, figs 238 and 239 (on the subject of the signatures); Pope, A.U., 1964–65, pl. 1424D; Yücel, Ü., 1964–65; Köseoğlu, C., 1987, pl. 82

Photograph Jacqueline Hyde L.K.

52 CEREMONIAL MACE

Turkey, Istanbul, mid or late sixteenth century
Steel(?) covered in gold leaf and set with rubies and turquoise; l. 72.0

Istanbul, Topkapı Sarayı Müzesi, 2/715

The mace, made of forged steel, comprises a long handle and a spherical, almost pear-shaped head. It is covered in gold leaf panels which had first been fashioned over a mould. Flat gold bands define the sections and conceal the joins.

The surface of the head is divided into vertical panels separated by raised ribs. The panels are decorated with *ḫaṭāyī* motifs intertwining between rubies and turquoise set in wide petal-shaped mounts. The surface of the circular apex is decorated with thin sheets of turquoise in gold in a technique (called *fīrūzekārī*) developed in Iran during the Safavid era. The apex centre is topped with a gold relief flower, originally set with a jewel.

The handle, the surface of which is divided into five zones separated by small rings, is attached to the head of the mace by a moulded band. This band, the rings and the rounded terminal are set with gems.

The four upper zones are sub-divided by slightly raised ribs into vertical panels decorated with *ṣāz* scrolls. The ribs of the lowest zone of the handle are placed diagonally, creating a twisted effect.

The decorative techniques used on this mace are also used on a helmet from the Treasury of the Topkapı Palace[1].

1 cf. no. 49

Photograph Jacqueline Hyde L.K.

53 CAMPAIGN THRONE

Turkey, second half of the sixteenth century
Walnut with ebony veneer, inlaid with ivory, wood, mother-of-pearl, metal and one turquoise; painted on the seat; 129.0 x 163.5 x 75.0

Istanbul, Topkapı Sarayı Müzesi, 2/2879
Used by the Sultan Murad IV (1623–40) during the Baghdad campaign
Treasury of the Topkapı Palace

The rectangular throne consists of five main components — two sides, the back, an ornamental pediment and the seat — originally held together with wooden pins. It rests on four straight legs decorated with movable ivory-inlaid corner-panels.

The extremely delicate decorative motifs are borrowed from contemporary illuminations. On the sides and the back, framed by a wide key-pattern border, are alternating circular and oblong medallions decorated with *rūmī* arabesques. The pediment, the articulated edge of which is carved in the shape of trefoils and half-palmettes, evokes the facade of the Süleymaniye mosque. In the centre, in a large circular medallion inlaid with mother-of-pearl, radiate the shaped lobes of a rose, the heart of which is adorned with a turquoise mounted in a gold bezel. On either side of the central motif, two smaller medallions with trefoil pendants are formed by a play of intertwining circular lines. The rest of the ground is adorned with *çintemani* motifs in which three pearls form a triangle. Scalloped ivory mouldings cover part of the collapsible arm-rests, the ends of which are mounted with ornamental finials, each originally decorated with a turquoise.

On the periphery and on the edge of the different sections of the throne, small geometric medallions of walnut with delicate inlays of wood, ivory and metal alternate; bands of clouds unfurl on the corner-pieces. The seat is decorated with double wavy black lines, called "Tiger stripes", on a yellow ground. The outer faces of the sides and back present a more geometric decoration based on a twelve-pointed star.

Although the Topkapı Palace archives mention that this throne was used by Murad IV (1623–40) during the Baghdad campaign, it was probably made at an earlier date. The decorative vocabulary used — *rūmī* and *çintemani* motifs — and the moderate use of mother-of-pearl relate it to artistic production of the sixteenth century. The piece probably dates from the end of the reign of Süleyman or that of Selīm II. A similar throne is illustrated on a page of the Süleymannāme of Lokmān dated to 1578[1], in which a Persian messenger brings a present to the sultan, who sits on a backed throne with a pediment. Although the arm-rests carry the same adornments, in the miniature the seat rests on a solid base, not on legs.

1 Dublin, Chester Beatty Library 413 f. 14v, illustrated in Minorsky, V., 1958

Bibl.: Arseven, C. E., n.d., fig. 570

Photograph Jacqueline Hyde T.B.

54 ATLAS by ʿAlī Macar Reʾis

Turkey, Şafer 975/August 1567
Watercolour and gold on parchment; binding 30.0 x 21.7; unfolded map 29.2 x 42.7

Istanbul, Library of the Topkapı Sarayı Müzesi, 644 f.4v°–5r°
Topkapı Palace collection

This atlas, executed on parchment, comprises nine pages which include seven geographical maps executed on double pages. In order, the seven maps are:

1 The Black Sea and the Sea of Marmara (f. 1v°–2r°)
2 The Eastern Mediterranean and the Aegean Sea (f. 2v°–3r°)
3 The Central Mediterranean, Italy and the Adriatic Coast (f. 3v°–4r°)
4 The Western Mediterranean (f. 4v°–5r°)
5 Western Europe, Great Britain and Ireland (f. 5v°–6r°)
6 The Aegean Sea and the Sea of Marmara (f. 6v°–7r°)
7 The map of the world (f. 7v°–8r°)

The atlas is bound in brown leather, without a flap. Medallions with a gold ground are embossed on the boards and decorated with *ṣāz* style motifs. The inside of the boards is covered with abrī paper of the sixteenth century. On the inside facing of the cover, the name of the author is given: "bu harita ʿAlī Macar'indir gaflet olunmaya".
The pages shown (2v°-3v°) represent the Eastern Mediterranean Sea and the Aegean including the Sea of Marmara as well as the islands of Crete, Rhodes and The Cyclades.

All the maps in this atlas, other than the map of the world, are coloured in the same way. The coasts are blue and different colours have been used to differentiate the islands. Inland and the seas are not coloured. Navigation lines are traced in red, green and black.

On the continents, the significant towns are shown amid clusters of green trees. The most important represented is the city of Toledo. The names of ports and towns are written, and several places which had significance in Ottoman history and geography are inscribed in Turkish.

The inscriptions on the side of the map show that this atlas was completed in 1567 by ʿAlī Macār, a captain of the Ottoman fleet. Of Hungarian origin, he had settled in Gallipoli as a mercenary. His name appears in a text by Süleyman in 1565[1].

It is likely that the drawing and colouring, of the same type as in Italian or Catalan nautical atlases, were executed by Battista Agnese or Freducci and that only the texts are the work of ʿAlī Macar Reʾis[2]. However, the technique used was not foreign to the palace workshops. The tones

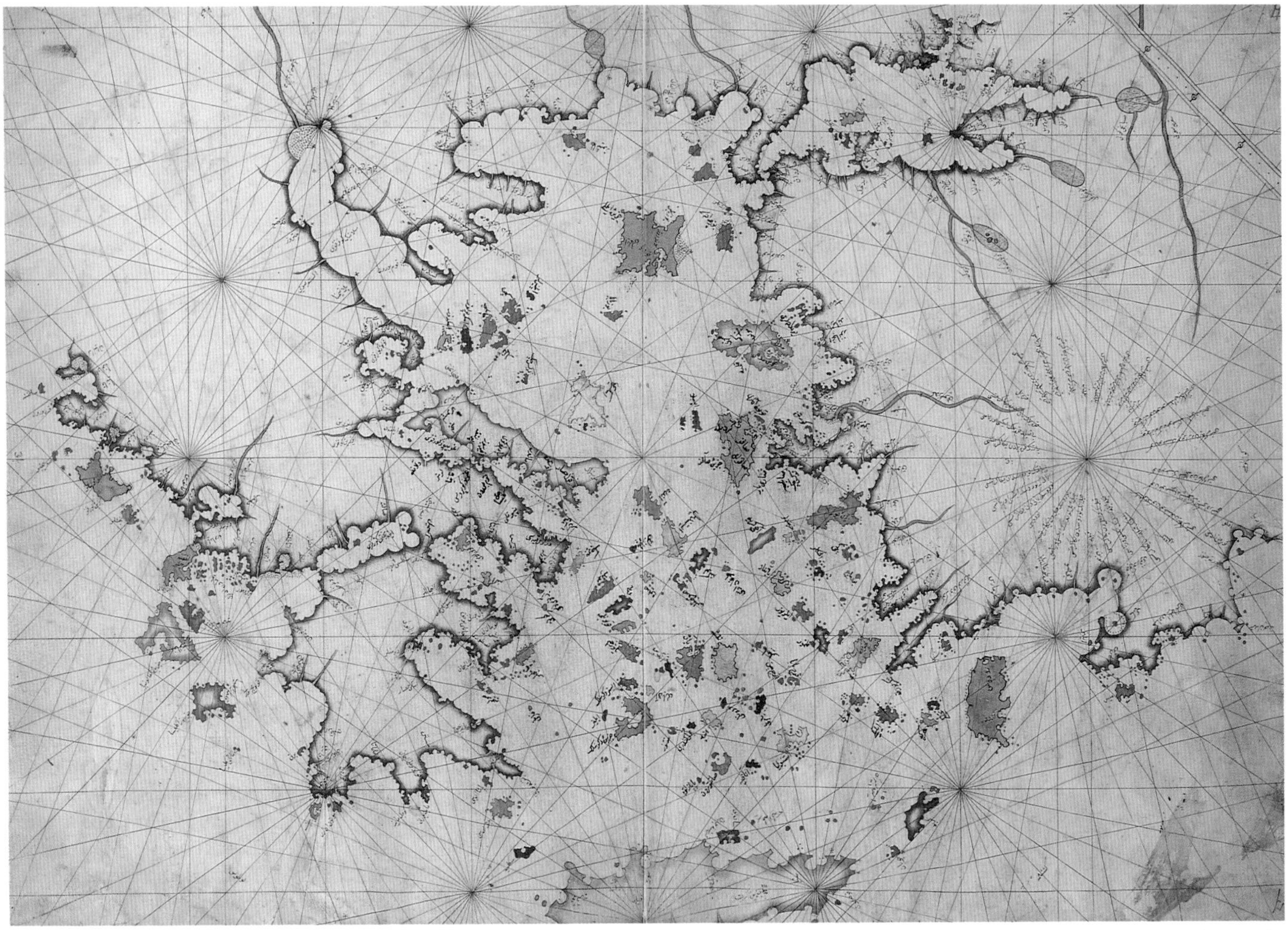

of green, used to represent the cities on the maps, as well as the shading, are very close to the rendering of trees in some miniatures which are found in the *Süleymannāme*, a work written in 1558 by the historian ʿĀrifī[3].

Another important Ottoman atlas, closely related to this one, is in the collection of the Walters Art Gallery of Baltimore. In that atlas some of the representations of cities are identical and may have been executed by the same person[4]. A third, less detailed, atlas is in the library of the Archaeological Museum of Istanbul[5].

In all these atlases, the oval map of the world closely resembles the one executed by Gastfaldi in 1561. The Ottoman sailors who prepared these atlases were therefore closely following European cartography.

1 *Kurtoğlu, 1935, p. 19; Konyali, 1936, pp. 241–42*
2 *Soucek, 1971*
3 *Third miniature of the Süleymannāme (Library of the Topkapı Palace H 1517): Atil, E., 1986, pp. 98–99*
4 *The Baltimore Atlas is discussed in Renda, G., "The Atlas of ʿAlī Macar, and the others",* Communication to the symposium Mimar Sinan, Association for Turkish language and history, *Ankara, 1988*
5 *Goodrich, 1987*
6 *Goodrich, 1987, pp. 91–92; Goodrich, 1987a, p. 99*

Bibl.: Kurtoğlu, 1935; Konyali, 1936, fig. 5; Karatay, in Turkish, no. 1410; Van de Waal, 1969, fig. 23; Soucek, 1971; Goodrich, 1987, p. 86 v.d.

Photograph Jacqueline Hyde F.Ç.

55 THE PORT OF MODON

Turkey, c.1540
Ink, opaque colours, silver and gold on filigreed prepared paper; miniatures 17.0 x 25.3; pages 26.7 x 25.3

Istanbul, Topkapı Sarayı Müzesi, R 1272 f. 24v°–25r°
Topkapı Palace collection, from the library founded in the pavilion of Revan. Stamp of the foundation of Sultan Mehmed I.

This work comprises 82 pages of 13 lines each, written in the *naskhī* style.

The *cedvel* are gilded and outlined in blue with the titles in red. The first pages are illuminated but unadorned. The cover with flap is original, of claret-coloured leather. The medallions and corner-pieces on a gold background are ornamented with Chinese clouds and various *ṣāz* style motifs.

The work includes representations of the towns of Navarin, Coron, Modon, Lepanto, Guler, Akerman and Kili, conquered during the reign of Bayazid II (1481–1512). There is also a miniature of a line of boats on the open sea at Modon. No human figures are represented.

It is now known that the calligrapher of this work, Maṭrāḳçi Naṣūḥ, also executed the illustrations.

The two pages shown represent the port town of Modon and its fortress, conquered on 10 August 1500. This fortress, south-west of Morea, is drawn in a realistic and detailed fashion, clearly indicating the position of the walls, towers and battlements. In the foreground opposite the fortress are the galleons of the Ottoman fleet; on the other side in the background are the Venetian boats.

The fortress and the buildings are very lightly coloured, the roofs generally painted in shades of maroon and red. The roof of the basilica on the port is painted in blue and filigreed.

The most prominent touches of colour in the miniature are the boats with their black hulls, the large white sails, red oars, flags and the silver sea. The skilful placement of the boats gives perspective to the picture.

Another depiction of Modon, housed in the Landesmuseum für Geschichte,

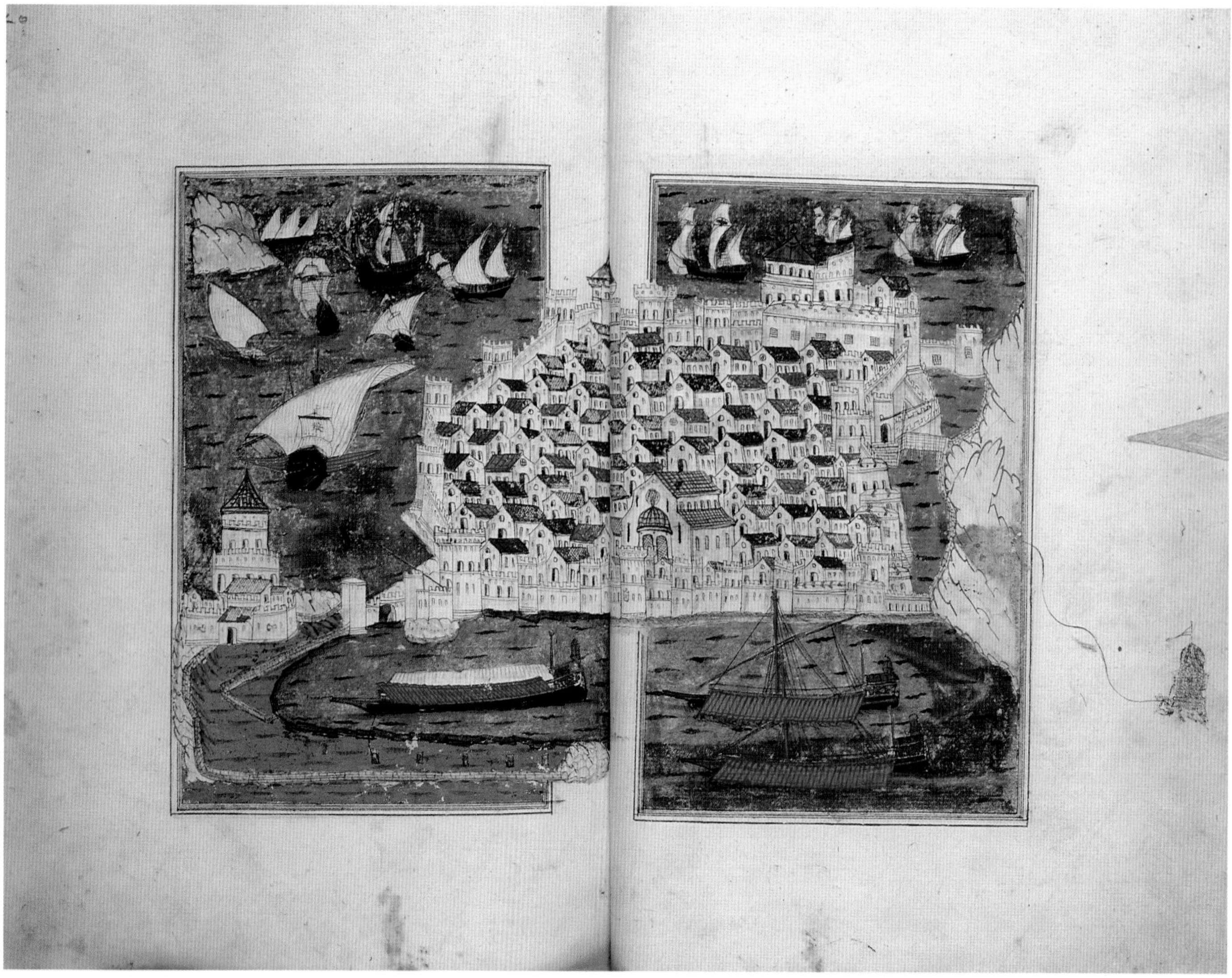

55

Dresden (E 391a), and formerly attributed to Kemal Paşazade but now acknowledged as the work of Maṭrākçi Naṣūḥ, could easily be mistaken for this work[1]. The only differences are that in the Dresden work there are no gilded *cedvel* outlined in blue; the sea and the earth surrounding the fortress are not coloured and there are no boats at sea. On the other hand, the fortress and buildings it protects are drawn in greater detail. The basilica situated by the port has a minaret[2].

It appears that the picture of the fortress of Modon housed at Dresden was a preparatory study for the final work, and that it was inserted into part of the work concerning fortresses[3]. Furthermore, the fact that the seas which have not been coloured are noted as *derya* (the sea) supports this theory.

It would be quite unusual that in a miniature of the capture of Modon, executed retrospectively, the basilica would have a minaret. In the present example, the absence of the minaret is due to a desire on the part of the artist to remain true to history by representing Modon exactly as it appeared during the battle for its capture.

1 Ugur, 1977; Çağman, 1980, p. 225
2 Rührdanz, 1988, pl. 4
3 Berlin, 1984, p. 127

Bibl.: Karatay (in Turkish) no. 624; Yardaydin, 1963, figs 41–48, 1964, figs 5–6; Akalay, 1969, figs 7–10; Reindl, 1974, figs 1–3; Çağman, Tanindi, 1986, pls 145–46

Photograph Jacqueline Hyde F.Ç.

56 THE PORT OF LEPANTO (INEBAHTI)

Turkey, c. 1540–50
Opaque pigments on paper; 57.5 x 75.5

Istanbul, Topkapı Sarayı Müzesi, 17/378
Topkapı Palace collection

The strategic Port of Lepanto, in the Gulf of Corinth in Greece, was conquered by the Ottomans in 1499 during the reign of Sultan Bayazid II.

This large painting, a topographical representation of the town, is a beautiful example of the paintings of towns executed by the Ottomans for documentary purposes. The date is not known, but according to information given by Evliya Çelebi on the position of Lepanto in the seventeenth century, the inscriptions, the types of buildings and the style indicate that it was executed towards the middle of the sixteenth century[1].

To the left of the fortified port, which faces onto the gulf, is the *hassahane* (hassa: the house of the sovereign); and on the right is the mosque of Fāthiyi, built by Bayazid II and also mentioned by Evliya Çelebi.

Right behind the port are two Turkish baths and a fountain. Towards the upper part of the city is the place where the Imperial music (*Mehter*) was played, and further up is the citadel. All these details are indicated by the captions which form part of the design.

The walls are surrounded by a water-filled moat. To the left, in front of the gate of Yeniburgaz, one can see a person holding a falcon, and above him a *janissary* drawing a bow and arrow. In front of the gate on the right of the wall another *janissary* holds a gun.

56

The inscriptions indicate that the group of red houses to the left of the walls is the Aksolfi quarter. Still on the left hand side, beyond the two walls of the gulf, it is inscribed that the fortresses were built by Kasim Bey and that they house the provincial guards. On the dwellings to the right of the city, one can read "houses of the Ṣūfī (mystic)". To their right is the small mosque of Şeyḫ Endere.

On the right side of the drawing are canals, dams and mills constructed by Muṣṭafā Paşa, Governor-General of Roumelie, who played a key role in the conquest of Lepanto. In the same section stands out the little monastery of Aylaku Ḥasan Paşa. Between this and the walls are vines, the mill of the *hassa* and tanneries.

Kasim Bey, who is mentioned in the text, was a vizier during the time of Süleyman. He was third vizier in the campaign of Iraq in 1535 and was subsequently made governor of Morea. He left the post in 1541. It was Kasim Bey who constructed the fortresses along the straits of Corinth.

This drawing, of such great documentary interest, was probably executed during the time when Kasim Paşa was about to leave Morea.[2]

It is understandable that this painting, which served as a topographic plan, should later have been partly restored and repainted.

1 *The Guide of Evliya Çelebi: Vol XVIII, Istanbul, 1928, p. 612 ff.*

2 *Encyclopedia of Islam "Kasimpacha (Gezelce)"; vol. 6, pp. 386–87*

Photograph Jacqueline Hyde F.Ç.

57 THE DEATH OF HÜSAYN PAŞA

from the *Süleymannâme* by 'Ārifī (died 1561–62)

Turkey, 965/1558
Opaque colours, gold and silver on prepared paper; page 36.8 x 26.0; miniature 23.0 x 14.7

Istanbul, Topkapı Sarayı Müzesi Library, H 1517, f. 235 r°
Treasury of the Topkapı Palace

Fāthullāh 'Ārif Çelebi, who was named historiographer of the palace, an official posting in Süleyman's time, wrote under the name of 'Ārifī. This miniature is part of his work, the Süleymannâme, which relates the events between 1520 (date of the accession of the sultan to the throne) and 1558.

This book, a representative example of the art of the book from the workshops of the Ottoman court, contains 617 pages; each page carries 15 lines of *nasta'līk* calligraphy in four columns.

The frontispiece (f. 2v°-3r°) and the presentation pages on which the genealogical tree and the sultan's titles are recorded (f. 1v°-2v°) are among the most prestigious examples of Ottoman illumination, certainly created by the artist Ḳaramemī, who was the *naḳḳaşbaşī* (head painter).

The beginnings of the chapters and some blank triangular parts of the pages are very elegantly illuminated; the *cedvel* are gold. The introductions of chapters are written with a ruby-red ink. On the colophon of the book it says that the calligraphy was finished in the middle of the *Ramaḍān* 965/1557 (f. 617v°) by 'Alī b Amīr Beg Ṣīrvānī. The work has a remarkable black leather binding with, on its medallions, its corner-pieces and its wide borders, motifs in the *ṣāz* style in many shades of gold. It contains 69 miniatures explaining and illustrating the texts; they were created by a team of decorative painters (*nakkaş*) of the palace.

Their varied style reflects the heterogeneity of the Palace *nakkaşhane*. The miniature exhibited illustrates an episode of the repression of the revolts in Anatolia. Ḥüsayn Paşa, Governor of Sivas, first gained a victory over the rebels on 26 September 1526 at Hoyoklu. The rebels, after their chief Zunnun Baba died, carried out a surprise counter-attack during which Ḥüsayn Paşa was mortally wounded.

Ḥüsayn Paşa is represented as he lies dying, his head on the lap of Khusrev Paşa, the prefect of Dyarbakir, who is seated beneath a gnarled tree. Around them are two guards (*peyks*) watching the event, as well as the bodies of those who died during the attack.

Ḥüsayn Paşa and Khusrev Paşa's horsemen, in line on either side of the composition, contemplate this event. Behind the hill, facing one another, are the horsemen carrying the banners and the instruments for Imperial music (*Mehter*).

The grand tree which forms the central axis of this more or less symmetrical composition comes from a *mise en page* style used as well in the work called *Futūḥat-i Jamīla*, and in particular in the miniature representing the headquarters during the siege of Temesvar (Timisoara) (compare no. 59) where the essential characters of the subject stand out.

The Süleymannâme miniatures often feature compositions where the motif of the tree magnifies the principal theme by delineating a central axis.

As well, in some Iranian calligraphic works, especially in those of Firdawsī and Niẓāmī, are often found miniatures representing the death of Dara (Darius) in the lap of Iskender (Alexander). The iconographical resemblance is undeniable. In the exhibited miniature all the colours are enhanced against the brilliant blue of the background and the gold of the sky. It was executed by an artist whose brushstroke is delicate and refined. His name unfortunately is unknown.

Bibl.: Ögümen, 1966, pp. 26–27; Çağman, 1986, p. 12; Atil, 1986, pl. 21 (of the work); Karatay, F. E., no. 160; Stchoukine, 1966, pp. 59, 111–13, pls XIX–XXII; Atasoy, 1970; Akalay, 1970; Sohrweide, 1971; Atasoy-Çağman, pp. 28–29, pls 7–9; Feher, 1976, pls VII–XII, XIV, XVII, XVIII, XXII, XXXI, XXXV; Çağman, 1980, p. 225, figs 162–64; Akalav, 1976, pp. 14–23; Akalav, 1978; Atil, 1980, ills 80–83; Atil, 1986; Çağman-Tanindi, 1986, pls 152–54; Renda, 1987, pls 3–10

Photograph Jacqueline Hyde F.Ç.

58 SÜLEYMAN RECEIVES HAYREDDIN BARBAROSSA PAŞA

Süleymannāme of Ārifī
Turkey 965/1558
Opaque colours, gold and silver on prepared paper; page 36.8 x 26.0; miniature 26.0 x 14.5

Istanbul, Topkapı Sarayı Müzesi Library, H 1517; p. 360
Treasury of the Topkapı Palace

This page is part of the Süleymannāme of "Arif Çelebi the Şehnameçi", the historiographer of the palace who used the pseudonym "Ārifī". Upon Süleyman's invitation the lord of Algeria, Barbarossa, arrived in the port of Istanbul with his fleet on 27 May 1533. He moored and brought as gifts hundreds of slaves and captive women, gold and silver objects, jewellery and silk fabrics, laden on 100 camels and several animals from Africa. The next day he was received at the palace by Süleyman. Barbarossa and his captains were wearing the *ḫil'at* (a valuable fur coat given by the sultans as a mark of distinction). Barbarossa then asked for the ratification of the binding of Algiers to the empire, although it had in fact already been in the sphere of Ottoman domination since Sultan Selim. Süleyman accepted this important gift and nominated Barbarossa Beylerbey of Algeria, which then became an Ottoman province. On 6 April 1534, Barbarossa became grand admiral, Kaputan Paşa, of the Ottoman war fleet.

The miniature exhibited here represents the interview at the palace between Süleyman and Barbarossa. The sultan is seated on a gold throne set in precious stones. In front of him Barbarossa, also seated, has white hair and a white beard. He is already old. Behind the Sultan and Barbarossa are the *ağa* of the private chambers, Hasoda.

The welcoming ceremony is represented in a portico with coloured marble columns. The verandah opens onto a garden where different kinds of trees can be seen. This garden is separated from the following courtyard by a door framed with white-veined marble columns and high walls. At the door and all around it, the "*ağa* of the door" (*Kapi ağalari*) wait in little groups. The site where the action takes place could be the court-room or the Hasoda portico overlooking the Golden Horn, which, according to Gunay, were called Dīvānhane in the sixteenth century.

This composition, in which horizontal and vertical lines balance one another and the pictorial technique (delicacy of detail and good distribution of colour) is harmonious, is a total success. The miniature, which serves as a prelude to the classical period of Turkish miniature painting (the second half of the sixteenth century) is also of great historical interest.

1 *Recalling Dīvānhane the* taslik *of the Hasoda, see Necipoğlu: Kafadar, 1986, pp. 395–428; to determine the locality, see Gunay, 1987, pp. 80–81*

Photograph Jacqueline Hyde F.Ç.

بزیر سپهبد بغلطید اسب زمین شد ز خون خوان آذرگشسب
جدا شد ز زین نامدار بلند ولی بر وجودش نیامد گزند

59 SIEGE OF THE FORTRESS OF TEMESVAR (TIMISOARA)

Futūḥat-i-Jamīla

Turkey, 964/1557
Opaque colours, gold and silver on light beige prepared paper; page 33.0 x 22.7; miniature 28.7 x 18.3

Istanbul, Library of the Topkapı Sarayı Müzesi H 1597, f. 18v°-19r°
Treasury of the Topkapı Palace
A seal on the 1r° folio shows that the work belonged to Sokollu Mehmed Paşa; on folio 7r° is affixed the seal of Sultan Ahmed III, dated 1703.

facing pages of manuscript, see also page 24

In 1551, while the Ottoman's powerful forces were campaigning in Iran, another army, commanded by Sokollu Mehmed Paşa, Beylerbey of Rumeli, was given the task of solving the problem of "Erdel". After having succeeded in seizing the fortresses of Beese, Becskerek, Csanad and Lipp, Sokollu beseiged Temesvar; but winter was coming and the Ottoman army had to retire. After Lipp was recaptured by the enemy, the second vizier, Ḳara Ahmed Paşa, was charged in 1552 with reconquering the region. With the help of Sokollu Mehmed Paşa, Lipp and Temesvar were conquered and the whole region passed into the hands of the Ottomans.

The manuscript deals mainly with the events of 1551-52. It is mostly Sokollu Mehmed Paşa's role and deeds which are described here. The text is in Persian in the *mesnevi* form. On the first page (f. 1r°) is the title: *Futūḥat-i-Jamīla*. Certain passages are identical to the *Sūleymanname* of ʿĀrifī, the historiographer of the palace, notably the one of the siege of Temesvar, but with more details. The manuscript, which is of undeniable historical value, was certainly written by ʿĀrifī. It comprises 30 pages of 12 lines, disposed into four columns and inscribed in *nasta'lik*. The work is ornamented with a total of seven miniatures.

The frontispiece is illuminated, the *cedvel* are gilt, the titles are coloured in blue, and inscribed by Abū Turāb Şah Abū Turab al-Ḥasanı al Ḥusaynī, known under the name of Hobi of Shiraz, at the end of the *Ramaḍān* of 964 (July 1559). The flap binding is authentic. The dark cherry-red leather boards carry a medallion and four embossed corner-pieces ornamented with *ṣāz* style leaves and flowers, on a gilt ground. The linings are in leather, light brown and ornamented with an oval medallion and little engraved corner-pieces.

The seal on the first page is dated 972 /1565. It contains commendations and he was probably made for Sokollu the year became prime minister[1].

The siege of Temesvar is represented on the exhibited miniatures. On the right (f. 18v°) can be seen, among others, the tent of Ahmed Paşa, who commanded the army. There are sentries around the main tent and behind the hill, facing each other, are groups of *sipahis* waiting to go into battle. All these characters are integrated in a representation of a seemingly peaceful headquarters. The colour of the ground, a very pale pink, and the tree placed at the top of the hill define the main axis and highlight Ahmed Paşa's empty display tent which is placed in the middle of the drawing.

On the left (f. 19r°) appears the fortress of Temesvar with its buildings, inside fortifications, towers and walls surrounded by trenches drawn in detail. At the bottom of the miniature, the incident which is the subject of the composition is represented in a realistic way. Cannon-fire from the fortress has shot off the head of Ahmed Paşa's horse. The second vizier, bow in hand, is facing the soldiers who are bringing him another mount. Beneath this scene, a soldier fights with the enemy. The background of this part is coloured in pale pink to distinguish it from the green area surrounding the fortress.

The same scene is illustrated in the *Süleymannāme* of ʿĀrifī[2]. In that version the fortress of Temesvar and the events which occur in front of it are illustrated with no background differences. On both miniatures are the same number of characters, but they face in different directions

In this *Süleymannāme* the accent is on the horse's decapitation; the fortress is seen from another angle and drawn in less detail. Nevertheless, the style is very similar on both miniatures, which must have been painted by the same artist. The precise detailing of the miniature exhibited reflects the topographical and documentary approach which characterises Ottoman pictorial art.

1 *There is no name on the seal. The only date is that of the year Sokollu Mehmed Paşa became* viziriazumm *972/1565. An undated seal of Sokollu Mehmed Paşa before he became* Sadruzam *(grand vizier) has been discovered in the archives at the Palace of Topkapı (E5484). The two seals are very alike in their form and in the praises they contain.*
2 *See Atil, 1986, pl. 55*

Bibl.: Karatay, F. E., no. 164; Atasoy, N., Çağman F., 1924, pp. 29-30, pl. 10; Fener, 1976, pls XXIX-XXXIV V° XXXVI; Çağman, F., Tanindi, Z., 1979, no. 147; Atil, E., 1986, figs 37-38; Çağman, F., Tanindi, Z., 1986, pl. 151

Photograph Jacqueline Hyde

F.Ç.

SÜLEYMAN THE MAGNIFICENT

The epithet "magnificent", attached since the sixteenth century by the Italians and the French to the name of Süleyman, echoes the ostentation of the Sultan's court and the grandeur of Istanbul. The sixteenth century represented the apogee of Ottoman civilisation, doubtless due to economic factors and to the exceptional personality of the sovereigns, Süleyman in particular.

Sultan Süleyman, extraordinary administrator, great conqueror, defender of the faith, was also a patron of the arts and a collector. Among other things he enriched the collection of Chinese porcelain started by the sultans at the end of the fifteenth century and which had grown considerably after 1514 with the addition of spoils taken by Selim I during the sack of Tabriz. These porcelains were a source of inspiration for the Iznik potters in the first quarter of the sixteenth century; but some of them, especially the delicate pure-white Ming pieces, were highlighted by the jewellers of the Royal Palace with gold networks punctuated with precious stones.

In the precinct of the Topkapı Sarayı were workshops of artisans recruited for their skills. They were trained in Turkey or brought from elsewhere as conquests progressed. The workshops were closely supervised and employed artists who had been strictly graded and who were paid according to a system of daily salaries known to us from the records of the palace archives. They received an extra salary for work done for the sultan and were provided with the raw material which the Treasury stored in great quantity. It was traditional for the sultans to learn a manual skill. Süleyman was trained in the art of jewellery-making; he was also an accomplished poet who wrote in Persian and in Turkish under the pseudonym "Muḥibbī", and many members of his entourage shared his taste for poetry and beautiful manuscripts.

Among all these workshops, the one concerned with the art of the book, the Imperial painting studio, the *nakkaşhane*, was undoubtedly the most important. It was established during the reign of Bayazid II and welcomed, after 1514, artists brought from Tabriz by Selim I (some of whom had formerly worked in the Herat Court). In the workshop, Iranians, rather than artists from Anatolia and the western provinces, played a predominant role until about 1560. This explains the importance of the Timurid and Safavid contributions to the art of book-binding and illumination, drawing and miniature. Most motifs and ornaments sprang from the *nakkaşhane*, which allowed considerable latitude to the painter's creativity. Then the different trades adapted motifs to their own needs and techniques and thus created the particular style of the period.

Among the styles popular in the sixteenth century, the *ḫaṭāyī* decorative repertory, derived from Chinese models, should be distinguished from the *rūmī* repertory, drawn from the palmette and arabesque; but the two styles are often found intermingled on the same object. In addition to the completely Chinese-influenced motifs — tchi (clouds), çintemani (a group of three sequins arranged in a triangle, with two undulating lines) — the elements used were usually derived from plant forms (stylized, naturalistic and imaginary), occasionally gathered in particular patterns as in the "four flowers motif" or the *ṣāz* design, which was brought into fashion by the painter, Şahkulū, around 1530.

The great manuscripts of the history of the reign were illuminated in the *nakkaşhane*, as were the sumptuous Korans, some with calligraphy by the celebrated Ḳaraḥiṣārī: literary works with exquisite illuminations and deliciously fresh miniatures. Many calligraphers worked for the chancellery, specialising in the drawing up of imperial *fermans*, written in *divani* script, to which the majestic imperial *tuğra* was affixed.

The precinct of the Topkapı Sarayı also included the jeweller's workshops. Many of the most beautiful objects preserved in the Treasury of Topkapı Sarayı were created there. Most are in jade with a colour ranging from black to white in rock crystal, gold or zinc, enhanced with precious stones and varying in shape. Their shapes repeat those of Timurid, Iranian or Syrian models of the sixteenth century, or even Western forms. Their elaborate decorations show the extraordinary technical virtuosity of the court jewellers. The background materials are covered by a fine network traced by narrow gold threads, not twisted, as has often been said, but in fact very finely notched and inlaid in relief, a technique which sometimes creates a contrast, on the same object, with the ordinary technique of inlay which leaves the surface smooth. The network is dotted with flowers made from precious stones set in bezels and mounted on gold corollas with lobed petals. Many other decorative techniques are often found on the same object.

The sixteenth century marks the golden age of production at the Iznik workshop. Wall tiles played an important role because they enhanced with colour many of the architect Sinan's great creations, thus establishing a chronological foundation for the study of the various styles. From the end of the fifteenth century, the potters perfected a technique which gives objects a remarkably white and shiny appearance. The range of colours, first limited to blue and white on large objects, is associated with stylized motifs made of angularly outlined florets, of *rūmī* and *ḫaṭāyī* motifs and of interlacings taking the shape of knots. It was enriched with turquoise blue and then with soft shades which are combined in delicate harmonies in large compositions, often in the *ṣāz* style: deep blue, turquoise blue, lime green, grey and mauve. Finally, towards 1555, red was added to the existing range of colours.

Another important industry developed in the sixteenth century in Turkey and enjoyed an increasing success: textiles. Its principal centres were Bursa and Istanbul. Before the culture of silk worms in the Bursa region, silk had long been imported from Iran. Imperial edicts regulated the production of silk and the weight of the threads, the fabrics and their price. Besides textiles for ordinary use, the main luxury products were silk fabrics, particularly lampas and velvet, enriched with gold and silver threads, with plant motifs, often against a red background, their monumental size emphasised by the simple cut of the kaftans men and women wore over their other clothes.

Decorations changed with fashion and were related to the other decorative techniques of the time; the most common composition, from the second quarter of the sixteenth century, was a network of almond shapes ultimately derived from imported Chinese models or Egyptian Mamluk models of the fourteenth century. In addition, a number of fabrics were patterned with waving stems from which sprang forth, in undulating curves and counter-curves, tulips, hyacinths and pomegranates giving the rather stiff garments a sense of flexibility and movement. The motifs, on a large scale, seem upon close attention to be in continual metamorphosis because of the unceasing movement of the lines and of the work which, like chasing, underlines each element with a different colour, transforming the *mandorla* into lotus flowers with dishevelled petals, or animating the inside of a pomegranate decoration or other motifs with tiny bouquets.

M.B.T.

61 PLATE WITH PEONIES

Turkey, Isnik, c.1520–35
Fritware with underglaze decoration over a white slip; 9.4 x 36.5

Istanbul, Arkeoloji Müzesi Çinili Kösk, 41/155
Transferred to the Yildiz Palace, 1912

This plate faithfully reproduces a Chinese Ming dynasty prototype: a foliate rim plate, the cavetto moulded in a series of gadroons and entirely decorated with patterns of foliage and floral bouquets[1]. For example, the way the three bands of parallel lines which divide the composition scrupulously follow the outline of the foliate rim, and the alignment of the motifs, are according to the rules of Chinese composition, rarely respected by the Ottoman potters. Similarly the large blooms scrolling around a central peony, the bouquets in the cavetto and the undulating border scroll of lotus, peonies and pomegranates are very close to their models. The only digression the artist has allowed himself is the division into 13 panels instead of 12.

1 *For example, pieces belonging to Ardebil Shrine in Pope, J. A., 1956, pls 34, 35, 36*

Bibl.: Soustiel, J., 1985, no. 373

Photograph Jacqueline Hyde G.J.

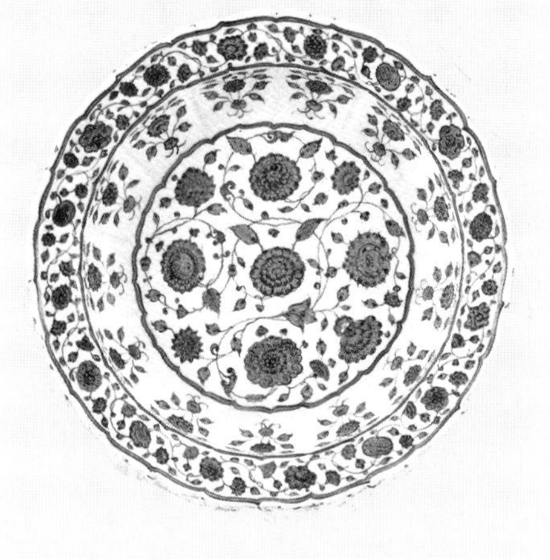

60 PLATE WITH ARABESQUE DECORATION

Turkey, Isnik, 1510–20
Fritware painted over slip under a lead glaze; 8.0 x 44.2

Paris, Musée du Louvre, Islamic section, 7449
Bequest of Baroness Delort de Gleon, 1914

This deep dish with a wide, slightly inclined rim, as with the lamp (no. 19) belongs to a group of Iznik ceramics produced during the first quarter of the sixteenth century, in which the white surfaces harmoniously alternate with the blue-painted surfaces on which the reserve decoration is emphasised by the deep-blue underlining. In this decoration, motifs used at the end of the fifteenth century — interlacings of leaves carrying half-palmettes, simple or bifurcated, and oriental floral scrolls of *rūmī-ḫaṭāyī* style — are mixed with new elements such as the festooned cloud which is derived from Chinese clouds[1].

The round medallion which decorates the centre is ornamented by arabesques with crescent clouds, or with inter-twining palmettes, which form a rigorously axial cruciform. The cavetto is not decorated. On the rim, between two thin blue lines, four blue panels with floral scrolls alternate with four white panels, decorated with a rosette in an oval vegetal medallion as well as two triangular florets.

The reverse side of the cavetto is adorned with a floral scroll similar in style to the one on the rim.

Although some plates have the same imposing size, tones of blue, style and skilful decoration[2], these marvellous pieces are rare.

1 *This motif, used frequently in the international Timurid style in the sixteenth century, only came into the Ottoman decorative vocabulary at this time. Brilliantly developed, it can be found on a variety of objects such as bookbindings and carpets.*
2 *Cf. Victoria and Albert Museum, London (inv. 986–1884), Arkeologi Müzesi of Bursa (inv. 814) or Çinili Köşk, Istanbul (inv. 41)*

Bibl.: Migeon, G., 1922, vol. II, no. 205; Atasoy, N. and Raby, J., 1989, no. 83

Photograph Jacqueline Hyde M.C.

62 MONOCHROME PLATE WITH MOULDED DECORATION

Turkey, Iznik, c.1535–55
Fritware ceramic with moulded decoration under a lead glaze; 9.0 x 42.5

Istanbul, Library of the Topkapı Sarayı Müzesi, 15/6086
Topkapı Palace collection

Monochrome Ottoman ceramics are rare, and this plate, with a moulded relief decoration covered with a pale grey-green glaze, is unique. Nevertheless, white Chinese porcelain, and celadons with incised designs, were greatly appreciated in the Ottoman court, as proven by the collection of the sultans in the Topkapı Sarayı Müzesi. This predilection for celadons, already established in the Islamic world, particularly at the court in Cairo, is thought to be related to their supposed ability to expose poisoned food by changing colour, or even breaking, upon contact with poison.

But the rarity of these locally produced monochrome pieces also demonstrates the Ottoman preference for polychrome decoration as illustrated in this exhibition. There are documents, however, attesting to the local manufacture of monochrome imitation celadons, but their quality did not reach a standard high enough to interest the court, and hence their disappearance. The recent discovery[1] of this plate in the basement of the Topkapı Palace enables us to fill this gap.

A graceful scroll of half-palmettes runs along the rim, following the foliated edge. In the centre, the radiating design is set in a hexagonal medallion recalling the shape of a tile. It is possible that this composition was traced from a pattern originally conceived for a hexagonal tile[2] and used indiscriminately on both types of objects. A plate housed in the British Museum in London[3], ornamented with the same design of poly-lobed medallions and lotuses around a central rosette, but painted in blue, turquoise, purple and grey-green, confirms this.

1 *Raby, J. and Yücel, Ü., 1983, pp. 45–46 and figs 11–13*
2 *Cf. Atasoy, N. and Raby, J., 1989, no. 50b*
3 *Inv. G 1983.47; cf. Atasoy, N. and Raby, J., 1989, no. 50a*

Bibl.: Atasoy, N. and Raby, J., 1989, no. 50c

Photograph Jacqueline Hyde

G.J.

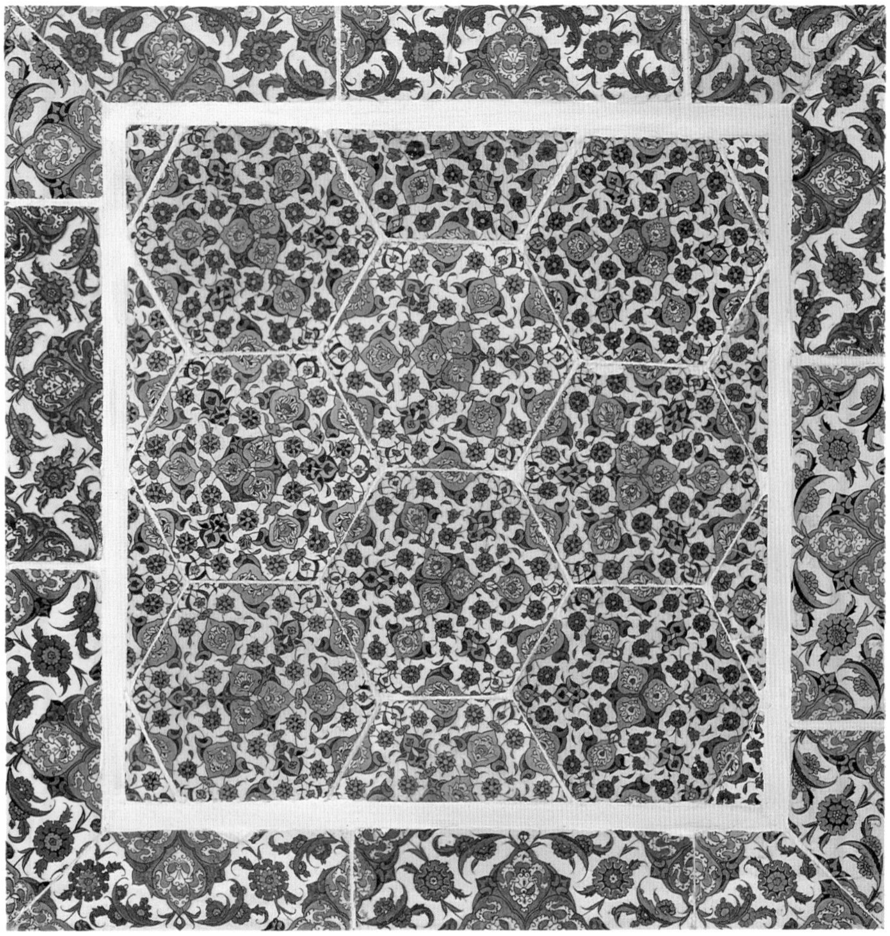

63 WALL TILE PANEL

Turkey, Iznik c.1530–40
Fritware painted over slip under a lead glaze; 101.0 x 99.0

Paris, Musée du Louvre, Islamic section, 7456
Bequest of the Baroness Delort de Gléon, 1914

On this square panel are juxtaposed tiles which were probably not fired or painted at the same time. This is suggested by the differences in tone, variations in detail and choice of colours. The hexagonal tiles follow a module which varies from 24.5 to 25.0 centimetres between two opposite tips and from 21.0 to 21.7 centimetres between two opposite sides.

The arrangement of the rather small motifs is tripartite and radiates, in a kaleidoscopic way, with stylised lotus flowers bound by very thin arabesques, decorated with little flowers, leaves and rosettes.

The border is made up of narrow, elongated modules (length 33.5 to 34.0; depth 10.0 centimetres). It presents half and quarter sections of diamond-shaped medallions decorated with Chinese clouds between which undulate very supple leaves and ṣāz style rosettes. The abundant use of bright turquoise and a cameo of blues ranging from lavender through rich cobalt to blue-black, gives this decoration on a white ground a vibrant clarity and an impression of gaiety.

This type of hexagonal blue-glazed tile was already popular during the previous century (Mosque of Murad II in Edirnoe). However, the floral decoration is of Chinese inspiration and the technique (a combination of siliceous clay and lead glaze) is different.

Bibl.: cf.: Lane, A., 1971, no. 32a; Vente, 1989, London, Sotheby's expert; Stephen Wolff, no. 66, p. 28; Atasoy, N. and Raby J., 1989, no. 52b; Istanbul, 1983, no. E45

Photograph Jacqueline Hyde A.L.

64 TILE WITH CYPRESS DESIGN

Turkey, Iznik, 1545–50
Fritware painted over slip under a lead glaze; 27.4 x 27.0

Paris, Musée du Louvre, Islamic section, 3919–102
Ex. collection Sorlin-Dorighy, acquired 1895

A cypress growing from a large bush is the axis of this rigorously symmetrical blue and turquoise floral composition: on its sides, branches of flowering "eglantine" (sweet briar) and wild hyacinths arch in an oval relating to the shape of the hexagonal frame.

This Iznik tile is a rare example of a limited type of production: the naturalistic floral decoration appeared towards the middle of the year 1540[1]; the hexagonal shape disappeared towards 1550[2]. There were some Iznik blue and white tiles previously in Bursa (*Turbe* of the princes Mustafā and Mahmud, 1511–13) and at Manisa (Valide Camī, 1522–23)[3], but all the major buildings were decorated, until the middle of the sixteenth century, with polychrome tiles in *cuerda seca*[4]. Thus, under Süleyman, this technique was used by 'Acem 'Alī the architect and by Sinan in his earlier works. The Iznik potters at that time concerned themselves more with the manufacture of everyday utensils.

It seems that the hexagonal tiles were decorated only in blue or turquoise (at this time, however, the Iznik palette was extending towards light green or mauve); their contour did not allow the decorative composition to spread onto other tiles. Therefore each tile was usually decorated with a complete motif which was often radial (compare no. 63) or symmetrical; rarely asymmetrical. Use was often made of a pounced drawing. The decoration of this tile can be compared with one belonging to the Musée des Arts Decoratifs in Paris (inv. 3556). The juxtaposed tiles formed a panelling which was bordered by narrow and long decorated tiles in a frieze.

1 *Atasoy, N. and Raby, J., 1989, p. 222*
2 *Atasoy, N. and Raby, J., 1989. p. 220*
3 *Lane, A., 1971, pp. 48–49*
4 *With this technique, a thick wire of manganese is used to separate the coloured glazes to prevent them from running*

A.L.

64

65 PLATE WITH DESIGN OF GRAPES

Turkey, Iznik, c.1545
Fritware painted on slip under a lead glaze; 7.1 x 40.0

Paris, Musée du Louvre, Islamic section, 2402
Acquired 1875

Through the colours used (blue and white but also green and mauve), we can see that this plate at the Louvre is still faithful to a Chinese prototype: the early fifteenth century Ming dish with a design of grapes. It is later than no. 61.

The theme of vine-branches deployed on the surface of the dish was used in China at the time, either on pieces with foliate rims and a cavetto moulded in panels (often 12) with bouquets aligned with the lobes, or on pieces with plain rims and cavettos adorned with floral scrolls.[1]

In Iznik, the potters often tended to imitate the earlier version, with their particular treatment giving the work a certain relief by superimposing vine leaves over the stems including those of the three bunches of grapes. The cavetto is smooth, with 12 bunches of flowers.

The pattern of "waves and rocks", which decorates the rim between two bracket lines, does not exactly correspond to the standard border of the Ming pieces, but consists of a new Ottoman interpretation of the Yuan pattern that was constantly used afterwards. This association of elements from different periods on the same piece shows how indifferent the ceramic painters were to the Chinese subtleties of treatment or rules of composition. Thus, without formal constraint, they were able to design freely while still copying some of the motifs.

1 cf. Pope, J. A., 1958, pl. 38

Photograph Jacqueline Hyde

M.C.

66 PLATE WITH BOUQUET

Turkey, Iznik, c.1550–55
Fritware painted on slip under a lead glaze; 7.0 x 36.5; diam. of base 18.3

Paris, Musée du Louvre, Islamic section, 6643
Formerly in the collection Sechan-Lahens (uncle of the donor); donated by H. Lahens, 1912

This plate with a softly foliated rim is decorated with a design in reserve on a ground of a superb brushed cobalt blue.

The design is arranged on a vertical axis, more apparent than real, punctuated in its centre by a large white multi-lobed medallion with a turquoise heart embellished by coils of blue-black clouds.

From a tuft of green leaves grow two white tulips which frame three stems, each crowned with two white flowers with purple hearts and separated by two unusually big green hyacinths. The whole composition is also decorated with purple rosettes and small green or turquoise flowers.

On the rim, eight purple rosettes with turquoise hearts and eight little white hyacinths are separated by 16 olive-green quatrefoil medallions with small black flowers.

On the back, on a white ground, five purple tulips, framed by thin blue leaves, alternate with five blue rosettes with green hearts.

Bibl.: Migeon, G., 1922, II, no. 196, pl. 37; Atasoy, N. and Raby, J., 1989, no. 363

Photograph Jacqueline Hyde

M.C.

67 PLATE DECORATED WITH COMPOSITE BOUQUET

Turkey, Iznik, c.1550–55
Fritware painted on slip under a lead glaze; 6.7 x 39.0

Paris, Musée du Louvre, Islamic section, 7590
Bequest of the Baroness Salomon de Rothschild 1922

The bowl and the cavetto of this large plate are entirely decorated with an imposing floral design enhanced by a few clouds and scrolls. The softly foliated rim is adorned with a motif of "waves and rocks".

A large bouquet grows from two leafy branches which are horizontally placed near the rim and bound by a thick turquoise loop. The central element of the bouquet is formed by two large roses with a turquoise heart. Two supple stems, carrying long curvy *ṣāz* leaves and blue and turquoise rosettes, cross in front of the roses. Other stems carry pomegranates (arrayed with scales), tulips and other flowers and buds. The scale, the exuberance and the vividness of colours — predominantly cobalt blue, turquoise blue and lime-tree green on a white background — are striking.

Bibl.: Atasoy, N. and Raby, J., 1989, no. 353

Photograph Jacqueline Hyde M.C.

67

68 LID WITH SCROLL DECORATION

Turkey, Iznik, 1550–60
Fritware painted over slip under a lead glaze; 1.8 x 20.5

Paris, Musée du Louvre, Islamic Section, 5960
Gift of Auguste Chabriere 1940

Some Iznik ceramics, such as this small, slightly domed lid, offer a striking proof of the harmonious co-existence of tradition and innovation in Moslem decorative art.

The central boss, encircled with a plain band, is decorated with *rūmī* motifs reserved on a cobalt-blue ground like late fifteenth century pieces: stems carrying half-palmettes intertwined around a six-petal rose. However, these elements are enhanced with dots of bole red, a colour which appeared only in the middle of the sixteenth century.

On the surrounding white field is deployed a supple coil, carrying the same elements arranged in a more elaborate pattern. Some half-palmettes, their stems studded with little dots, expand and contract, creating lambrequin or medallion motifs. Red is also present in all these motifs but it is a thin red, perhaps indicating the first experiments of the Iznik potters with this colour. The narrow straight border is lightly decorated in reserve.

This decoration of interlacings and stems with palmettes is present during the second half of the sixteenth century. We find it on wall panellings and especially on the designs which border large tiled panels.

Bibl.: Migeon, G., 1922, vol. II, no. 215; Atasoy, N. and Raby, J., 1989, no. 376

Photograph Jacqueline Hyde M.C.

69 PITCHER DECORATED WITH FLOWERS

Turkey, Iznik, 1560–70
Fritware painted over slip under a lead glaze;
25.0 x diam. belly 16.5

Paris, Musée du Louvre, Islamic Section, 7595
Legacy of Salomon de Rothschild 1922

This pitcher, with pear-shaped body on a slightly flared pedestal foot, is adorned with a delicate multi-coloured floral design in red, blue and green outlined with thin black lines and divided into two zones bordered by braid of different motifs.

On the flared neck between a band of half-rosettes and a band of chevrons surmounting a row of elongated leaves, four stems bearing three blue flowerettes of decreasing size separate four predominantly red groups, each comprising one tall flower with heart-shaped petals framed by small tulips or crocuses. The same alternation appears all around the body in a more elaborate composition; four groups of three stems with blue flowers (one large, one framed by two small ones) alternate with four groups of large red roses. The latter are made up of two stems, one vertical and crowned by the rose, the other broken and behind or in front of the first, bowed towards the base of the body, as if weighed down by the weight of the flower. This motif of broken stems, which often appeared in floral compositions after the 1540s, together with the slight curve of the vertical stems which seem to wave in the breeze, maintain the spontaneous and lively character of this repeated pattern. Other details also contribute to this effect: for example, in each red group one flower differs from the others and the blue flowerettes are not all the same shape.

The rounded handle, curved like a bracket, is adorned by a row of small horizontal blue marks between two lines of the same colour.

Photograph Jacqueline Hyde M.C.

70 PLATE DECORATED WITH SEVEN BOUQUETS

Turkey, Iznik, 1565–75
Fritware with underglaze decoration over slip under a lead glaze; 5.7 x 29.0

Paris, Musée du Louvre, Islamic Section, 7880-70
Acquired in Rhodes by the Consul Aug. Salzmann between 1865 and 1878; then acquired by the Cluny Museum (inv. Cl. 8465) and deposited in the Louvre in 1926

The bottom of this deep plate with softly foliated rim is decorated with seven evenly spaced small alternating blue and red bouquets, all vertically aligned. Six half-bouquets on the edge of the *cavetto* and a sprinkling of small green triple balls complete the design. This repeated pattern of small sprays of five to seven blossoms on stems bound by delicate three-lobed clips, found more often on textiles than on ceramics, is nevertheless found on several pieces, such as the plate preserved in the Museum of Ecouen[(1)].

On the rim, between two foliated lines, ten pairs of blue tulips are separated by ten red fleurets with heart-shaped petals and green centres. On the back, six bouquets of blue balls with red centres alternate with six green rosettes also with red centres.

The piece is distinguished by the high quality of the execution, the precision of the motifs (sharp without being stiff) and the brightness of the colours. This same care is demonstrated with the softly foliated rim, a refinement which had become rare by this time, and by the careful alignment of the curved line with the scallops of the rim.

1 *inv. Cl. 8125; however, the rim is ornamented with rock and cloud motifs*

Bibl.: Du Sommerard, E., 1883, p. 190, no. 2596; Atasoy, N. and Raby, J., 1989, no. 425

Photograph Jacqueline Hyde M.C.

71 PLATE DECORATED WITH BOATS

ill. page 86

Turkey, Iznik, c.1570–75
Fritware with painted decoration over slip under lead glaze; 5.0 x 28.0

Paris, Musée du Louvre, Islamic section, 7880.82
Acquired in Rhodes by the consul Aug. Salzmann between 1865 and 1878; then by the Musée de Cluny (Cl 8527); deposited in the Louvre in 1926

This plain-rimmed plate revives a form often used during the second quarter of the sixteenth century. Around the straight edge runs a band of small black spirals.

The entire inner surface of the plate is decorated with a flotilla of 11 small boats with black and white striped blue lateen sails arranged in four rows and all facing the same direction.

The gunwhales on the pointed black hulls are painted green. The white ground is ornamented with a series of red, green and blue horizontal festooned wavelets and some minute blue leaves and palmettes.

The remarkable illusion of movement engendered by these repeating motifs is achieved through the treatment of the fully-blown sails, which seem to be irresistibly pushed by a violent wind.

Bibl.: Du Sommerard, E., 1883, p. 186, no. 2204; Atasoy, N. and Raby, J., 1989, no. 753

Photograph Jacqueline Hyde M.C.

72 PITCHER DECORATED WITH BOATS

ill. page 87

Turkey, Iznik, c.1570–75
Fritware with painted decoration on slip under a lead glaze; 21.7 x diam. mouth 7.4

Paris, Musée du Louvre, Islamic section, 7880.61
Acquired in Rhodes by the Consul Aug. Salzmann between 1865 and 1878; then acquired by the Cluny Museum (inv. Cl 8403); deposited in the Louvre in 1926

The boat motif, often used on plates, is also found on vessels, tankards or large bottles. It appears here on a bulging pear-shaped pitcher with a broken handle.

The decoration is organised in three zones, each separated by a series of braids; the one encircling the top of the neck is adorned with a succession of white half-rosettes with red centres on a blue background.

On the body, four large boats with blue and white striped lateen sails travel across a ground strewn with green spots and small red shapes which evoke small stylized waves. The middle zone is decorated with a crown of elongated blue and white petals; in the neck zone are two boats identical to those on the body.

Bibl.: Du Sommerard, E., 1883, p. 192, no. 2660

Photograph Jacqueline Hyde M.C.

71

72

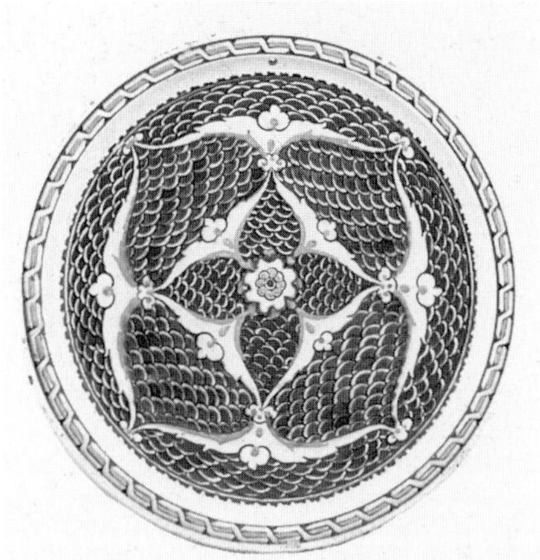

73 PLATE WITH DECORATION OF SCALES

Turkey, Iznik, c. 1575–80
Fritware painted on slip under a lead glaze; 4.7; diam. 29.6

Paris, Musée du Louvre, Islamic Section, 7880–28
Brought from Rhodes between 1865 and 1878; then acquired by the Cluny Museum which deposited it in the Louvre in 1926

This straight-rimmed plate stands on a small round foot. Its entire surface is covered with a decoration of scales drawn in black and compartmentalised by elongated white half-palmettes, highlighted with red. In the centre is an eight-petalled rose around which is a four-point blue star and four large heart-shaped emerald-green palmettes. The remainder of the space is covered with blue scales and bordered with a festooned line. Each coloured scale is underlined by a thin white line left in reserve.

During the years 1570–80 the scale style, created half a century earlier, became particularly fashionable. The scales were arranged in panels of blue or green, drawn in black and defined by white and red motifs: elongated clouds, half-palmettes, *ṣāz* leaves and fleurets.

They appear on plates but just as frequently on vessels such as ewers, large bottles and pitchers. There is a lamp, decorated in this way, which also carries a rather clumsy Hebrew inscription, probably commissioned from potters who were unfamiliar with the language[1].

The flat rim is adorned with a geometric band of blue, white and red. On the back, between two double blue lines, seven circular motifs, blue spotted with white, alternate with seven small irregular multi-lobed elements.

1 *cf. Atasoy, N. and Raby J., 1989, no. 731*

Photograph Jacqueline Hyde M.C.

74 TANKARD WITH DESIGN OF SERRATED LEAVES

Turkey, Iznik, second half of the sixteenth century
Fritware painted on slip under a lead glaze; 21.7; diam. mouth 21.0

Paris, Musée du Louvre, Islamic Section, AA403
Gift of Chompret, 1939

A lavender blue creates the ground for the black, white and brick-red decoration of this cylindrical tankard, with its flat, angular handle.

Four long serrated leaves painted in red with black spines are superimposed obliquely over a supple and light floral motif. Undulating black stems, with leaves occasionally studded with red, carry carnations, small tulips or crocuses; irises enliven the whole surface between two bands of motifs derived from the *çintemani* bordering the rim and the base. The inside is undecorated.

Developed during the Ottoman era (second half of the sixteenth century), this form of tankard may have been adapted from wooden[1] or leather prototypes. It was also used for jade or metal pieces, sometimes fitted with a lid[2].

1 *Similar vessels were used in Greece as grain measures or as wine mugs*
2 *Cf. Istanbul, Topkapı Sarayı Müzesi, inv. 2/3832 in jade, and Baltimore, Walters Art Gallery, inv. 54512 in copper gilt (tombac)*

Bibl.: Öz, T., 1957, p. LXXI, no. 130

Photograph Jacqueline Hyde M.C.

75

75 VASE *ill. page 89*

Turkey, Iznik, third quarter of the sixteenth century
Fritware under a lead glaze; 25.0 x diam. base 9.5

Istanbul, Türk ve Islam Eserleri Müzesi, 816
Transferred from the Kulliye of the Selimiye Mosque, Edirne, 1922

This pear-shaped vase with a high flaring neck is related to the series of ceramics from Iznik covered in a coloured slip. In most cases such pieces are also adorned with a painted design over the coloured ground.

The originality and rarity of this Iznik vase stem from the fact that it is a monochrome, apart from thin white mouldings on the lip and at the base of the neck. This feature allows us to fully appreciate the degree to which the potters of the second part of the sixteenth century had been able to perfect a ferruginous, siliceous slip which produced superb red tones enhanced by a brilliant glaze.

Because of its general shape and certain details such as the moulding at the junction between the neck and the belly, this piece is related to contemporary metal ware. The preference for simplicity and spareness in the decoration is evocative of certain silver bottles of rare elegance.

As in several of the ceramic lamps, the centre of the base of this vase is pierced with a hole, the function of which is undetermined.

The fact that this vase comes from an imperial foundation, the Kulliye of the Selimiye of Edirne, seems to indicate that the taste of the privileged classes for extremely decorated objects did not exclude pieces such as this, which were to be appreciated for their restraint and their rare technical quality.

Bibl.: Carswell, J., 1982, pl. 88; Atasoy, N. and Raby, J., 1989, fig. 710

Photograph Jacqueline Hyde G.J.

76 VASE WITH VERTICAL LINE DECORATION

Turkey, Iznik, third quarter of the sixteenth century
Fritware with underglaze slip decoration painted on slip under a lead glaze; 25 x diam. base 9.5; diam. lip 9.5

Istanbul, Türk ve Islam Eserleri Müzesi, 817
Transferred from the Kulliye of the Selimiye, Edirne, 1922

Several features of this vase enable us to link it to another similar one in the Victoria and Albert Museum (inv. C2003. 1910): the shape, the red ground and the provenance (the Kulliye of the Selimiye in Edirne). They differ in their decoration: painted in white and lavender blue slip (in slight relief) on the British example; in black on this vase.

The simple design consists of a series of vertical lines alternatively white, blue, white, black, around the body and neck. They are interrupted at the base of the neck by a slight ribbing decorated with a festooned ribbon dotted with black. The shape of the body forces the lines to contract towards the base of the neck. The lines along the neck are reduced in number (halved) relative to those on the body. At the edge of the neck the lines terminate in white arches enhanced with black dots, crowned with the same ribbon as that on the slight ribbing. The centre of the base is pierced with a hole.

Bibl.: Atasoy, N. and Raby, J., 1989, fig. 711

Photograph Jacqueline Hyde G.J.

77

77 WALL TILE

Turkey, Iznik, c.1570–80
Fritware painted on slip under a lead glaze; 62.3 x 34.2

Paris, Musée du Louvre, Islamic Section, 3919/2287
Ex. Collection Sorlin-Dorigny; acquired 1895

The complex decoration of this panel fills the area with a floral style and a soft palette enriched by coral red and a tender emerald green. Delicate flowering branches are coiled up in the *ṣāz* leaves from which grow the spirals. Along with other leaves which grow from the top and the bottom of flowers cut in half, they create a meandering motif of curves and counter-curves. The panel is bordered with lappets.

Whereas on the formal pieces the *ṣāz* style often gives way to a less complicated floral style (after 1570), it continued to appear on tiles and wall panelling until the seventeenth century[1], with other decorative motifs.

According to some, this style was generally less elaborate on ceramics than on miniatures or fabrics[2]. However, the panel represented here can well sustain any comparison with the most beautiful creations on textiles, for example.

This panel and an identical one in the collection of the Harvard University Art Museum were probably part of a series of decorative panels intended for a building (now unidentified)[3].

1 Atasoy, N. and Raby, J., 1989, p. 133
2 id., p. 142
3 Washington, 1987, p. 278

Bibl.: Migeon, G., 1922, II, no. 246

Photograph Jacqueline Hyde

A.L.

78 WALL TILES

Turkey, Iznik, c.1580
Fritware with underglaze decoration painted on slip under lead glaze; 55.0 x (max.) 109.5

Paris, Musée du Louvre, Islamic Section, AA 405
Deligande Bequest 1940

This decorative panel differs from no. 77 in its more brilliant glaze, brighter colours, sharper decoration and the division of composition into tiles: each repeating motif is spread over four tiles, producing two complete motifs where roses alternate in quincunxes with a large almond-shaped cartouche decorated with tulips, carnations and roses reserved against a red ground. The long, almost straight *ṣāz* leaves give a horizontal emphasis. These serrated leaves are embellished with white tulips: this superimposing of floral and vegetal elements was very common in late sixteenth and early seventeenth century Ottoman art, particularly in textiles. From 1544, designers sometimes added a wild rose or plum branch to the *ṣāz* leaf, but around 1580 this was replaced, as in this example, with a tulip[1].

78

In Iznik tile production from about 1551 the square format completely supplanted the earlier hexagonal shape (in the mosque of Ḳādim Ibrahım Paşa, built by Sinan in the Silivrikapi quarter in Istanbul)[2]. This format made it possible to extend a decorative theme over several tiles. It was also in the early 1550s that the technique of *cuerda seca* was abandoned in imperial buildings; the Süleymaniye mosque in Istanbul (1550–57), in particular, marks the beginning of the large-scale use of Iznik ceramic decoration[3], this technique generally having been used for the interiors of buildings. Mosques, mausoleums and palaces were decorated in this manner, and the production of tiles and panels gradually overtook the production of three-dimensional objects.

While the invention of new colours such as sage green and aubergine inspired the creativity of potters, it had little effect on Iznik tile production, which continued to be ornamented principally in cobalt blue and turquoise. From the 1550s, new colours (firstly bole red, then during the late 1560s, emerald green) were developed to enhance patterns which had to be viewed from afar[4].

The tiles presented here are identical to others housed in the Louvre (inv. 3919-2, No. 247E), the Museum of Islamic Art in Cairo (inv. 6321), the Çinili Köşk in Istanbul, the David Samlung in Copenhagen (inv. 41/1968) and the Gulbenkian Foundation in Lisbon (inv. 1709). They may have come from the Mosque of Eyüp. This sanctuary was redecorated in 1798–99 with earlier tiles and panels: one can therefore not date these accurately. According to J. Raby, close examination of certain details suggests that they were made around 1580, during the reign of Murad III (1574–96), the grandson of Sultan Süleyman[5].

Until about 1585, Sultan Murad gave numerous orders to the Iznik workshops, as all his edifices, even boat-houses, were decorated in this type of ceramic[6]. This abundant use ensured a consistently high quality. Foreigners also appreciated and bought vessels and tiles, as indicated in a letter dated 1577 from Gerlach, Secretary of the Austrian ambassador in Istanbul[7]. From about 1585 until the ascension of Ahmed I in 1603, architectural activity was practically limited to the construction of mausoleums and went into decline: the Court was spending less, resulting in a decline in quality. After a reprieve under Ahmed I (with the "Blue" mosque project, completed in 1617), Iznik production sank to the point where, by the first quarter of the seventeenth century, the number of workshops fell from over 300 to just nine[8].

1 Atasoy, N. and Raby, J., 1989, p. 249
2 Atasoy, N. and Raby, J., 1989, p. 220 (a single exception is noted in south-eastern Anatolia at the end of the 1550s)
3 The restoration of the Cupola of the Rock in Jerusalem from 1545–46 to 1551–52 revived the need for diverse ceramic techniques
4 Atasoy, N. and Raby, J., 1989, p. 221
5 Atasoy, N. and Raby, J., 1989, pp. 246–48
6 Arseven, C. E., 1952, p. 162
7 Lane, A., 1971, p. 59
8 Carswell, J., 1982, pp. 87–88

Bibl.: cf. Atasoy, N. and Raby, J., 1989, no. 477; Arseven, C. E., 1952, pl. 8; Frankfurt, 1985, no. 2/77

Photograph Jacqueline Hyde A.L.

79 PAIR OF SPANDRELS WITH FLORAL SPRAYS

Turkey, Iznik, c.1570–80
Fritware with underglaze decoration on slip;
57.9 x (max.) 29.5

Paris, Musée du Louvre, Islamic section, 3919-56 and 3919-57
Ex. Sorlin-Dorigny Collection; acquired 1895

These two spandrels, cut out to form a poly-lobed arch, the contours finely outlined in red and blue, are decorated with floral sprays which face each other in mirror-image. Springing from a turf are red carnations and red-spotted blue tulips on long and fine turquoise-green twigs which curve and bend for the flowers to spread harmoniously in the poly-lobed space; a blue hyacinth and small carnations spring from the lower part of the spandrel. A few minute cloud-scroll motifs are placed along the inner poly-lobed contour.

Decorated spandrels were already in use in Turkish architecture during Seljuk times, as for example those from the Kubadabad palace at Beysehir in stucco decorated with peacocks. In the form of glazed tiles, several Iznik examples can be found in various museums (Istanbul, New York, London, Copenhagen, Kuwait).

Ornamented corners also appear frequently in Ottoman bookbindings and textiles, particularly velvet cushion covers.

Photograph Jacqueline Hyde A.L.

80 BOWL

Turkey, first half of the sixteenth century
Tinned copper, chased decoration; 25.0 x 47.5

Istanbul, Topkapı Sarayı Müzesi, 25/3216

The hemispherical body of this bowl is somewhat flattened at the base. The sides flare slightly outwards towards a narrow out-turned rim. The chased decoration is in slight relief against a matt ground. The decoration covers the exterior of the bowl beneath a smooth band separated by two parallel lines. A foliage scroll bearing leaves, lotus flowers and other flowers of the *ḫaṭāyī* type springs from large blooming palmettes. The circumference loops are linked together by rings and the base is adorned with lambrequin-shaped motifs. The inside wall on the slightly flaring sides (the external wall is undecorated) is decorated with alternating multi-lobed arches, within which the supple stems and tapered leaves of a *rūmī* design are inscribed.

Tinned copper objects were in vogue in Mamluk Egypt during the fifteenth century and later, generally for pieces in everyday use. Tin which was imported from England had a double advantage: it protected the food from the noxious effects of copper and gave to the object the luxurious aspect of silver. It was applied with the aid of a dabber impregnated with hot ammonium salts. The volatile salts cleaned the surface of the copper, allowing the molten tin to be deposited in thin layers on the object[1].

The decoration of this bowl links it to the artistic production of the first half of the sixteenth century.

1 *Allan, J., Raby, J., 1962, p. 33*

Photograph Jacqueline Hyde T.B.

79

81 SILVER TRAY

Turkey, mid sixteenth century
Turned, hammered and engraved silver; traces of gilding; 2.0 x 29.0

Istanbul, Library of the Topkapı Sarayı Müzesi, 23/1625
Topkapı Palace collection

This silver plate is characterised by its low sides, a narrow, rounded and grooved rim and a flat bottom. The rim is gilded and traces of gilding also remain on the engraved area.

The decoration plays on the opposition between the filled and the empty spaces, on the contrast between the central engraved circle and the wide smooth ring surrounding it, between the motifs treated in light flat relief and the very finely ring-punched ground. Three fine lines circumscribe two superimposed scrolls radiating from a central blossom. The scrolls interweave and entangle their stems which bear elongated *rūmī* flowers or *ḫaṭāyī* flowers and lotus buds, in a very dense design, built around a central point. The monogram of Sultan Süleyman is stamped into the smooth ring. The reverse of the plate is stamped with the Arabic numerals 383.

This small plate is one of the few silver objects from Süleyman's time still in existence, not because this precious metal was not prized in the Ottoman court but because over the centuries these objects were melted down as demanded by financial exigencies. Royal patrons and the taste for luxury favoured prolific production, and the fact that Selim I and Süleyman, following in the tradition of Ottoman princes, chose to learn goldsmithing, also contributed to the development of this art. In the early sixteenth century, there were some 70 goldsmiths in Istanbul; counting master apprentices and artisans by the end of the century[1], the number grew to more than 500.

Silver objects influenced the shapes of ceramic objects; certain large plates have the same shape as this silver plate.

1 Raby, J., Allan J., 1982, pp. 19–20

Photograph Jacqueline Hyde

T.B.

82 PITCHER

Turkey, second quarter of the sixteenth century
Cast zinc set with gold, rubies, turquoise, diamonds and a peridot; 17.5; diam. mouth 8.4; diam. base 7.5

Istanbul, Topkapı Sarayı Müzesi, 2/2856
Treasury of the Topkapı Palace

This pitcher is similar in shape to those with serpentine handles ending in a dragon's head. However, in this example the handle is simply curved.

The slender neck bears a domed cover with a wide flat border and is ornamented by a gold knob set with a peridot mounted in little claws. This lid is attached to the handle by a small silver-gilt chain.

The decorative motifs, inlaid in gold, are set in relief against a background which is entirely matt apart from two thin bands at the base and rim of the neck which emphasise the structure of the piece. The body is decorated with a network of *rūmī* arabesques of engraved leaves punctuated with gold five-petalled turquoise-centred flowers. This pattern is interrupted by four large oval multi-lobed medallions between which are knotted cloud bands alternating with half-medallions spaced around the perimeter. Executed in slightly thicker and more raised gold strips than those used in the arabesques, the medallions are ornamented by cabochon rubies and turquoise in claw-mounts on a wide gold collar. Connected by circular stems bearing little leaves, these gems surround a central facet-cut diamond.

The ornamentation of the neck and the dome of the lid is similar to that of the body, but without the clouds. On the flat edge of the lid undulates a fine stem with leaves and fleurets with turquoise and ruby centres. A foliage scroll coils around the small annular foot; on the interior of the neck is a gold filter with *ḫaṭāyī* and *rūmī* motifs ornamented with the same gems.

Objects of Iranian origin, made of zinc highlighted with gold and precious stones, enjoyed great popularity in Turkey in the sixteenth century and the Ottoman artisans assimilated the decorative techniques of their Iranian counterparts. However, although the shapes of the pitchers, bowls and ewers which dominated production were similar to those of the Persian examples, the decorative motifs differed greatly. The Safavids favoured animal themes or figurative scenes, often accompanied by epigraphic motifs; the Ottomans used only plant motifs.

Photograph Jacqueline Hyde T.B.

83 PITCHER DECORATED WITH CARNATIONS AND TULIP *ill. page 96*

Turkey, last quarter of the sixteenth century
Cast zinc, chased and inlaid with gold, emeralds, rubies and turquoise; 15.0; diam. opening 8.0; diam. (max.) 34.0

Istanbul, Topkapı Sarayı Müzesi, 2/2836
Treasury of the Topkapı Palace

The pear-shaped body of this pitcher extends without interruption into a tubular neck which flares slightly at the mouth. A small ring placed on top of the baluster handle suggests there was originally a lid to match (cf. no. 84).

An embossed striated relief gold thread delineates three multi-lobed medallions on the body, a motif repeated as half-medallions at the base and neck of the pitcher. The medallions are decorated with stems in the shape of a figure-eight bearing finely veined leaves slightly curved at the tip and small flowers with grooved gold petals and hearts of emeralds, rubies or turquoise set in bezels. In between the medallions, long supple branches are deployed gracefully, their leaves equally veined and curved at the tip and bearing flowers such as tulips and carnations with two stamens. A large turquoise gem marks the intersection of the branches.

The thicker rim of the neck, slightly convex, is defined by two gold bands and inlaid with small elongated gold leaves alternating with pairs of dots. The same leaf motif occurs on the handle of the pitcher.

There is a subtle contrast here between the "classical" jewelled design of the medallions and the naturalistic motifs curving freely over the body of the pitcher, reminiscent of Iznik ceramics enriched with red, of the second half of the sixteenth century.

A small zinc tray with a similar motif is in the collection of the Topkapı Sarayı Müzesi (inv. 2/2844).

Photograph Jacqueline Hyde T.B.

83

84 PITCHER

Turkey, second quarter of the sixteenth century
Moulded zinc inlaid with filigreed and chased gold; rubies, emeralds, turquoise and pearls; 13.2; diam. lip 7.1; diam. base 6.4

Istanbul, Topkapı Sarayı Müzesi, 2/2873
Treasury of the Topkapı Palace

The slightly flattened globulous belly of the pitcher rests on a very small annular base decorated with a simple geometric pattern. It is adorned with six large slightly convex oval medallions of gold, chased and filigreed and inlaid with a ruby surrounded by four turquoise and applied over a light moss-green painted background. These medallions stand out on a vegetal network punctuated by five little petalled flowers decorated at their centre with pearls, rubies, emeralds or turquoise set in small claws. This decoration is repeated on a smaller scale on the cylindrical neck. A gold thread meanders down the baluster handle, which is furnished with a thumb-rest in the form of a clover-leaf.

The flat lid is topped with a prehensile button in the shape of a lotus in which a turquoise is set. It is also decorated with three filigreed gold medallions, but some variations in the decorative technique indicate that it may come from another piece. The bottom, for instance, is finely matted; there is no trace of paint under the three medallions, and a cloud frieze in pronounced relief adorns the rim.

Persian influence is very noticeable, not only in the shape of the pitcher but also in some of its technical characteristics: the use of filigreed medallions, the presence of pearls, and the setting of the stones in claws instead of bezels. Nevertheless, as a whole the decoration remains typically Ottoman.

Photograph Jacqueline Hyde T.B.

85

85 PITCHER

Turkey, second quarter of the sixteenth century
Cast zinc, engraved, inlaid with gold, turquoise and rubies; 13.5; diam. mouth 7.3; diam. base 6.7

Istanbul, Topkapı Sarayı Müzesi, 2/2842
Treasury of the Topkapı Palace

The characteristic shape and decoration of this zinc pitcher indicate a very strong Iranian influence. A small circular foot supports the bulbous body of the pitcher, separated from the wide cylindrical neck by a convex collar. The rounded lid is topped by a lotus-bud finial.

The volute end of the dragon-headed serpentine handle is not directly attached to the body but, in characteristic Timurid style, rests on a support fixed to the vessel.

The engraved gold decoration, executed in low relief, is concerned more with the delicacy of the motifs than with their energy. A cloud freize decorates the lower part of the body. Above is a network of *rūmī* arabesques with engraved bifurcated leaves and four-petalled flowers, each of which is set in the centre with a turquoise or a ruby in a bezel and placed horizontally in the centre of the composition.

Ottoman examples do not usually feature decoration on the convex collar. This pitcher follows the Iranian style, in which the collar is bordered with tooled narrow grooves and decorated with *rūmī* scrolls in eight elongated cartouches separated by a turquoise or a ruby mounted in a five-lobed collar.

The most characteristic decoration is found on the neck, where above the sparsely arranged *rūmī* arabesques, punctuated with little five-lobed flowers with ruby or turquoise hearts, a Persian poetic inscription is contained in four oblong cartouches, separated by turquoises set in bezels and mounted in lobed collars. The cursive graphics are of only average quality:

if you want to find
joy in your life
drink from this ewer of eternity
the Water [which gives life]
because all things in the universe
are [founded] on existence
so be happy while drinking! [1]

The lid is also decorated with an epigraphic frieze, but one with very clumsy graphics. The Ottoman text, interspersed with many Persian words, is difficult to decipher. It must have been executed by someone who had only a poor knowledge of the Ottoman language.

Whereas poetic texts are often part of the decoration on Iranian pitchers, the Ottoman braziers and goldsmiths rarely used epigraphic decoration on any item except arms. This zinc pitcher is one of the few known examples to make use of a poetic text placed exactly as on the Iranian works. Other decorative motifs used on this piece date it as an Ottoman production of the first half of the sixteenth century; however, the refined, low-relief treatment of these same motifs and the characteristics of the two inscriptions indicate this pitcher was executed in Istanbul, probably by an Iranian artist originally from Tabriz.

1 *Reading and translation by Shahriar Adle, for whose collaboration I am grateful*

Photograph Jacqueline Hyde T.B.

84

86 PITCHER *ill. page 98*

Turkey, mid sixteenth century
Hard stone (black onyx or obsidian?) set with gold, rubies and amethysts(?); gold, niello, turquoise, translucent enamel; 18.0; diam. mouth 9.1; diam. base 8.7

Istanbul, Topkapı Sarayı Müzesi, 2/3831
Topkapı Palace collection

This vessel has a gently-flared circular base, a slightly flattened globular body and a small cylindrical neck. It has a dome-shaped cover and a dragon-shaped handle.

The meticulous decoration is arranged in three principal bands, the cover, neck and body, separated by a row of stones arond the base and shoulder. Narrow engraved bands, set with stones, form in relief a network of overlapping *mandorlas* on the belly, a scroll around the neck and a network of ovals on the lid. All these lines are punctuated by flowers with six-lobed corollas of finely-striated petals, the centres picked out in table-cut rubies and amethysts(?) set in bezels, and small, finely-engraved leaves with curved ends. The handle, in the shape of a serpentine dragon with its tail twisted back, is set with small relief flowers, rubies and gold ocelli. The beast's head is minutely sculpted, its mouth biting the lip of the pitcher.

The cover and footrim have a gold mount highlighted with inlaid green, blue and yellow translucent enamel. The footrim is encircled by a fretwork band of small trefoils, ornamented on the reverse by a gold six-pointed rosette with floral motifs. A narrow fluted band emphasizes the contour of the lid, which is lined in a gold latticework radiating outwards from a central turquoise. The inside rim of the lid is enlivened with branches of tulips, hyacinths and enamelled carnations.

A gold fretwork filter covers the mouth of the pitcher. Around a central medallion composed of a turquoise set in a garland of leaf-shaped nielloed arabesques radiates, against a background of fine engraved plant motifs, an inscription from the Koran in cursive letters, invoking the pure waters of paradise (Koran LXXXVI, 21).

This object, which has been decorated with particular care using several decorative techniques, is one of a long series for which the prototype is a white jade example made for the Timurid Sultan Ulugh Beg (1417–49)[1]. Several of these

86

pitchers are attributable, from the fifteenth to the seventeenth centuries, to the Timurids[2] and the Safavids[3] as well as to the Ottomans. Executed in silver-plate, brass or zinc (cf. no. 85), they were also made of jade, as shown by the gold-inlaid pitcher of Iranian origin which was brought back to Istanbul among the booty seized by the Turks at Çaldiran following their victory over the Safavids in 1514, and now housed in the Topkapı Sarayı Müzesi (inv. 1814)[4]. These forms were imitated by potters in China, during the Xuande period of the Ming dynasty[5].

1 *Housed at the Calouste Gulbenkian Museum in Lisbon, inv. 328*
2 *Several examples, in brass with a finely engraved ornamentation on a striated background and inlaid with gold, bear inscriptions indicating their place of manufacture, Herat, date in the second half of the fifteenth century and the name of the craftsman; examples are housed in the Louvre (inv. MA0697), in the Victoria and Albert Museum in London (inv. 943-1886, dated 1461-62), and in the Berlin-Dahlem Museum (inv. 3606, dated 1456-57)*
3 *Cf., e.g., Victoria and Albert Museum (inv. 241-1896)*
4 *Dedicated to the Safavid Sovereign Shah Ismā'īl (1501-24); cf., Köseoğlu, C., 1987, no. 48*
5 *E.g., the blue and white porcelain pitcher in the British Museum, inv. OA 1950 4-31(57)*

Photograph Jacqueline Hyde M.B.T.

87 PITCHER

Istanbul, second half of the sixteenth century
Engraved gold and carved rock crystal inlaid with rubies and emeralds; colours and gold on paper; 20.0; diam. mouth 8.9; diam. base 10.0

Istanbul, Topkapı Sarayı Müzesi, 2/8
Treasury of the Topkapı Palace

The medallions of rock crystal set into the body make this gold pitcher unique. As a result of damage (it was crushed at one time), the original proportions have been altered and the bulbous body sits heavily on the base. The cylindrical neck widens slightly and is capped with a dome-shaped cover surmounted by a small pine-cone finial. The serpentine handle is shaped as a double-headed dragon; one head has a widely-opened mouth baring sharp teeth.

A decoration of finely engraved foliage enlivens the surface of the pitcher, which is studded with rows of regularly-placed rubies. The cabochon stones are set in bezels in high relief without collars and the same technique has been used for the eight gold-rimmed medallions on the body. The thick rock crystal, cut in wide facets with sloping slides, is inlaid with table-cut emeralds and rubies mounted in almost square bezels in the centre of wide striated collars. Between these gems is visible the night-blue paper decorated with illuminated motifs which serves as a background for the medallions. The base, which seems to be later in date, is decorated with an engraved design radiating from a central star.

A porcelain bowl (cf. no. 97) and a pen box (cf. no. 134), also kept in the Topkapı Treasury, apply the same style of decoration, combining gold, rock crystal and illuminated designs. The use of an illuminated paper lining to enhance the sparkle of the rock crystal could be an adaptation of the gold-leaf technique used by Ottoman jewellers to line mother-of-pearl.

Bibl.: Türkoğlu, 1985, p. 12; Köseoğlu, C., 1987, no. 52

Photograph Jacqueline Hyde T.B.

88 CUP DECORATED WITH FLORAL MANDORLAS

Turkey, mid sixteenth century
Jade inlaid with gold and rubies; diam. mouth 8.2; diam. foot 3.8

Istanbul, Topkapı Sarayı Müzesi, 2/3826
Topkapı Palace collection

The sides of this cup curve out gently from a circular foot to a double-grooved rim. The pale-green jade is translucent and the decoration is elegant and light.

A thin striated gold thread, inlaid in the jade surface, traces a pattern of three multi-lobed *mandorlas* each containing a rose marked at the heart and on the tips of its six petals with rubies. Six small elongated and slightly curved leaves, finely striated on only one side of their ribs, impart rhythm to the composition. Between the *mandorlas*, six rubies are arranged in two inverted triangles. The table-cut stones are set in bezels at the centre of six-lobed gold collars, the finely incised shapes of which repeat the style of the other gold outlines.

Photograph Jacqueline Hyde M.B.T.

89 LIDDED TANKARD

Turkey, second half of the sixteenth century
Jade, set with gold, rubies, emeralds, peridots and amethysts(?); 17.7; diam. base 10.9; diam. opening 10.0

Istanbul, Topkapı Sarayı Müzesi, 2/3832
Treasury of the Topkapı Palace

This tankard, with angular handle, has been cut from a single block of milk-white jade and is fitted with a lid in the shape of a flattened dome topped by a knob. The decoration is divided into three separate zones by a gold thread. Slender threads of notched gold corolla set into the jade define in shallow relief a network punctuated by small elongated leaves and flowers with gold corolla and centres of ruby or emerald. This is interrupted in the middle zone of the body to allow for four medallions in the shape of multi-lobed *mandorlas* ornamented with flowers spaced like a wreath around the central flower, which is larger and formed with a facet-cut ruby.

Each flower is made up of a stone (some rubies and emeralds seem to have been replaced by peridots and amethysts) set in a bezel on a gold lobed and striated collar. The small leaves are also striated. A thin zig-zag line encircles the lip of the tankard. On the lid, the knob, also topped with a ruby, is finely decorated with leaves and inlaid stems.

The interior of the receptacle is lined with gold leaf. The lid and underside of the base are also lined with gold leaf, which has been cut out and engraved to make a delicate pattern of arabesques of long leaves with elongated curved ends.

The shape of this tankard is undoubtedly derived from prototypes sewn in leather. Whether of German or Balkan origin, such tankards became very fashionable in Ottoman Turkey from the beginning of the sixteenth century and were also made in ceramic[1] and metal[2].

The Topkapı Sarayı Müzesi possesses another very similar tankard, slightly narrower, with the lid missing.

1 *E.g., a tankard unearthed in Iznik in 1989 with a blue and white floral motif dating from 1510–20; cf. in the Islamic section of the Louvre, AA403, 6323, 6324*
2 *Cf. the piece in the Walters Art Gallery in Baltimore (54.512), reproduced in Petsopoulos, V., ed., 1982, p. 20, fig. 4; or Wenzel, M., September 1988, p. 161, fig. V*

Bibl.: Köseoğlu, G., 1987, p. 209, no. 53

Photograph Jacqueline Hyde M.B.T.

90 MATARA

Turkey, second half of the sixteenth century
Chased, repoussé applied and nielloed gold, inlaid with rubies, emeralds and amethysts; nephrite jade inlaid with gold, emeralds, rubies and amethysts; pearls; 27.5 x max. 24.0; weight 640 dirham

Istanbul, Topkapı Sarayı Müzesi, 2/3825
Recorded on the inventory of the private imperial treasure of 1680

This gold gourd has a distinctive shape. The markedly flat pear-shaped body widens from a flared pedestal foot. Two dragon heads project from the shoulder, one holding a pearl in its mouth, the other an emerald. The curved spout terminates in another dragon head. A domed lid covers the thin cylindrical neck. The flexible handle, attached to the base of the neck, is made up of chevron-shaped links.

The centre of either side is set with a lobed medallion of light green nephrite, held in place by small gold tacks. At the heart of the medallion a large table-cut emerald is mounted in a lobed gold bezel set in a collar of striated petals. This type of setting, which transforms each stone into a flower, is called *gül resmi*, "in the shape of a rose", and was widely used by goldsmiths in the time of Sultan Süleyman. The emeralds and the rubies which alternate on the jade in a double circle are similarly set and linked together by a finely striated gold thread and occasionally punctuated with tapered leaves, curved at the tip. The medallion is surrounded by a row of similar stones set in thick lobed bezels. A frieze of large palmettes chased with fine floral motifs is applied in relief and follows the contours of the *matara*. Emeralds and rubies punctuate the heart of the palmettes and are interposed between them on a matt ground with a chased foliage design.

On the narrow sides of the gourd, gold medallions of decreasing sizes are applied, the lower half medallion in nephrite set with three stones. The neck and the pedestal are also matted, chased and decorated with rubies and emeralds set in thick bezels. Those adorning the lid are set in square or triangular bezels and the apex is crowned by a large ruby. The cylindrical lip which fits into the mouth of the gourd is decorated with engraved medallions on a nielloed ground.

The inventory of 1680[1] mentions that the *matara* is decorated with 370 rubies, 12 amethysts and 427 emeralds. Most of the stones are cabochon; some are cut and facetted, in particular the ruby which surmounts the lid. This discrepancy can be explained by the words engraved under the head of the dragon holding a pearl: "*tecdid*" (restored) and "640 *dirham*" (nearly two kilograms). This piece has therefore been restored, some of the stones have been replaced and the lid, of a different structure, probably dates from the time of the restoration.

The peculiar form of the *matara* copies that of the leather gourds of Central Asia, which have been recorded as early as the fifth century BC, as evidenced by the gourds found at Pazyrik and still found in the south of Anatolia. Gold vessels almost identical to the gold *matara* are illustrated in Ottoman manuscripts dating from the second half of the sixteenth century. The earliest date from 1569. On a miniature illustrating a funeral procession we can see a sword-bearer and the master of the wardrobe holding a gourd similar to that from the treasury of the Topkapı[3]. Two dignitaries and the *matara* are also depicted on a page of the *Tārīḫ-i Sultan Süleyman*, of Loḳmān, completed in 1579[4] describing the visit of the sovereign to the monastery of Eyüb Ansari. The *matara* was obviously a ceremonial object: water reserved for the sultan was kept in it and, as with the sword, it represented a symbol of sovereignty which was used exclusively in the Ottoman world. The last illustration of this type of *matara* appears on a manuscript dated 1597[5].

This gold gourd was probably made during the reign of Selim II or Murad III. It is known that the latter presented a similar leather gourd with appliqué leather decoration[6] to Emperor Rudolph of Austria in 1581. Another example in gilded and engraved copper is kept in the British Museum[7].

91

1 *Çağman, F., 1987, pp. 450–51*
2 *Çağman, F., 1987, p. 457 and note 22*
3 *Istanbul, Topkapı Palace Library H1339, f. 103v° and 184v°*
4 *Dublin Chester Beatty, Ms 413, f. 38r°*
5 *Istanbul Topkapı Palace Library, H-B 200, f. 28r°, 29v° and 32r°*
6 *Vienne Kunsthistorisches Museum, C. 20; ill. in Çağman, F., 1987, pl. 83*
7 *Ill. in Barret, D., 1949, no. 38a*

Photograph Jacqueline Hyde

T.B.

91 BOX FOR AN ANTIDOTE TO POISON

Turkey, mid sixteenth century *ill. page 103*
Perforated and engraved gold, with turquoise and ruby inlay; 3.6 x 5.5

Istanbul, Topkapı Sarayı Müzesi, 2/3725
Treasury of the Topkapı Palace

The technique used to decorate the perforated and engraved surface of this small round box with flat lid is called *firūzekārī*, in which thin sheets of turquoise are inserted under a thin mesh of latticed gold. This technique was popular in the second half of the sixteenth century. The structure of the mesh, geometric on the upper part of the lid but more supple on the remainder of the surface, is decorated with small six-petalled flowers and finely veined leaves.

Cabochon rubies set in bezels on a gold ground and linked by engraved bands form a braid around the rim of the slightly contracted opening of the box, as well as around the rim of the lid and its centre, which is made of a cabochon ruby with sheets of turquoise set in a large lobed collar. Bands of gold engraved in a zig-zag pattern emphasise the various sections of the design. The under-side of the box is decorated by a central rose with four oblong petals, stems and small flowers finely chased on a tooled background. There is no pattern inside the box.

This small gold box, easy to conceal in the folds of clothing, was supposedly used to carry antidotes for poison. The use of poison and antidotes was certainly not the monopoly of the Ottoman Court or of the sixteenth century, but a very ancient practice which explains, among other things, why theriac became so popular, first in the East and later in the West. Theriac was a universal antidote whose creation, according to tradition, dates back to the scholars of Ancient Greece.

Photograph Jacqueline Hyde T.B.

92

93

92 CASKET

Turkey, second quarter of the sixteenth century
Jade inlaid with gold, turquoise and rubies; wood, silver-gilt
7.2; diam. opening 15.3; depth 6.2

Istanbul, Topkapı Sarayı Müzesi, 2/2085
Treasury of the Topkapı Palace

Five plaques of dark jade make up the body and sliding lid of this rectangular box; the base is of dark wood. The plaques are joined together by a silver-gilt frame, the uprights of which include two pairs of lance-head braces. This frame is ornamented with a fine curvilinear tracery of chased curves, enriched with black paint and studded with precious stones set in bezels: rubies on the lower edges; turquoise on the vertical mounts and enclosing the clasp for the cover; turquoise and rubies elsewhere. The levered clasp fixed to the lid is treated in the same way, decorated with alternating turquoise and rubies; its end widens to form a cut-out lance head into which is inserted the ring attached to one of the small vertical sides of the casket.

The box rests on four small silver-gilt feet, each shaped like an arched dragon from which the head, with finely-engraved detail, projects at an angle.

The jade plaques are covered with a seeded pattern: five rows of alternating turquoise and cabochon rubies in claw-shaped mounts on gold plaques in the shape of five-petalled rosettes form the flowers. Between these are set tiny gold dots decorated with a spiral.

This box, which is particularly remarkable for the quality of its materials and the refinement and relative restraint of its decoration, was no doubt used, as suggested by Esin Atil, to hold objects such as jewels or precious stone seals[1]. There are several such boxes in the Treasury of the Topkapı Sarayı[2].

1 *Washington 1987, p. 132*
2 *Ref. no 2/2084 in Istanbul 1983, no. E82; Milan, 1987, no. 286; Tokyo, 1985, no. 313*

Photograph Jacqueline Hyde M.B.T.

93 CHESS PIECES

Turkey, sixteenth/seventeenth century
Carved rock crystal, gold, emerald and rubies; h. (max.) 4.0 (king), 2.6 (pawn); diam. (max.) 2.3 (king), 1.7 (pawn)

Istanbul, Topkapı Sarayı Müzesi, 1372–73
Treasury of the Topkapı Palace

The 32 chess pieces are made of smooth-carved rock crystal. Their shape is that of a slightly concave cylinder, flared a little at the top and crowned by a cap decorated at its apex with a ruby or emerald set in a bezel on a lobed striated gold collar. Only the rook piece, in the shape of a palmette atop a half-sphere, bears four gemstones. Certain details distinguish the pieces: the queen, identical in shape to the king, is slightly smaller; the knight, baluster-shaped, has two notches on its top. The pawn, smaller than all the others, has two grooved lines on its top.

The Topkapı Sarayı Müzesi has another chess board with pieces, taken as booty during the battle of Çaldiran against the Safavid Shah in 1514. The pieces for one side are made of turquoise sheets set in chased gold *cloisons*; for the other side of mauve agate[1].

The game of chess, probably of Indian or Iranian origin, was widely known early in the Islamic world. Often mentioned in contemporary literature and considered a noble game, the rules appear to have been variable in the Middle Ages.

The game is also represented in miniatures as exemplified by a *Shahnāma* page from the sixteenth century, which is attributed to Shiraz[2] and shows Nurşirvan, the Iranian Sovereign, receiving a chess game as a gift from the Raj of India.

1 *Inv. 1366–68, 1375; cf. Köseoğlu, C., 1987 no. 121*
2 *Copenhagen, David Samlings, inv. 45–1982; cf. Louisiana, 1987, no. 222.0*

Bibl.: Köseoğlu, C., 1987, no. 120; cf. Carra de Vaux, B., 1934, p. 350

Photograph Jacqueline Hyde M.B.T.

94 EWER CONVERTED INTO A MATARA

China, fourteenth century; Turkey, around 1600
Celadon; silver gilt; 20.5; base 6.5 x 7.9

Istanbul, Topkapı Sarayı Müzesi, 15/668
Treasury of the Topkapı Palace

This celadon ewer has an oval base, a pear-shaped body with two sides flattened as discs, and a flaring neck. The moulded decoration comprises on one disc a crane flying through clouds and on the other a ship riding the waves. Floral motifs cover the sides. A ewer with the same type of decoration was found during the excavation of a tomb dated 1418, just outside Nanjing[1].

The spout, the handle and the lid, perhaps deliberately broken off, have been replaced in such a way as to transform the ewer into a *matara*. At the two openings corresponding to where the spout and handle would have been are attached two large collars from which rise symmetrically two silver-gilt curving spouts with fine chased decoration of a trellis pattern enclosing flowers. The truncated neck is bound with a crown of lambrequin shapes decorated in the same style and topped by a domed stopper crowned with a coral pearl. Chains, attached to the upper part of the spout collars and to the stopper, link on a hook decorated with a fleuret.

1 *Property of the Cultural Conservation Committee at Nanjing; cf.* Longquan qinyci, *1966, pl. 65*

Bibl.: Krahl, R., 1986, vol. I, no. 219

Photograph Jacqueline Hyde M.B.T.

95 EWER WITH ORNAMENTED GOLD STOPPER

China, early fifteenth century; Turkey c.1600
Incised porcelain, open work, engraved gold set with rubies and a turquoise; 33.0 x diam. base 9.5

Istanbul, Topkapı Sarayı Müzesi, 15/2944
Treasury of the Topkapı Palace

This ewer with pear-shaped body and a slightly flared angular base has a long neck and a curved deeply grooved handle topped by a thumb-rest with a circular ring.

The long slightly curved spout is attached to the neck by a cloud-shaped strut. The quality of the extraordinarily white porcelain, the exceptional delicacy of the motifs incised on the body, handle and spout-arches, the interlacing plant motifs and chrysanthemums: all enhance the overall shape of the object, giving it great elegance.

Ottoman goldsmiths have encircled the (broken) mouth of the ewer with a serrated gold band, chased and set with rubies. This pattern is repeated in mirror-image around the base of the lid. The original lid has been replaced with a bulbous gold cupola finely engraved with small flowering stems and decorated with three circular medallions, each made up of seven rubies. All the stones are table-cut and set in engraved bezels without collars. The knob-shaped apex is set with a turquoise. The interior of the lid and lip are lined with gold leaf or silver-gilt.

Bibl.: Ünal, I., 1963, pl. 2; Jenyns, S., 1964–66, pl. 39b; Misugi, T., 1967, no. 3; Lunsingh Scheurber, D. F., 1980, pl. 582; Misugi, T., 1981(a), vol. I, p. 218 and vol. II, pl. T6; Krahl, R., 1986, I, p. 19 and II, no. 633

Photograph Jacqueline Hyde M.B.T.

96

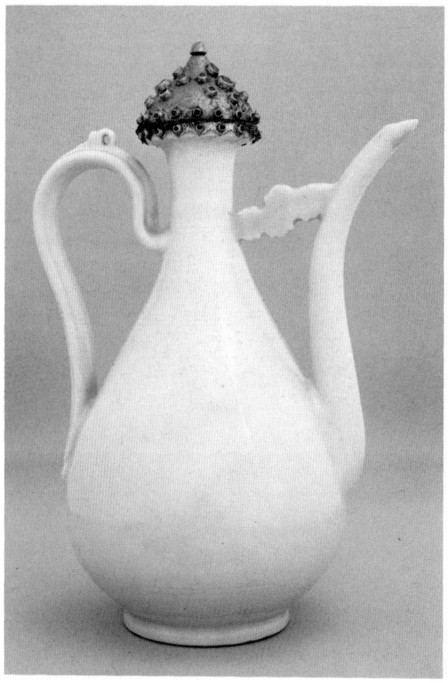

95

96 CUP DECORATED WITH FLOWERS AND TRELLIS WORK

China, Ming dynasty, Hongzhi period (1488–1506)
Turkey, second half of the sixteenth century
Incised porcelain, inlaid with gold and rubies; 7.2; diam. mouth 14.2; diam. base 5.7

Istanbul, Topkapı Sarayı Müzesi, 15/2762
Treasury of the Topkapı Palace

The elegance of this bowl lies in the simplicity of its shape and the pure white of its porcelain. A graceful lotus scroll is incised on the interior of the bowl. The exterior features six rows of diamond-shaped lattices defined by smooth, flattened gold wire inlaid in light relief. On the upper section of the bowl, tri-lobed *fleurons* complete the composition. At the centre of each lattice are flowers arranged in order of decreasing size. Each flower is made of a table-cut ruby set in a bezel, at the centre of a collar of finely striated gold. In the lower four rows, the flowers are six-lobed; in the top row they have a lotus shape within a garland of *fleurons* that forms lambrequins. On the base is a four-character mark in under-glaze blue: *da Ming Hongzhi nian zao*, meaning "made in the Hongzhi period of the Ming dynasty".

Other bowls in the same style are kept in the Topkapı Sarayı Müzesi[1].

1 For example, invs 15/3104, 15/3077, 15/3139; cf. Krahl, R., 1986, II, pp. 869–71

Bibl.: Zimmerman, E., 1930, pl. 70; Misugi, T., 1967, no. 3; Mikami, T., Cig, K. and Namikawa, B., 1974, fig. 44; Misugi, T., 1981, (a), vol. II, T108; Krahl, R., 1986, II, no. 1861

Photograph Jacqueline Hyde M.B.T.

97 COVERED BOWL DECORATED WITH MANDORLAS OF FLOWERS

China, mid sixteenth century; Turkey, late sixteenth century
Porcelain inlaid with gold, rubies and emeralds, chased gold; rock-crystal; paper; gilt paint; 17.0; diam. mount 14.7; diam. base 5.4

Istanbul, Topkapı Sarayı Müzesi, 15/2767
Treasury of the Topkapı Palace

Two bowls of white Chinese porcelain have been combined, undoubtedly in the workshops of Istanbul in the late sixteenth century, to form this work. Each bowl is decorated by six *mandorla* medallions, each formed by the curves of four serrated flowers enclosing a stem bearing three flowers. An inlaid flattened gold wire engraved with fine lines delineates the design in barely perceptible relief. The two flowers enclosed in each leaf and the three blooms in the centre of the *mandorla* are mainly rubies, interspersed with a few emeralds; it seems that the latter had been intended for the flowers of the *mandorla*. The table-cut stones are set in bezels on finely-engraved collars, cut in the shape of a lotus flower in a design seen on other Chinese porcelain pieces (cf. pen box no. 132) and less often on hard stones (cf. pen box no. 133). The base of the upper bowl has been replaced by a rock crystal crown decorated in the same manner, with three *mandorlas* enclosing five rubies alternating with three stems each bearing a flower. The whole is crowned by a crystal knob, which was originally adorned with three rubies.

A pale-yellow paper with a multicoloured floral pattern can be seen through the transparent crystal (as in pen box no. 134). A serrated and engraved gold band encircles the base of the cover; another similar band with double serrations, together with six rivets, holds the block of crystal onto the porcelain bowl (these are visible from the inside). Traces of gilt paint, mirroring the gold band, are found around the rim of the lower bowl and the base.

The interior of the lower bowl is ornamented with a chrysanthemum and blue leaves with traces of gilding. The two-character Chinese mark *jing zhi* ("exquisitely made") is inscribed in a square on the base. The interior of the upper bowl bears a design of a rocky landscape with a weeping willow and fishing boat executed in blue with gold highlights in a circular medallion. A pattern of lotus flowers in medallions and small flowers is moulded in light relief on the sides.

Bibl.: Zimmermann, E., 1930, pl. 70; Misugi, T., 1967, no. 3; Misugi, T., 1981(a), vol. II, pl. T/09; Krahl, R., 1986, vol. II, no. 1784

Photograph Jacqueline Hyde M.B.T.

98 TURBAN ORNAMENT

Istanbul, mid sixteenth century
Chased gold; l. 11.5; diam. collar 1.2

Istanbul, Türk ve Islam Eserleri Müzesi, 419
Transferred in 1911 from the Mausoleum of Hürrem Sultan (Roxelana), located in the graveyard of the Süleymāniye

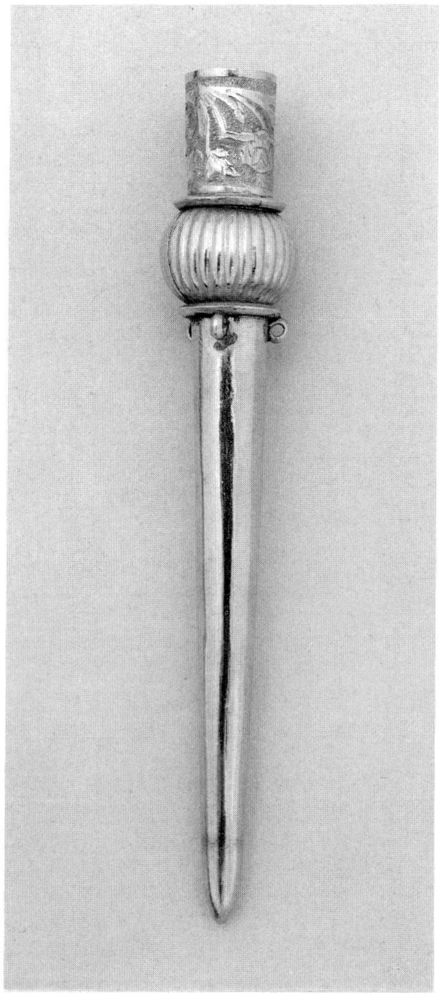

The jewels of the Süleyman period which have reached us are very rare and in order to obtain information on them we have to turn to Ottoman miniatures of the time, in particular to the illustrations of the *Süleymānnāme*.

In these illustrations, decorating clothes or hair styles are belts, kaftan clips, *sorguç* (turban ornaments) and, less frequently, as high-ranking women were rarely portrayed, ear pendants, necklaces and neck pendants[1].

The plume-holder was mainly used to decorate the male head-piece. The shaft was hidden inside the folds of the cloth, while the chains rested on the turban and secured the jewel with their hooks. This type of ornament, however, also appears on other types of head-gear such as the hat of the Flying Peri attributed to Şahkulu[2].

The plume-holder, which comes from the Mausoleum of Hürrem Sultan, is of great simplicity. The hollow shaft bears a large swollen fluted globe between two small pads. Above this the cylindrical ferrule is decorated with a foliage of *ṣāz* leaves and of stylized flowers on a ring-punched ground. Chains were probably attached to the four small rings at the base to steady the jewel and perhaps to hold other ornaments.

1 *cf. The Sultana looking at her reflection in a fountain, miniature of the* Ravzat al Usak *by 'Arīfī, illustrated in Atil, E., 1986, p. 71*
2 *Washington, Freer Gallery of Art, inv. 37.7*

Photograph Jacqueline Hyde T.B.

99 TURBAN ORNAMENT

Turkey, mid sixteenth century
Chased and nielloed gold; l. 15.5; diam. collar 1.4

Istanbul, Türk ve Islam Eserleri Müzesi, 421
Transferred from the Mausoleum (türbe) *of Sultan Selim II in 1914*

The ornament of gold has a hollow shaft, atop which is a small spherical ball faceted with lozenge shapes and a cylindrical ferrule. These are decorated with a simple, finely chased design on a nielloed ground. The half-palmettes and stylized clouds are adapted to the shape of the facets, elongated when necessary to fill the available space. A milled edge and an articulated ring encircle the collar. Four small rings are attached to the base of the spherical element, two bearing chains with double links and a final hook.

Photograph Jacqueline Hyde T.B.

100 TURBAN ORNAMENT

Turkey, second half of the sixteenth century
Chased gold, silver, rubies and turquoise; 1. 14.5; diam. collar 2.3

Istanbul, Türk ve Islam Eserleri Müzesi, 416
Transferred from the Mausoleum (türbe) of Sultan Selim II in 1914

The light flaring socket gives this *sorguç* the appearance of a torch. Its shaft is made of two parts: one tubular, in gold and ringed with a large spherical gadrooned collar; the other flat, in silver, and from a later period. The tubular section is decorated in vertical panels with foliage and stylized flowers in high relief. On the gadroons of the spherical collar, cabochon rubies and turquoise set in gold bezels are linked by branches. The collar, bordered with a row of turquoise, is not divided into sections like the other parts and the gems are inserted in a free-flowing design of leaves and stylized flowers. The ground is finely ring-punched.

Photograph Jacqueline Hyde T.B.

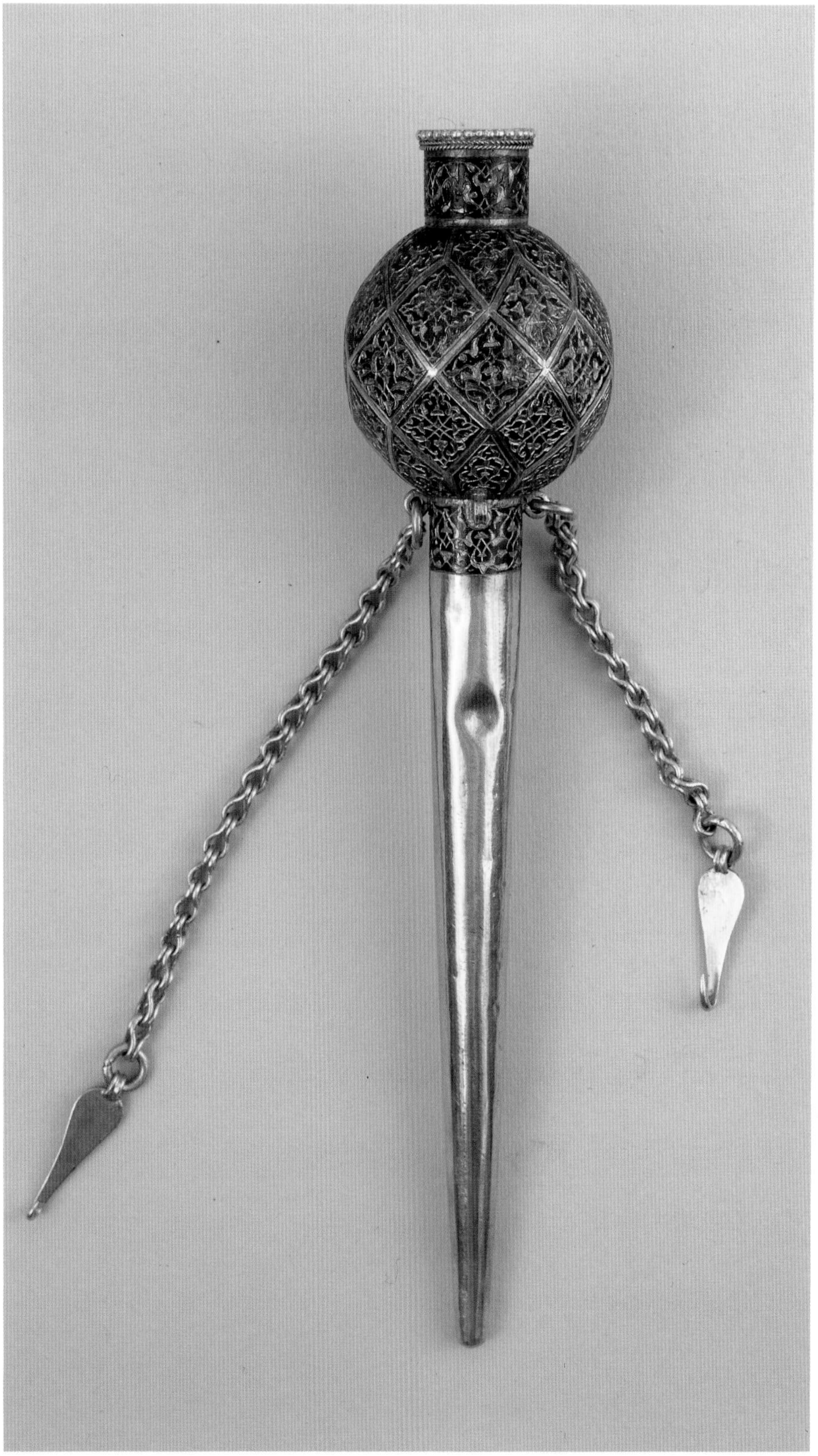

101 TURBAN ORNAMENT

Turkey, second half of the sixteenth century
Chased and nielloed gold; sapphire, diamonds, rubies and turquoise; 19.4 x (max.) 5.7

Istanbul, Topkapı Sarayı Müzesi, 2/2912
Treasury of the Topkapı Palace

A flat circular medallion with slightly lobed edges is mounted on a grooved bar ornamented with a small spherical piece holding two rings to which are attached two chains.

The front of the medallion is decorated with a large facet-cut sapphire surrounded by four diamonds (which were probably added later) alternating with cabochon rubies. Rubies and turquoise alternate around the perimeter. A very fine gold *rūmī* plant design is set against the nielloed background.

A similar decoration adorns both the small spherical piece and the back of the medallion. On the latter is a plume-holder decorated with nielloed clouds on a gold ground.

Each chain is ornamented a third of the way down with two turquoise set back-to-back in a gold bezel.

Photograph Jacqueline Hyde T.B.

102 MIRROR WITH CLOUD DECORATION

Turkey, first half of the sixteenth century
Steel(?) inlaid with gold, rubies, turquoise and diamonds(?); carved jade; 30.0 x 14.0

Istanbul, Topkapı Sarayı Müzesi, 2/1801
Treasury of the Topkapı Palace

The burnished steel mirror is set in a circular frame bordered by 17 festooned lobes. It is attached to a dark-green jade hexagonal handle ending in a gadrooned knob and a five-lobed flower. The handle is set into a gold filigreed band with alternating rubies and turquoise, surmounted by the mirror clasp: a pierced poly-lobed gold plaque with a turquoise in the centre and surrounded by four rubies. Most of the stones ornamenting this piece are cabochons, although some of the rubies are table-cut. All are set in clawed bezels, a type of mount used on certain objects during the first half of the sixteenth century, rarely thereafter.

The front of the mirror is bordered by a gold band decorated with a fine pattern of arabesques, highlighted with alternating rubies and turquoise, each separated by a table-cut diamond(?).

The back of the mirror displays a large disc marked in the centre by a star-shaped six-pointed rosette, of which the centre is a ruby. Six *mandorla*-shaped medallions, separated by small oblong cartouches, radiate from the rosette. Six half-lozenges encircle this composition. All these medallions are adorned by a fine engraved pat-

tern of Chinese clouds; they stand out from the dark-grey metal ground set with minute gold arabesques and highlighted by six turquoise. Around the rim, a band, divided into six cartouches each separated by a gold medallion decorated with either a ruby or turquoise, bears a Persian poem inscribed in *nasta'līk*. In each of the cartouches on the border is a minute leafed stem.

Translation of the Persian text:

1 *Oh you, whose mirror the sun holds [which reflects] your beauty*
2 *[and you whose] seed of beauty . . . black musk*
3 *Without being able to reflect your face, O you my well-beloved who resembles a cypress, my heart clouds over*
4 *Such a mirror tarnished by the breath of sighs*
5 *She has entrusted to this mirror that which has ravished my heart*
6 *Out of a calamity which has eaten away my existence, she has made two*

The decoration of this mirror is inscribed in the Timurid tradition and also reflects the art practised in the first half of the sixteenth century by the artists of the *nakkaşhane*, as evidenced also in lacquered book bindings and textiles.

A mirror treated in the same spirit is in the collection of the Metropolitan Museum of Art in New York[2].

1 *Reading and translation courtesy of Sharyar Adle*
2 *Department of Islamic Art, inv. 1982, 72-24*

Photograph Jacqueline Hyde M.B.T.

102

103 BELT

Turkey, mid sixteenth century
Engraved mother-of-pearl inlaid with gold and black organic material; silver-gilt(?), leather, velvet; 92.0 x 2.7 x 0.6

Istanbul, Topkapı Sarayı Müzesi, 2/575

This articulated belt comprises 42 links of mother-of-pearl mounted in metal (silver-gilt?) attached to leather which is lined in the exposed sections with garnet-coloured velvet.

Twenty circular links alternate with 21 oblong pieces. At each end of the belt is a rectangular lobed element, one of which is missing.

The decoration is extremely fine. The mother-of-pearl has been grooved so that it can hold small six-lobed gold fleurets, made up of three superimposed collars, which create the impression of flowers with serrated petals. A fine network of arabesques, punctuated with miniscule flowers and leaves and filled with black paste, forms the background. The general design is reminiscent of that of certain *tuğra* of Sultan Süleyman (compare no. 3) and of ceramics of the so-called "Golden Horn" series.

Two of the plaques are undoubtedly taken from another belt because the design of arabesques is ornamented with small tulips.

Five mother-of-pearl belts of this type, which were worn by men and women, are housed in the Topkapı Sarayı Müzesi.

Bibl.: Bilingen, E., 1989, fig. 4

Photograph Jacqueline Hyde M.B.T.

104 BELT

Turkey, second half of the sixteenth century
Ivory inlaid with gold, black paste, rubies and turquoise; 65.5 x 4.5

Istanbul, Türk ve Islam Eserleri Müzesi, 482
Transferred from the Mausoleum (türbe) *of Selim II in 1914*

This articulated belt comprises four square plates linked together by five rows of three or four (depending on the spacing) small rectangular elements with lobed centres joined by a system of pins. The polished ivory is decorated with delicate, precise motifs. Each square plaque displays a large central disc in slight relief. Two arabesques interlace on each disc: one, a design of volutes, is engraved in a fine line inlaid with a black paste and adorned with tiny flowers of various shapes, leaves and tendrils; the other, in relief, is made of gold wire inlaid in the ivory and bearing small fleurets, half-leaves, tendrils and fleurets with finely chased elongated lobes. The gold line forms a swirl of curving motifs and four overlapping palmettes which seem to issue from a six-petalled cabochon turquoise set in a bezel with a six-lobed gold collar. This flower is surrounded with four cabochon rubies set in bezels on five-lobed collars within the centre of the palmettes and linked together by curved lines which form a lozenge. A cabochon turquoise set in the same way marks each corner of the square plaque; two gold branches with flexible bifoliated branches, and fine stems inlaid with black paste radiate from these.

At each end of this square plaque, three oblong cartouches in chased gold with lotus scrolls accentuate the rectangular panels which start the articulated part.

A simlar design to that on the plaques is found on each of the small rectangular links: alternating rows of cabochon rubies and six-petalled turquoise, set in bezels on lobed collars with trefoil pendants in embossed gold, circled by a fine black line adorned with four trefoils. The clasp of the belt is missing.

The belt comes from the tomb of Selim II, within the precints of the Ayasofya. Built in 1577, this mausoleum, the work of Sinan, houses the sepulchre of 42 members of the families of Selim II and of Murad III. This belt probably served as an ornament to one of the deceased, but as men and women wore similar belts, it is impossible to be more precise.

Several belts of the same type are kept in the Topkapı Sarayı Müzesi and in the Türk ve Islam Eserleri Müzesi.

Photograph Jacqueline Hyde M.B.T.

105 THREE BELT COMPONENTS

Turkey, beginning of the sixteenth century
Carved ivory, engraved and painted
1: 7.8 x 5.2 x 0.6
2: 6.6 x 4.9 x 0.6
3: 5.1 x 3.6 x 0.5

Istanbul, Topkapı Sarayı Müzesi, (1) 2/627, (2) 2/628, (3) 2/629
Treasury of the Topkapı Palace

The three components, tongue, buckle and plaques, probably come from the same belt and would have been attached to a piece of textile or leather (cf. no. 103). Each is carved from a single piece of ivory. The tongue is rectangular with a multi-lobed end; the buckle is a rhomboidal crescent; the plaque is a multi-lobed oval shape. On the surface of each object, the decoration is deeply carved and engraved, and a thin strip of blue paint surrounds the edge; the tongue, which is the largest piece, bears a scroll with flowers and leaves of two types.

On each of the components, the dense decoration is centred on flowers with multi-collared hearts and curving disarrayed petals arranged like the blades of a vane. Double-grooved stems describe a circular movement, forming coils; pointed leaves, often curled and finely engraved, sometimes in the opposite direction, are wound around many of the stems.

Bibl.: Bilingen, E., 1989, fig. 6

Photograph Jacqueline Hyde M.B.T.

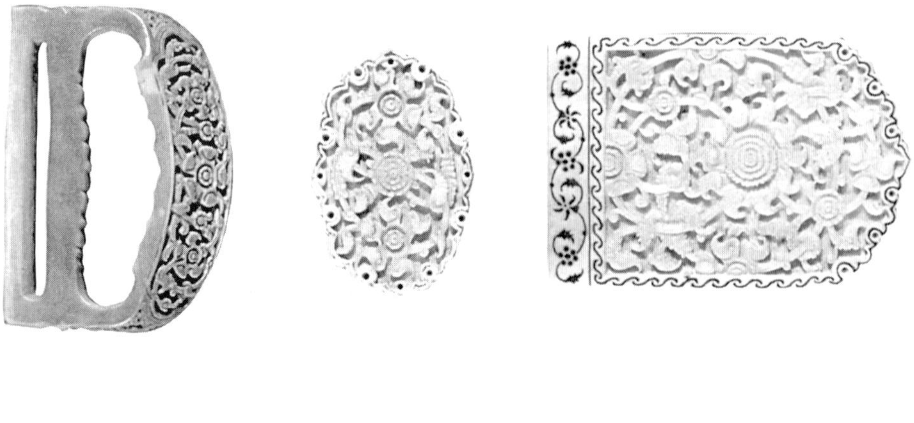

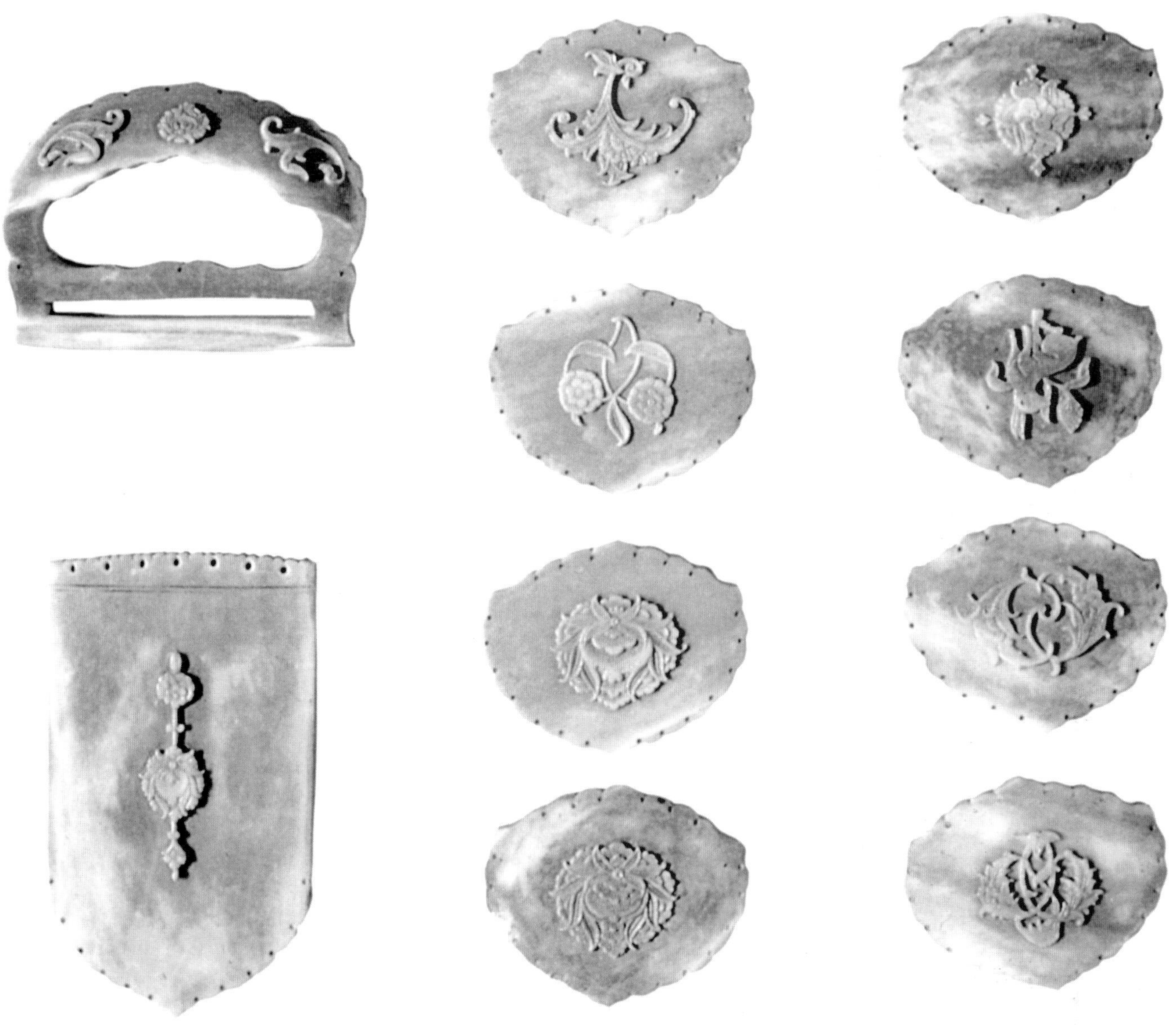

106 COMPONENTS OF A BELT

Turkey, mid sixteenth century
Carved ivory; (1) 4.8 x 4.8; (2) 6.0 x 4.8; (3) 5.6 x 4.1

Istanbul, Library of the Topkapı Sarayı Müzesi,
(1) 2/635; (2) 2/636; (3) 2/638
Treasury of the Topkapı Palace

These 10 components — eight medallions, one tongue, one buckle — were probably part of the same belt and would have been fixed to a strip of textile or leather. Each is carved from a single piece of ivory with a different design. The medallions are flat festooned lozenges; the tongue, rounded at one end, has some fastening holes on the other end; the buckle has a lobed crescent and a straight side with a slit into which the leather was inserted. Blue dots emphasize the grooves of the festoons, the medallions and the buckle. A motif carved in rather high relief decorates the centre of each component, rising clearly above the smooth surrounding surface. One medallion represents a hare (?) poised, its head turned, against a background of branches; the seven other medallions show motifs of flowers, stems or leaves: full lotus flowers, curved stems with two palmettes, supple indented leaves with or without half-rosettes, forming whirling patterns. On the tongue is an isolated but more elongated motif — a lotus flower with floral pendants; two incised lines emphasize the rectilinear end of the object. On the buckle, two small branches with curved leaves frame a lotus flower.

The extreme precision of the sculpting and the adaptation of the motifs for decoration give these plaques a high artistic quality. The elements of the decoration and their treatment are characteristic of the *ṣāz* style, perfected in the workshops of the minature painters in the second quarter of the sixteenth century.

A few rare examples of this type of ivory belt are kept at the Topkapı Sarayı Müzesi[1].

1 *For example, a tongue (inv. 2/599; Istanbul 1983, no. E90) decorated with a motif carved in the same manner as the one in the exhibition; a tongue, a buckle and a medallion (inv. 2/622, 2/623, 2/624) of the same shape but entirely covered with a finely sculpted ornamentation (Istanbul, 1983, no. E86). The Kuwait National Museum owns a buckle decorated with a lotus motif and ṣāz leaves (inv. LNS 461); another complete belt of this type is in the Metropolitan Museum, New York*

Bibl.: Bilingen, E., 1989, no. 12

Photograph Jacqueline Hyde

M.B.T.

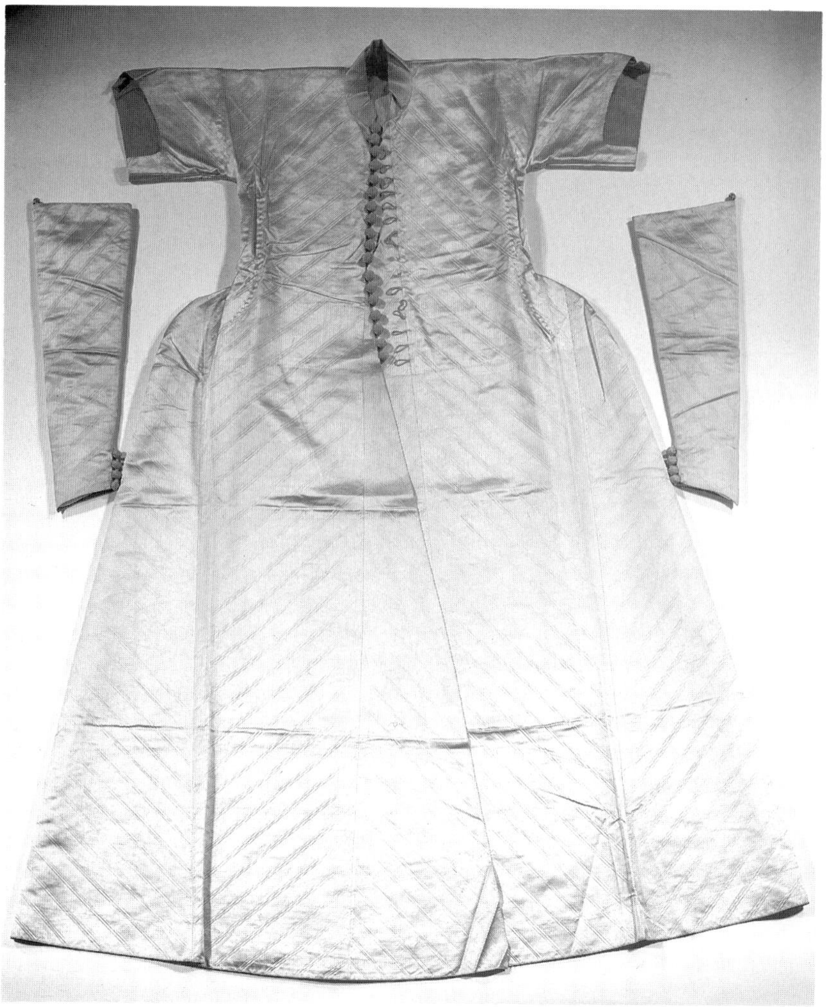

107 CHILD'S KAFTAN AND CULOTTES

Turkey, beginning of the sixteenth century
Silk satin, cotton; kaftan 72.0 x 65.5; l. culottes 70.0

Istanbul, Topkapı Sarayı Müzesi, 13/92 plus 13/93
Treasury of the Topkapı Palace

This outfit of a kaftan and trousers meant for a child of 8–10 years of age is made of pistachio-green satin. The kaftan, without pockets and with a small stand-up collar, widens at hip level and fastens with seven braided buttons in the same green. It is lined to the waist with white cheesecloth and bordered on the inside with a strip of mauve watered silk. The trousers, ornamented with socks and an attached white silk draw-string belt, are lined with white quilted cotton.

The kaftan is labelled as having belonged to Sultan Süleyman. The Topkapı Sarayı Müzesi has about 80 pieces of clothing which belonged to the sovereign. They bear witness to his extremely slim frame and his taste for plain, unpatterned cloth, particularly in pistachio-green.

Photograph Jacqueline Hyde M.B.T.

108 KAFTAN WITH DETACHABLE SLEEVES

Turkey, mid sixteenth century
Silk, goffered satin for the kaftan and the internal borders, cotton for the lining; l. 146.0; (max.) width with the short sleeves 8.5; l. sleeves 49.0, 45.0; w. 16.5

Istanbul, Topkapı Sarayı Müzesi, 13/100

This long kaftan with short sleeves and a stand-up collar, narrow in the bodice and wide at the hips, is fastened with 18 braided buttons with loops. Long sleeves with four buttons at the wrist can be attached; a round button with beige, white and blue chevrons is still attached to the upper part of the sleeve but the corresponding loop inside the armhole of the kaftan is missing. This garment is made of a beige-pink satin, goffered to create a pattern of triple line stripes. Lined to the waist with white cotton, it is edged on the inside by a band of pistachio-green satin goffered with patterns of four or five lines; the seams are covered by a silk ribbon in the same colour.

A blue ink circular stamp on the hem is illegible, but one can assume it indicates the taxes paid on the silk (production of silk was a state monopoly and strictly controlled). The material (plain satin), the cut and the shape of the collar of this kaftan are similar to those in the child's outfit (no. 107), also thought to have belonged to Sultan Süleyman the Magnificent whose austere taste, which was not without elegance or refinement, is well known.

Photograph Jacqueline Hyde M.B.T.

110

and encircling trefoils. The whole pattern is emphasised by fine *ḫaṭāyī* motifs in light blue, pistachio-green and red.

The kaftan is lined with apricot-coloured quilted cotton with a pattern of vertical stripes giving to the other side of the material a fluted appearance.

A wide silk ribbon of pistachio-green, goffered in groups of four stripes, edges the lining.

According to the label of the Topkapı Sarayı Müzesi, this garment belonged to Selim I (1512–20), but a stylistic study of the motifs, similar to those found on illuminations and ceramic tiles of the period 1520–60, places it at a slightly later date.

Bibl.: Öz, T., 1950, pl. 91 and pl. XXIV, no. 3432; Mackie, L. W., 1980, no. 201; Tezcan, H. and Delibas, S., 1986, pl. 7

Photograph Jacqueline Hyde M.B.T.

109 KAFTAN

Turkey, mid sixteenth century
Wool, cloth, silk; l. 133.0; w. (shoulders and sleeves) 140.0

Istanbul, Topkapı Sarayı Müzesi, 13/145
Treasury of the Topkapı Palace

This kaftan, made of dark green cloth, opened by two slits on the sides and with two straight pockets, is made of several patches of material delicately sewn together. With a small stand-up collar, it is fastened by 12 braided buttons attached to frogs of a pistachio-green colour.

On the inside this robe is lined with black cloth to the waist and bordered with a wide strip (12 centimetres) of purple silk with a goffered satin design of lines grouped in fours.

This kaftan, which belonged to Süleyman, was not for ceremonial wear. It corresponds to the sultan's austere taste, or what we know of it from numerous portraits of him. Many other kaftans which are thought to have belonged to the sultan are often made of material of a plain colour (cf. nos 107 and 108).

Photograph Jacqueline Hyde M.B.T.

110 KAFTAN WITH A NETWORK DECORATION *ill. page 115*

Turkey, second quarter of the sixteenth century
Silk, gold thread, cotton; lampas on satin ground, quilted; 137.0 x 130.0

Istanbul, Topkapı Sarayı Müzesi, 13/46
Treasury of the Topkapı Palace

This kaftan with short sleeves, which is wider at the shoulder and has no collar, is fastened by 15 braided buttons attached to braided frogs, at the end of which are small pompons in the same colour as the cloth or in red, gold or white. Two slitted pockets are placed at hip level.

The remarkable condition of this robe emphasises the weaving technique which gives a relief effect to the decoration. The cerise ground weave is fashioned with a repeating pattern of half hexagonal motifs, giving a variegated appearance reinforced by the padding underneath. The cut of the garment relates to the large continuous motif, undulating and ascendant, in gold on a red field, which covers the whole surface.

The long arms of the volutes contain patterns of palmettes laid out in quincunxes

111 KAFTAN WITH A TULIP DECORATION

Turkey, second half of the sixteenth century
Silk brocaded satin (serenk), *weft patterned, cotton lining; l. 86.0 (back), 76.0 (front); w. 99.0 (max.)*

Istanbul, Topkapı Sarayı Müzesi, 13/38
Treasury of the Topkapı Palace

This short kaftan without a collar, with three-quarter sleeves, longer at the back than at the front, fastened on the chest by six braided silk buttons, has only one pocket. The pattern, made up of rows of alternate motifs arranged in quincunxes, is yellow with touches of pale blue and red, on a red damask ground ornamented with scrolls bearing tiny leaves and flowers with hearts of yellow and blue.

Two large almond-shaped leaves decorated with overlapping scales encircle a large stylized tulip decorated with a small network of flowers. Two smaller leaves, attached to the larger ones by a stem, hold an almost full-blown lotus flower of which the heart matches that of the tulip.

The reverse side of the material, quilted and lined with unbleached cotton, is bordered by a wide green silk band. This type of kaftan was worn over wide trousers by horse-riders and sportsmen.

According to the inventory of the Topkapı Palace, this garment belonged to Bayazid II (1481–1512) but, from the study of its pattern, it is probably a few decades later.

Bibl.: Öz, T., 1950, p. 47 and plate X, no. 5674; Tezcan, H. and Delibaş, S., 1986, no. 6

Photograph Jacqueline Hyde

M.B.T.

113

112

112 PAIR OF DETACHABLE SLEEVES

Turkey, mid sixteenth century
Silk and metallic thread; lampas, ground tabby twill (kemha); 95.0 x 29.0 x 13.0

Istanbul, Topkapı Sarayı Müzesi, 13/72
Treasury of the Topkapı Palace

These two wide sleeves could be buttoned to the inside of the shoulder of the kaftan. A button trim is visible in the top corner; three others, matched with loops, enable the cuff to be tightened around the wrist. The decoration, executed with extraordinary delicacy, stands out in silver on a rosewood-coloured ground. Lengthways it repeats in six vertical rows a *ṣāz* motif of rare elegance, combining feathery leaves, *ḫaṭāyī* flowers and lotus in the style of those produced by artists of the *nakkaşhane* in the second quarter of the sixteenth century and of those which decorated bindings such as the *Khamsa* of Mīr 'Alī Shīr Nevā'ī in 1530–31 (cf. no. 130). The sleeves are bordered on the inside with an embossed green silk ribbon.

Photograph Jacqueline Hyde M.B.T.

113 BELT WITH LOTUS DESIGN

Turkey, mid sixteenth century
Linen with silk and gold thread embroidery; 174.0 x 28.3; h. embroidery 12.2

Istanbul, Topkapı Sarayı Müzesi, 31/50
Mausoleum (türbe) *of Prince Şehzade Mehmed (died 1543)*

This belt is made of a long band of unbleached linen, folded in two, lengthwise. Only the ends are decorated with a very heavy gold thread embroidery covering the whole surface, imitating scales and serving as a backdrop to a delicate floral motif of lotus in bloom, flower buds, lilies, leafy stems and Chinese clouds. These motifs, which are outlined, depending on their size, with stem-stitching made up of one to three threads, have a variegated appearance. They are embroidered in light blue, green, pink and yellow, with a running stitch.

In some miniatures, such as the portraits of Süleyman and of Selim II by Nīgārī for instance[1], the dignitaries accompanying the sovereign wear this type of accessory, passed as an ornament through a belt.

1 Both kept at the Topkapı Sarayı library

Bibl.: Arseven, C. E., n.d., fig. 1575

Photograph Jacqueline Hyde M.B.T.

114 and 115

114 HANDKERCHIEF

Turkey, c.1540
Printed muslin, embroidered with silk and silver threads; 55.0 x 53.0; border 3.6

Istanbul, Topkapı Sarayı Müzesi, 31/53
Mausoleum (türbe) *of Prince Şehzade Meḥmed (died 1543)*

This handkerchief, in fine cinnamon-coloured muslin, is decorated with a black printed border on which a frieze of octagons stands in reserve. The reversible design is embroidered with extreme fineness in stitches and on some parts in openwork, in red, yellow, green, white and light-blue silk; the pattern is highlighted by a tinsel effect produced by fine silver threads knotted around the linen thread. Inside these tinsel-outlined rosaces around the border is a blue and green cruciform design and four white and yellow *fleurons* highlighted with silver. Red almond-shaped motifs set point-to-point and stemming from two half-leaves in green and blue flank these octagons.

Several other handkerchiefs of the same type, kept in the Topkapı Sarayı Müzesi, come from the mausoleum of Şehzade Meḥmed and from that of Roxelana(1) and Aḥmed I.

The ceremonial handkerchief has always been, it seems, a symbol of royalty in the Islamic world; it may be a legacy of the Byzantine *mappa*. In many miniatures, the throned sovereign holds this accessory in his left hand(2). They were often presented as royal gifts and sometimes deposited in mausoleums where they were laid on the cenotaph.

1 *Inv. 31/1473*
2 *E.g., the frontispiece page of the* Maqāmat of al-Ḥarīrī *in the Nationalbibliothek in Vienna, which was made in Egypt in 1334; the portrait of Süleyman painted by Nīgārī and kept in the Topkapı Sarayı Müzesi*

Bibl.: Tezcan, H. and Delibaş, S., 1987, no. 88

Photograph Jacqueline Hyde M.B.T.

Note: nos 114 and 115 illustrated on page 119 are placed on top of each other.

115 HANDKERCHIEF

Turkey, c.1540
Printed linen muslin with a border of silk and gold threads; 50.0 x 48.0; w. border 5.2

Istanbul, Topkapı Sarayı Müzesi, 31/54
Mausoleum (türbe) *of Prince Şehzade Meḥmed (died 1543)*

As with the previous handkerchief, this one is in fine cinnamon-coloured linen muslin, but printed in black; only the border, which is decorated with a frieze of lozenges in reserve, allows the original colour to be seen. It is also embroidered with red, pistachio green, white and light blue; gold tinsel punctuates the design of imbricated triangles set around a cruciform motif of fleurons in the centre of the lozenge and adjacent to its external sides.

Bibl.: Arseven, C. E., n.d., fig. 601; Tezcan, H. and Delibaş, S., 1987, no. 88

Photograph Jacqueline Hyde M.B.T.

116

116 TEXTILE FRAGMENT WITH FLOWERING ROSES PATTERN

Turkey, second half of the sixteenth century
Cut silk velvet on satin lame foundation; 81.0 x 67.0

Istanbul, Topkapı Sarayı Müzesi, 13/1466
Treasury of the Topkapı Palace

Two floral compositions are arranged in alternate rows to form quincunxes: a rosace encircled by stylized tulips and hyacinths; four carnations arranged as a cross around a crown. The motifs stand out in garnet red and green on a background which must have been gold or silver in the past: the silk core around which the metallic thread was twisted is white inside the rose motif and yellow elsewhere.

Though very worn, cut without much care and mounted as a cushion cover with a *bayadere* (contrasting stripes) border, this piece of material nonetheless features an interesting ornamental pattern evocative of certain Ushak carpets from the seventeenth century.

Bibl.: Öz, T., 1951, pl. CXIII

Photograph Jacqueline Hyde M.B.T.

117 TEXTILE WITH FLOWERING CLOUDS

ill. opposite detail

Turkey, Istanbul or Bursa, sixteenth or seventeenth century
Silk, metallic thread; velvet: cut, voided, satin foundation, faced with foil-wrapped silk wefts and embellished with loops of a foil-wrapped silk; 156.5 x 119.0

Collection Rifaat Sheikh El-Ard, Riyadh

The ensemble is made of two widths with green satin selvedges. Joined at the selvedge, they constitute a large decorative composition in which the pattern repeats twice, in both length and width, in a mirror-image. Large golden poly-lobed cartouches in a shape of a bulging "S", reminiscent of Chinese clouds, stand out against a background of garnet red velvet, outlined by a narrow fillet of looped gold thread and enhanced by scrolls with carnations, tulips, florets and small leaves unfolding on the golden background in an ascending layout. These cartouches, facing each other obliquely in twos, are assembled in groups of four around a diamond-shaped space decorated by a large gold rosace highlighted with gold thread loops on the garnet-red background: from a central flower in full bloom radiate four straight stems and four flowers which give rise to supple and curving twigs bearing lotus flowers and florets. A similar blossoming flower occupies the space where the tips of the four cloud-like cartouches come together.

This textile, for which there is no known equal, is striking for its high-quality craftsmanship: the different ways the gold thread is treated, flat or looped to bring out the relief, and the shades in the colour. The decorative motif is typical of the sixteenth century, as can be seen in other art forms and techniques.

M.B.T.

118 MATARA COVER

Turkey, late sixteenth–early seventeenth century
Leather, silk, gold and silver threads, embossed embroidery on velvet, stamped leather; 40.0 x 33.0

Istanbul, Topkapı Sarayı Müzesi, 31/169
Treasury of the Topkapı Palace

This cover for a *matara* (a bulbous gourd-shaped container for the sultan's water) is made of two parts linked by a cream-coloured ribbon decorated with red and blue cartouches (made at a later date?) which allows the top of the flask to slide off and on. It is made of beige leather which has turned brown on the outside; a thin ribbon of blue leather, sewn to the leather on the two sides of the cover, emphasizes the contour. Inside, the leather has retained its beige colour and is stamped with motifs: indented leaves and pomegranates surrounding a hyacinth flower.

The two parts fit together to form a multi-lobed silhouette. The floral decoration stands out in gold and silver on a background of red velvet; the pattern, created in running stitch over paste-boarded motifs, is secured in cross-stitch with thicker gold thread. The upper part, which is normally covered by the lid, retains freshness of colour; it is decorated with a scatter of 12 flowers each with five or six petals, and gold with silver hearts. The decoration on the cover and the lower part of the case is treated in the same spirit and comprises: a palmette of indented half-leaves enclosing a flower around which is organised, in a symmetrical fashion, a pattern made of stems with small indented curved leaves; small and large flowers reminiscent of lotus flowers, embroidered in gold thread with some of the details in silver thread.

Photograph Jacqueline Hyde M.B.T.

119 CARPET WITH MEDALLIONS

Turkey, Ushak, sixteenth century
Wool, symmetrical knot; 610.0 x 315.0

Istanbul, Türk ve Islam Eserleri Müzesi, 36
Transferred from the Ibrahim Paşa Mosque in 1911

Carpets in the Orient were works of art, the particular expression of a tribe or ethnic group, as well as objects of daily life. Indispensable to a nomadic society, they were often the only piece of furniture in a dwelling. Women were particularly adept at weaving them. In ancient times carpets were generally of rather small dimensions; later, workshops were established in urban centres where larger carpets could be made.

In these urban centres the huge Anatolian carpets of the sixteenth century were manufactured. It is still hard to pinpoint their place of origin, but carpets with medallions such as the one presented here are thought to come from Ushak. Similar pieces can be seen in European paintings from the middle of the sixteenth century, a fact which establishes a guideline for dating.

Their decoration, inspired by Safavid Persia, is distinguished by its supple lines and curvilinear motifs. The more strictly geometrical compositions are of Turkoman origin and characterize those Anatolian carpets known as "Holbeins" or "Lottos". In the centre, on the red ground, a large oval medallion decorated with lotus and other floral motifs on a blue ground projects vertically into two pendants of lozenge shape. At the extreme ends of the field appear the edges of two other medallions severed by the wide dark-red border and decorated with large open flowers. Lengthwise on both sides two pendant stars, halved by the border, are decorated with fine arabesque motifs in an ivory colour on a blue ground.

In this pattern, characteristic of the best Ushak work, the sides of the medallions featured at each end of the design and the truncated stars seem to prolong the composition to infinity and give it a dynamic

120

121 HANCERI LEAVES AND PHEASANT

Turkey, 1550–75
Black ink on prepared paper; page 37.0 x 20.0; drawing 13.2 x 7.5

Istanbul, Library of the Topkapı Sarayı Müzesi, H.2135 f. 14i
Treasury of the Topkapı Palace

This drawing, executed in ink with a brush, is from an album compiled in the ateliers of the Topkapı Palace at the end of the seventeenth century or the beginning of the eighteenth century.

This perfect rendering of the *ṣāz* style represents pointed leaves which, starting from a common point, curve, twist and pierce themselves. On one of these leaves is perched a pheasant.

The pheasant motif is common among the bird images used in compositions of the *ṣāz* style, which was influenced by the "forestry" themes of central Asia and the Far East. In Chinese mythology, the pheasant replaces the *zümürüdüanka* (the legendary bird of the fables), which is the symbol of beauty and good fortune.

It appears that in sixteenth-century Ottoman art, and particularly in *ṣāz* illustrations, the pheasant carries a symbolic meaning identical to the one he has in Chinese art[1].

1 Mahir, B., 1987, p. 130

Bibl.: Mahir, B., 1987, fig. 16

Photograph Jacqueline Hyde F.Ç.

character not seen in Persian models. A carpet in very similar style is kept in Paris at the Musée des Arts Décoratifs (inv. 14.428).

Bibl.: cf. Mackie, L., 1980, pp. 299–343; London, 1983, pp. 73–74

Photograph Jacqueline Hyde T.B.

120 ḪAṬĀYĪ FLOWER WITH LEAVES

ill. page 123

Turkey, second half of the sixteenth century
Black ink, watercolour and gold on prepared paper; 35.2 x 21.5; drawing 14.5 x 8.7

Istanbul, Library of the Topkapı Sarayı Müzesi, H 2168, f. 15a
Treasury of the Topkapı Palace

This drawing dates from the second half of the sixteenth century and is characteristic of the *ṣāz* style, recognised as influential in the painting and decoration which emerged from the ateliers of the palace during the early years of Sultan Süleyman's reign.

The most frequently used motifs in the *ṣāz* style are:

1 The *ḫaṭāyī* flower, a mixture of lotus and peony
2 The *hanceri*, long, slender leaves with serrated edges on broken stems.

The drawing shown is executed with a brush in black ink. In some places it is coloured with an ink which has turned pink through the application of water and by gilding.

The work is attributed to the artist known as Velīcān, who worked after 1583 in the *nakkaşhane* (design atelier) of the palace. The signature is at the bottom of the drawing.

Photograph Jacqueline Hyde F.Ç.

122 HUNTING HORSEMAN AND LION

Turkey, mid sixteenth century
Black ink, blue watercolour paint and gilding, on prepared paper; page 30.8 x 22.0; drawing 12.8 x 19.5

Istanbul, Library of the Topkapı Sarayı Müzesi, H 2163 (f. 7v°)
Topkapı Palace collection

This album of 10 pages, comprising mostly ink and brush drawings of the Safavid era and examples of calligraphy, must have been compiled in the palace ateliers late in the seventeenth century.

The drawing shown illustrates the struggle between a horseman armed with bow and arrows, and a lion. The background of this brush and ink drawing is a large branch describing a circle embellished with leaves and *ṣāz* style flowers.

The horse's saddle and blanket and parts of the leaves and flowers are highlighted in blue. The quiver, the horseman's belt, the stirrup, the harness and the eye of the lion are gold. The horseman's clothing, particularly his turban, is in the style fashionable at the time of Sultan Süleyman the Magnificent.

Bibl.: Mahir, 1987, fig. 7

Photograph Jacqueline Hyde F.Ç.

123 PHOENIX AND LION *ill. opposite*

Turkey, mid sixteenth century
Black and gold ink on prepared paper;
page 41.4 x 27.9; miniature 19.0 x 12.5

Istanbul, Library of Topkapı Sarayı Müzesi,
H 2169 f. 37r°
Topkapı Palace collection

This brush drawing is from a compilation probably executed in the palace workrooms during the years 1600–25. The main motif is a large Phoenix perched on a long stem which bears ṣāz flowers and leaves coiling to the bottom of the composition to encircle a small lion, seen in profile turned towards the fabulous bird. Small Chinese clouds are strewn across the top of the page. The style of these motifs, especially the shape of the clouds, indicates that the drawing dates from the end of the reign of Sultan Süleyman the Magnificent.

The fabulous bird, which plays an important role in the mythology of Asia, bears the name of *anka* in Arabic, *simurğ* in Iranian mythology and *garuda* in Indian mythology. It was thought to live in the mountains of Elbūrz or of the Kaf and it was believed that if a person could obtain a feather, they would learn the secret of immortality[1].

The diverse motifs — lion, lotus flowers, stems carrying long ṣāz leaves, *simurğ* — are characteristic of ṣāz compositions which evoke a mysterious forest.

1 Ögel, 1971, p. 108; Mahir, B., 1987, p. 129

Bibl.: Mahir, B., 1987, fig. 5

Photograph Jacqueline Hyde F.Ç.

124 PERI

Turkey, c.1550–75
Black ink, watercolour, opaque colours and gold on prepared paper; page 36.2 x 26.0; drawing 18.7 x 11.6

Istanbul, Library of the Topkapı Sarayı Müzesi,
H 2162 f. 8r°
Topkapı Palace collection

This drawing is part of an Ottoman album compiled in the eighteenth century. In front of a blossoming bush kneels a *peri* (an angel or fairy) holding in her hands a golden bowl and carafe decorated with ḫaṭāyī flowers. One wing is folded, the other open; she wears on her head a head-dress in the shape of ṣāz leaves, which is very characteristic of this style. On the collar of her costume is drawn a *zümürüduanka* (phoenix) fighting a dragon among ḫaṭāyī flowers and leaves. A lion, which is difficult to see, is placed at the bottom of the collar. On the buckle of the belt is a horseman using his bow and arrow.

All the motifs are typical of the ṣāz style, which uses the forest as subject matter, and this drawing cannot have been executed after 1575. Furthermore, the part of the blouse visible near the collar of the costume is decorated with spirals adorned with small flowers which were particular to the workrooms of the palace at the time of Sultan Süleyman. This type of ornament, originally employed for the decoration of *tuğra*, was often used after 1530 to adorn manuscripts.

The ground on which the *peri* is sitting has been painted dark green, probably at a later date. Clouds have also been added.

The inscription at the bottom of the drawing states that the work is attributable to Bihzād, the famous artist of the Herat school, in the Timurid era. This erroneous claim, encountered on many drawings, must have been added at the time when the anthology was assembled.

Bibl.: Denny, W., 1983, pl. 23

Photograph Jacqueline Hyde F.C.

125 YOUNG EUROPEAN *ill. opposite*

Turkey, second half of the sixteenth century
Black and gold ink on prepared paper;
page 35.3 x 22.0; miniature 13.4 x 7.0

Istanbul, Library of the Topkapı Sarayı Müzesi,
H 2168 f. 14v°
From the Treasury of the Topkapı Palace

This drawing is from a compilation, probably executed in the middle of the eighteenth century, which includes Safavid, Uzbek and Ottoman miniatures as well as ink and brush drawings.

This ink and brush drawing represents a young European standing upright, wearing a cape, a hat and a sword on his hip. In the background are scattered tulips and other flowers highlighted in gold. There is no trace of paint.

In the lower left corner of this drawing, which is a beautiful example of the art of the brush, is inscribed the name of Velīcān, a famous painter of the end of the sixteenth century.

Velīcān, born in Tabriz, was a student of Siyavuş and came to Istanbul[1] in his youth. After a period of working independently, he joined the painters of the palace in 1583[2]. From this date, he worked on drawings and calligraphies decorated with miniatures. A number of ink drawings signed by Velīcān are in existence. The delicacy and skill of execution of the *Young European* evoke the art of Velīcān and probably led to the drawing's being attributed to him in the eighteenth century.

1 *Muṣṭafā ʿĀlī, p. 67*
2 *According to a document dated sevval 991 H (30 October 1583) concerning the illustration of the* zübdet ü-tavarih *of Sayyed Loḳmān, Velīcān was requested especially for this work and began being paid as a* janissary *on its completion (Archives of the presidency of the council, filing of Repeci, Ruus 242; Renda, 1977, p. 65)*

Photograph Jacqueline Hyde F.Ç.

126 QUATRAIN

Calligraphy by Aḥmed Ḳaraḥiṣārī
Turkey, c.1525–50
Black ink, opaque colours and gold on prepared paper
Page 19.5 x 29.2; frame 9.8 x 19.2

Istanbul, Library of the Topkapı Sarayı Müzesi,
GY.323/158
Topkapı Palace collection

This work, which comprises three lines with three calligraphies of different styles, *çeli sülüs, muḥaqqaq,* and *naskhī,* is signed at the bottom of the page by the famous calligrapher who worked during the reign of Sultan Süleyman: Ahmed Ḳaraḥiṣārī.

It consists of a *Kalām-i Kibar* in Arabic (a saying by a holy person belonging to a *Sufi* order). It means:

126

The first modesty is to speak little and the first remedy is to eat little. The first of all rites and prayers is to commit as few sins as possible. The first of vows is to be patient.

The frame and the internal lines are made up of a gilded ribbon delineated by two black lines. At each end of the internal lines is placed a hexagonal illuminated rosette.

The frame of the calligraphy was executed at a much later date, in the eighteenth or nineteenth century, and is covered with dark beige coloured paper decorated simply with classical stencilled motifs.

Bibl.: Rado, S. D., p. 80

Photograph Jacqueline Hyde F.Ç.

127 SŪRA FROM THE KORAN *ill. page 130*

Calligraphy by Aḥmed Ḳaraḥiṣārī
Turkey, 961/1554
Black ink, opaque colour and gold on prepared paper;
page 29.4 x 20.3; frame 17.0 x 11.2

Istanbul, Library of the Topkapı Sarayı Müzesi,
E/H 416, f.1v°–2r°
Topkapı Palace collection; from the Library of the Hasoda (the Sultan's private apartments); an inscription on page 1 indicates that the work belonged to Beşir, the Ağa of Darüsaade

The work comprises the *sūra* I, VI, XII, XVIII, XXXIV, XXXV, XXXVI, XLVIII, LXVII and LXXVIII of the Koran.

The leather binding, with a flap, is black. Its medallions and corner-pieces are decorated in the *ṣāz* style on a gilded background. The work has 79 pages and the colophon (f. 70r°) carries the signature of Aḥmed Ḳaraḥiṣārī, a disciple of Sayyid Asadüllah al-Kirmānī, and the date 961/1554. The whole is written in the *naskhī* style.

Each page comprises nine lines written in *naskhī,* in black ink. The *cedvel* and the rosettes are golden. The beginning of the *sūra* is written in *sülüs,* the letters gold outlined in black ink. The illuminated rosettes *ḥizb* and *ʿaṣār* (signs concerning the rules of reading) are found in the margins.

On the pages displayed, the *serlevha* (f. 1v°–2r°), the title of the *sūra* and the last lines are written in gold letters outlined with black. Each text is surrounded on three sides by illuminations: on the top and bottom, they form rectangular panels; on the large vertical side, three festooned half-medallions resemble cupolas. From these illuminated frames project fine motifs in the shape of needles. Red, white, light blue or turquoise flowers highlight these decorations, with blue and gold dominating tones. The decorations include Chinese clouds and arabesques of the *rūmī* style.

The shape of the half-medallion which can be seen on the sides of the pages can also be found in some superbly illuminated works of the time. For example, on the frontispiece of the *Vakfiye* of Hürrem Sultan, dated 1540[1], and on the illuminations of the frontispiece of the copy of the *Dīvān-i Muḥibbī,* created by Ḳaramemī (Kara Meḥmed Çelebi) in 1554[2], we can admire the same type of decoration.

The motifs and the choice of colours reflect the classical Ottoman taste. The quality of the illumination and the characteristics of the composition evoke the pieces signed by Ḳara Meḥmed Çelebi, the most famous artist of his time, and are probably his work.

1 *Istanbul, Turk ve Islam Eserleri Müzesi no. 2191; cf. Washington, 1987, no. 6*
2 *Hamburg; cf. Haase, 1987, fig. 1*

Bibl.: Karatay, 1962–69, no. 451

Photograph Jacqueline Hyde F.Ç.

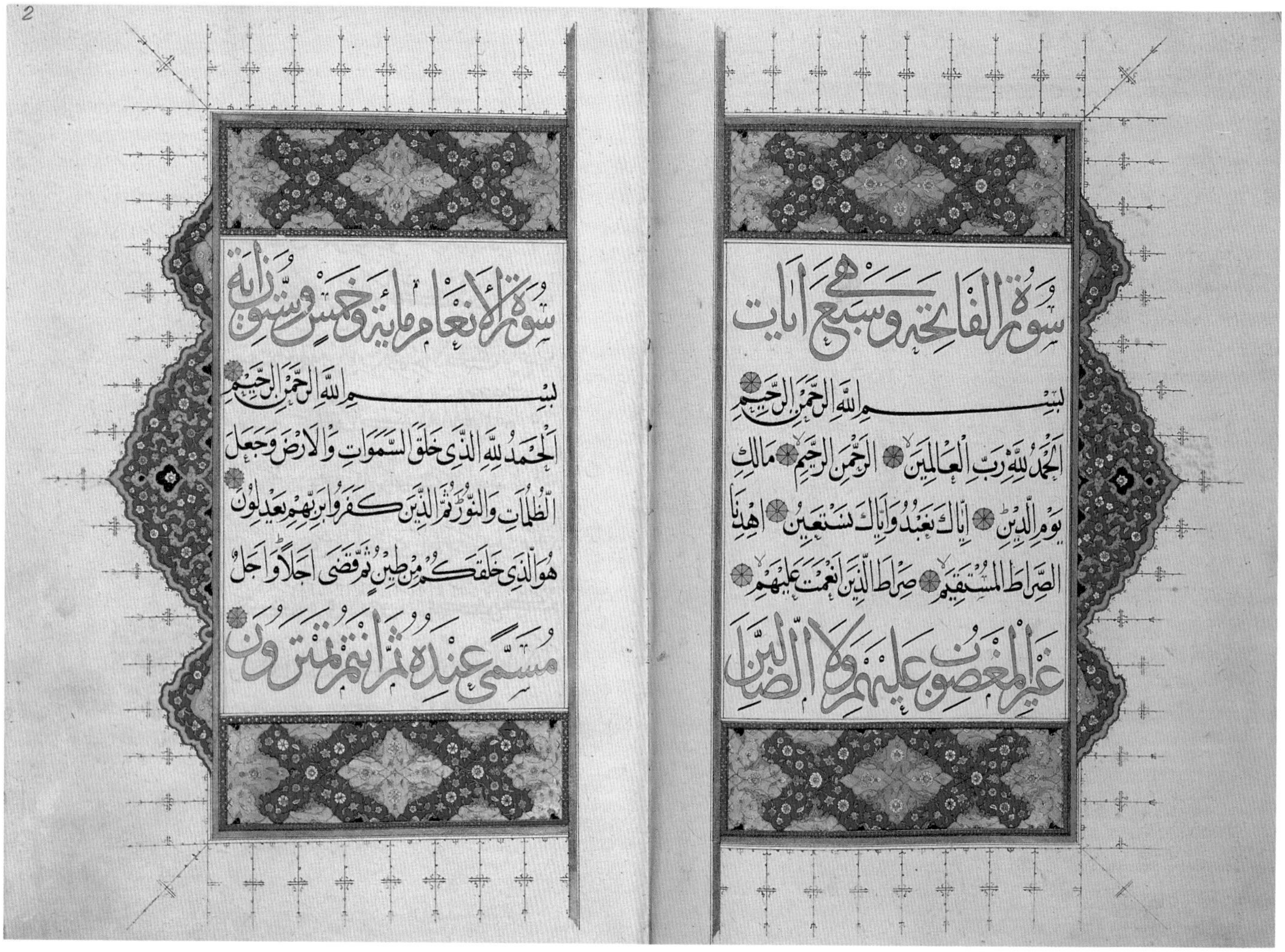

127

128 CALLIGRAPHY ALBUM *ill. opposite*

Turkey, c.1540
Coloured papers, opaque and gilded paint, paper-cut calligraphy; page 30.2 x 19.4; calligraphy f. 2v° 13.6 x 8.0; f. 3r° 16.8 x 8.2

Istanbul, Library of the Topkapı Sarayı Müzesi, H 2177 (f. 2v° and 3r°)

This album is a compilation of calligraphies which are all paper-cut, with the exception of the five calligraphies of the *ta'līk* type executed by the calligrapher Imad, the most recent of which is dated 1017/1608–09. Among the paper-cut pages are found some *ta'līk* (male and female cuttings) by the Safavid artist 'Alī Katib (f. 3v° 4v°) and by the famous Ottoman artist Faḫrī of Bursa, as well as a *ta'līk* calligraphy cut out by 'Abdu'l-Karīm b 'Alī, a calligrapher from the time of Sultan Süleyman the Magnificent.

The flapless leather binding of this compilation, probably executed in the seventeenth century, is decorated with a gilded background carrying large embossed medallions. The two pages exhibited are unsigned *ta'līk* paper-cut calligraphy pasted on paper. One of these comprises two *rubā'ī* (quatrains) in Persian, cut out in white paper and pasted on pink paper. Some parts of the letters are missing. The dots are in light-blue paper. One of the *rubā'ī* is written diagonally, the other vertically.

The corners and spaces between the *rubā'ī* are delineated by gilded lines and adorned with fine gilded stems carrying pastel coloured leaves and flowers in red, blue and green. These floral compositions are also found around and between the entries. In addition, almost invisible gilded motifs (*zerefşan*) are scattered over the whole page.

The second page shown (f. 3r°) contains an *asikane ghazal* written by Süleyman, who used the pseudonym "Muḥibbī" in his poems. The letters have been cut out in white paper and laid onto dark-blue paper. The four lines of the section on the right are alternately written diagonally and horizontally. The three lines of the section on the left are written vertically. Some dots are gilded. In the *mahlas* verse, where the name of the poet is found, "Muḥibbī" is written entirely in gold:

In the rosary of your beauty
Muḥibbī until morning
like a nightingale
sings your praise.

The background is divided by gilded lines. One corner and three spaces of triangular shape are decorated with *rūmī* motifs and fine gilded stems on a dark-blue background.

These two pages are not signed, so we cannot be sure who executed the paper-cut calligraphy of the poems. The decoration, however, reflects the art of the first half of the sixteenth century, as it was practised in the workrooms of Sultan Süleyman. The graphics are very similar to the works of some artists of the same period who specialised in cut-outs on paper. It is probable that these two pages were executed by Benli 'Alī Çelebi or his son 'Abdül-Karīm.

Photograph Jacqueline Hyde F.Ç.

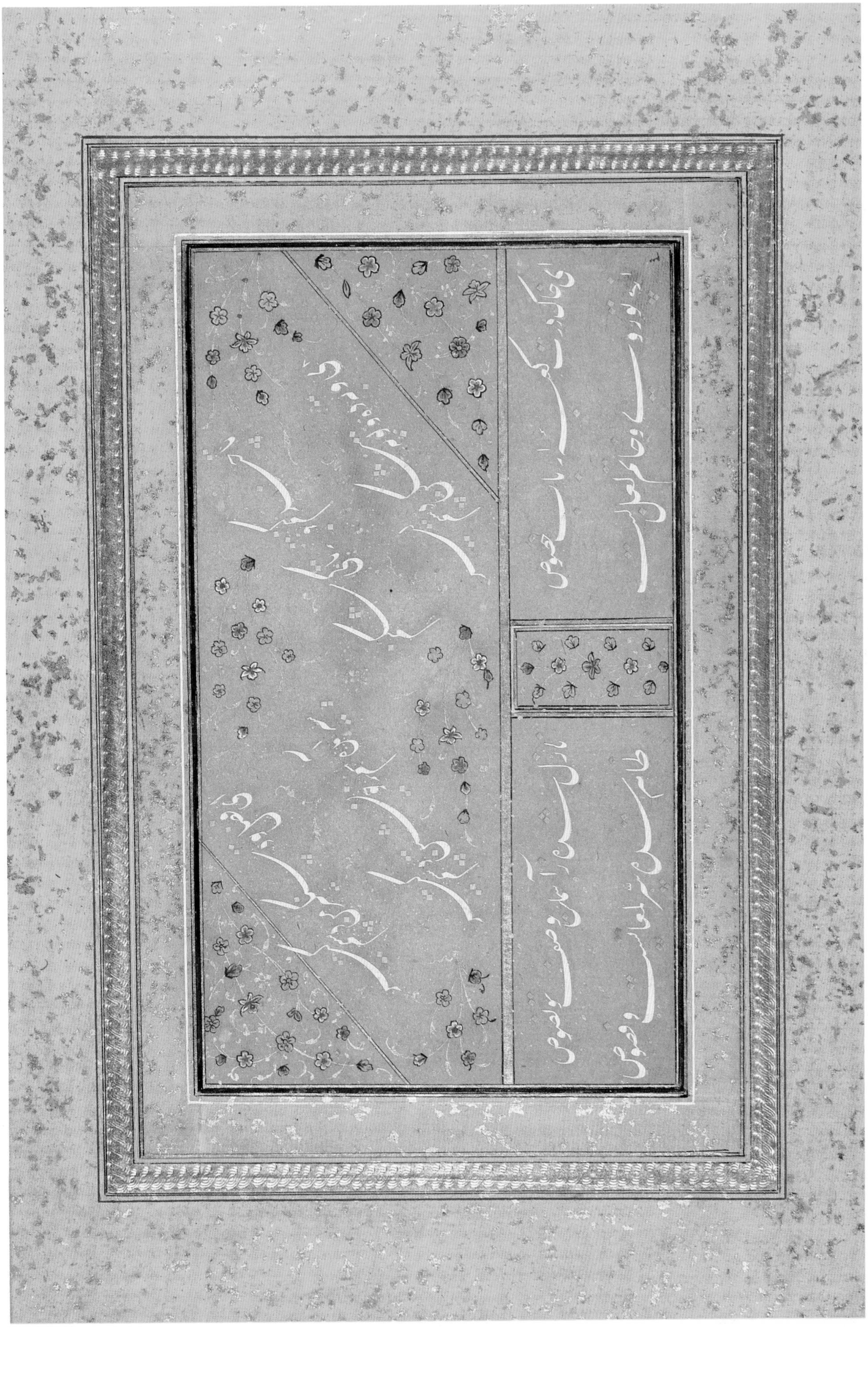

The pages are in mauve, beige, cream and straw-yellow coloured paper. All the *cedvel* are gilded. Some pages, within the text or below the *cedvel*, are decorated with stencilled birds, flowers and plants coming up from a vase. On other pages appear painted and gilded dragons, mythical birds (*zümürüduanka*) lions, peacocks, gazelles, hares and birds. The margins are embellished with gold (*zerefşan*) or are decorated with plant motifs in *rūmī* and *ḫaṭāyī* styles as well as Chinese clouds. The anthology contains five miniatures. On one of the exhibited pages (f. 57r°), a bird rests on a flowering branch inside an elongated oval medallion. It is painted with a brush and has gold contours. In the miniature on the facing page (f. 58r°) a young man, seated at the foot of a flowering tree, takes the hem of the garment of the sultan who is standing and speaking to him. Behind blue hills, two men are looking at them with surprise. The theme illustrates the line of the text: "Take your hands away from the bottom of my clothes."

The margins of these two pages present a theme frequently used in Ottoman decoration after 1515: the trunk and leaves of the blossoming trees, as well as the nearby bushes, seem to move[1]. The miniature and the decoration of the margins are typical examples of the palace school of painting influenced by the artists of Tabriz brought to Istanbul by the Sultan Yavuz Selim. The decoration and miniatures most resembling those of this anthology are found in the *Dīvān-i Selīm*, produced around 1520, probably by the same artist[2]. A very similar miniature is found in the *Amīr Ṣahī Dīvān*, preserved in the collection of the Osterreichische National Bibliotek (cod. mixt. 399) which contains a number of miniatures[3].

1 *For similar forms see Rogers, 1983, nos 20, 40*
2 *Library of the University of Istanbul, for the work catalogued F1330, see Washington, 1987, fig. 28a-b*
3 *Duda, 1978-79; Duda, 1983; Abb. 326-32*

Bibl.: Kataray, F. E., in Persian, no. 647; Atazoy, N., Çağman F., p. 25; Çağman, F., Tanindi, Z., 1979, no. 133

Photograph Jacqueline Hyde F.Ç.

130

129 POETIC ANTHOLOGY *ill. page 138*

c.1520–30
Opaque colours and gold on prepared paper; page 21.6 x 8.3; miniature 6.9 x 3.8

Istanbul, Library of the Topkapı Sarayı Müzesi, YY 846 f. 57v°–58r°
Acquired in 1957

This anthology is composed of pieces chosen from *ghazal* and Persian *rubāʿī* of Iranian poets such as Ḥāfiẓ Shīrazī, Şeyḫ Kamal (*Huçan di*) and Haçu ʿImadet Salman (*Savaci*). Its long, narrow format is typical of this type of anthology, called *cönk*. As they open from bottom to top, such anthologies are also known as "bull's tongue".

The claret-coloured leather binding dates from the nineteenth century. This anthology of elegant calligraphy, bound without order and lacking a beginning or end, comprises 85 pages. Each page contains no more than 12 lines of calligraphy in *nastaʿlīk*. The lines are written vertically or diagonally.

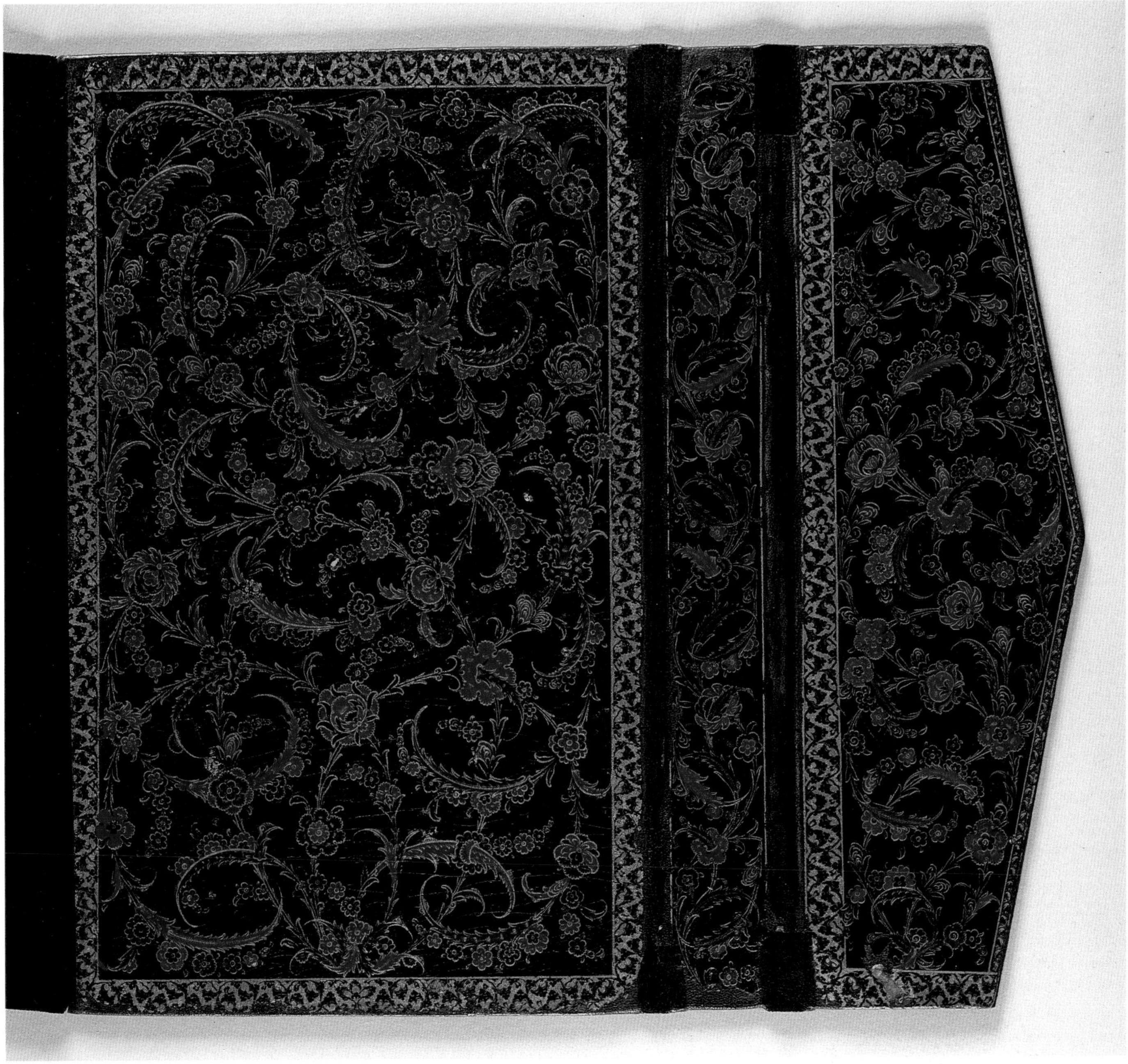

130 THE MEETING OF LAYLĀ AND MEJNŪN Khamsa-i Nevā'ī

Turkey, 937/1530–31
Opaque colours and gold on prepared paper; leather, opaque colours, gold and varnish; binding 29.3 x 18.5; page 29.2 x 19.0; miniature 14.7 x 11.7

Istanbul, Library of the Topkapı Sarayı Müzesi, H 802 f. 134r°
Topkapı Palace collection

This work is provided with a lacquered binding typical of the era of Sultan Süleyman. It is adorned with motifs of the *ṣāz* style which developed in this period under the influence of the artist Şahkulu, who was then head of the *nakkaşhane* of the palace. The boards and the flap are completely covered with a decoration of supple stems which, starting from one point at the bottom of the boards, curve and intertwine. They bear long curving leaves (*hanceri* in the shape of a dagger) crossed by half-rosettes and large *ḫaṭāyī* flowers. These motifs are traced in gold and highlighted with different tones of red on a black-painted ground.

Around the borders runs a wide gilded band featuring black *rūmī* motifs. The inside of the boards is in claret-coloured leather embossed with a gilded background, adorned with corner-decorations and a little medallion in the *ṣāz* style.

The work consists of five *mesnevi* poems made up of inter-rhymed couplets in *Çağatay* Turkish by Mīr 'Alī Shīr Nevā'ī, Hayretü' l-Abrār (f. 1r°), Ferhād-ū Şīrīn (f. 51v°), Mejnūn-u Laylā, Sab'a Sayyāra (f. 176v°) and Iskendernāme (f. 225).

The volume consists of 309 pages, each of 23 lines of calligraphy in *nasta'līk*. The beginning of the text and the *cedvel* are gilded. The name of the author and the title of the work are inscribed in a medallion (1r°). The frontispiece and the beginning of the other *mesnevi* are illuminated in the purest Ottoman style (f. v°–2r°). The colophon (f. 309v°) gives the name of the copyist, Pīr Aḥmad b Iskander, and the date, 937/1530–31.

The 16 miniatures scattered through the work seem to be by one artist: the same highly decorative coiling of clouds with long tails, the same background treatment, notably the ground with clumps of flowers and foliage, and a figurative style not unlike that found in the miniatures of Shiraz of the years 1500–25[1].

Another Ottoman manuscript, the *Yūsuf*

131 *greatly enlarged*

ve Zulaykhā of Ḥamdī (Munich, State of Bavaria Library, codex 183) is illustrated with miniatures produced by the same artist[2].

On the page exhibited, Laylā and Mejnūn are standing face-to-face in a flowering garden, to the left of a small pavilion. Nearby, a fountain supplies a stream which meanders down the foreground. Water gushes from another place at the lower left side of the page.

This miniature, like most of the other works in the book, offers a perfect synthesis of the decorative tradition of Shiraz — seen in the treatment of faces, clouds, and flowering bushes — and of the established Ottoman taste for realistic architectural representations.

1 cf. Guest, 1949, pl. 27A; Stchoukine, I., 1959, pl. VIII
2 Söylemezoğlu, 1974, fig. 2, p. 477

Bibl.: Tanindi, Z., 1984, fig. 18; Atil, E., 1986, fig. 6 (binding); Karatay Türkçe, no. 2299; Stchoukine, I., 1966, pls X–XI; Atasoy, N. and Çağman, F., pl. 3; Çağman, F. and Tanindi, Z., 1979, no. 136, fig. 48; Atil, E., 1980, ill. 74; Grube, E., 1981, figs 14–16; Atil, E., 1986, fig. 12; Çağman, F. and Tanindi, Z., 1986, pls 135–39

Photograph Jacqueline Hyde F.Ç.

131 BINDING OF A "BANNER KORAN"

Turkey, c.1530–40
Stamped and gilded leather; 5.7 x 4.6 x 2.2

Istanbul, Library of the Topkapı Sarayı Müzesi, E H 522
From the Library of the Hasoda

This undated Koran is complete. It comprises 286 pages containing 17 lines in *ğubarī* script, inscribed in a circular frame 4.1 centimetres in diameter. The page surrounding the *serlevha* is gilded.

The artistic value of this small Koran rests in its full leather burgundy-coloured binding. A decoration of embossed *ṣāz* style covers the boards and the flap. The floral decoration is conceived without any clear beginning or end, not as a self-contained composition. On the fine stems which twist, intertwine and break are *ḥaṭāyī* flowers and tapering leaves. All the motifs are in black leather relief against the recessed gold-stamped ground.

This small Koran is the only example of binding ornamented in the *ṣāz* style (most common on Ottoman bindings) worked in this way. The back has been restored.

The "Banner Korans" were small and round, hexagonal or rectangular. They were sometimes wrapped in parchment, generally protected by metal cases and hung at the tip of banners used during campaigns.

The Topkapı Sarayı Müzesi holds a rich collection of Banner Korans from the Ottoman empire and from other regions of the Islamic world.

Bibl.: Karatay, 1962, no. 638

Photograph Jacqueline Hyde F.Ç.

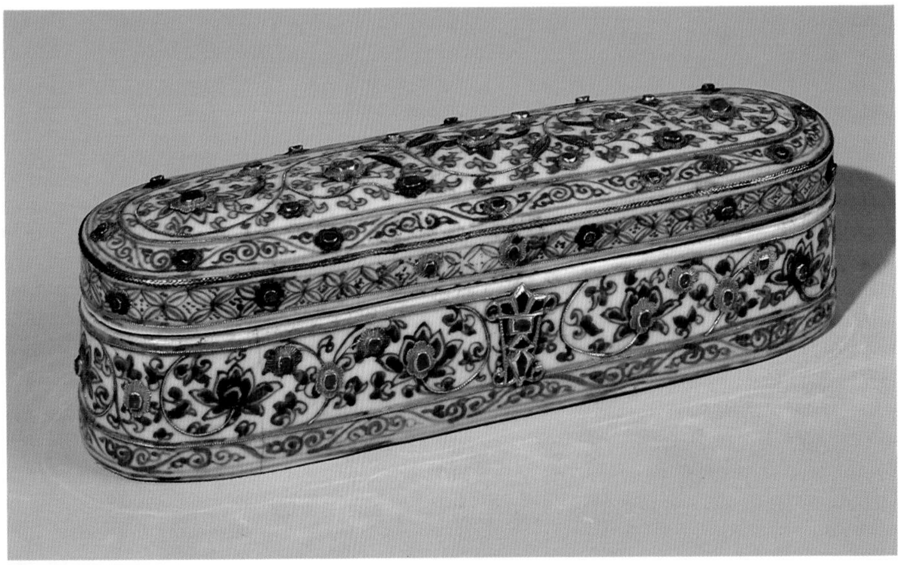

132

132 PEN BOX WITH LOTUS DESIGN

China, Ming dynasty, late fifteenth - early sixteenth century; Turkey, late sixteenth century
Porcelain inlaid with gold, rubies and emeralds; paint; gold inlaid with rubies; jade inlaid with gold; 7.5 x 27.5 x 7.7

Istanbul, Topkapı Sarayı Müzesi, 2/894
Treasury of the Topkapı Palace

This pen box, with its oblong body, straight sides and slightly domed cover, revives the shape of the brass pen boxes fashionable in Iran and the near East during the fourteenth century. Along with several other Chinese porcelain objects in the Palace collection, it has been enriched with gold ornamentation, in line with the prevailing taste of the period.

The object itself, made of white porcelain decorated in under-glaze blue, is ornamented on the cover and around the outside of the vessel with a graceful scroll of lotus flowers and small leaves. Bands of undulating floral scrolls encircle the bottom of the box and the upper part of the cover; another band covered in quatrefoils surrounds the base of the lid.

The gold decoration emphasises the pattern of the porcelain. A thin grooved thread set in relief with fine elongated leaves, follows the scrolling stems exactly and bears blooming flowers superimposed on the centres of the lotus-flowers and on some of the leaves within the foliage.

A gold thread also emphasises the three bands encircling the box and cover. The two bands on the cover are punctuated by isolated flowers. Each flower is made up of a table-cut ruby set in a bezel on a wide collar of six striated lobes. The clasp, in the shape of an angular floret set with rubies and emeralds, was undoubtedly added at a later date.

The interior of the pen box is equally ornate.The cover is held to the body by a gold chain attached on the right side. The inside of the lid is decorated with fine gilt arabesques with red highlights within a central oblong multi-lobed medallion; two floral cartouches at the ends are painted. The well is divided into compartments and adorned with a pierced palmette.

Three receptacles in gold, finely engraved with scrolling leaves and dating from the Ottoman period, occupy the left side. The ink-well is covered with a lotus-shaped plaque made of grey-green jade inlaid with gold arabesques. A flower adorns the centre of the circular cover, which is articulated by two small gold bars. The sand-shaker is covered with a pierced dome-shaped lid of green jade set with gold. The receptacle to hold the small pad of silk used as a blotter is covered with a circular engraved gold stopper marked in the centre by a flower, articulated by two small bars and surrounded by a wreath of tiny flowers.

Bibl.: Hobson, R. L., 1933–34, pl. IX; Unal, I., 1963, pl. 9; Krahl, R., 1986, II, no. 666

Photograph Jacqueline Hyde M.B.T.

133 PEN BOX WITH LOTUS DECORATION

Turkey, second half of the sixteenth century
Gold, jasper inlaid with gold, rubies and emeralds, translucent enamel; 2.6 x 27.0 x 3.7

Istanbul, Topkapı Sarayı Müzesi, 2/2111
Treasury of the Topkapı Palace

The body of this narrow, oblong pen box is made of a single piece of a translucent, yellow-brown coloured stone called *balgami* (jasper), which was seldom used. The lid, a thin sheet of stone, slides along grooves cut into the gold frame that surrounds the upper edge and has a fine incised decoration of small intertwined leaves.

The same decoration is repeated on the lid and the exterior walls: a thin, engraved gold ribbon, inlaid into the jasper, forms in relief an ornamental scroll of large lotus-type flowers alternating with delicate serrated leaves. A fine engraving highlights the veins of the leaves and the superimposed collars of the flowers. Table-cut stones, mounted in bezels, give brilliance to the centre of each of the plant motifs: rubies for the leaves, alternating rubies and emeralds for the flowers.

Inside, at one end, the jasper has been cut out in a lobed form to provide for a small ink-well, with its cap in the form of a flower with the centre highlighted by a square emerald and the eight petals rendered in translucent red enamel.

The material used (*balgami*), the presence of translucent enamels and the interesting shapes of the collar and the leaves determine the originality and refinement of this elegant piece. The same treatment of the lotus decoration is also found on the porcelain cup (no. 96).

M.B.T.

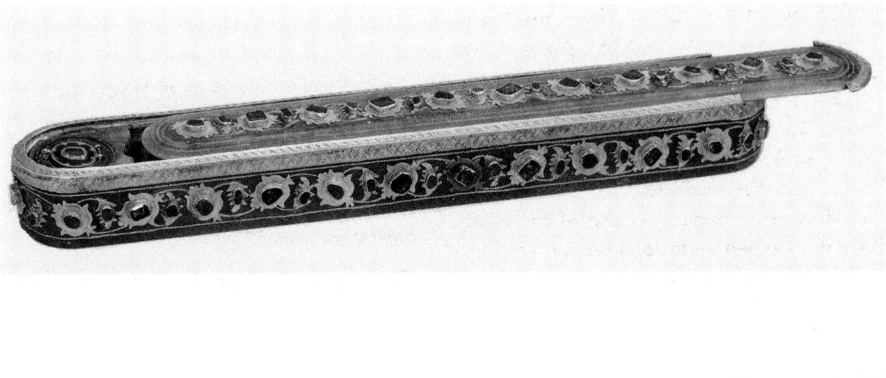

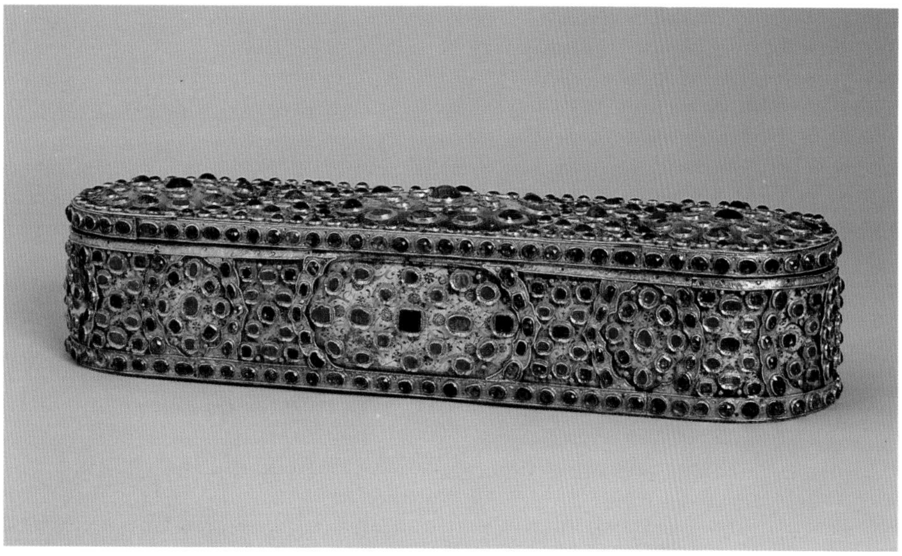

134 PEN BOX

Turkey, second half of the sixteenth century
Engraved gold and rock crystal inlaid with rubies and emeralds; lacquered wood; illuminated and gilded paper; 8.2 x 40.0 x 10.5

Istanbul, Topkapı Sarayı Müzesi, 2/22
Treasury of the Topkapı Palace

The pen box is rectangular with rounded ends. On the sides and the flat lid are alternating oval and circular rock crystal medallions, framed by wide gold bands corresponding to their slightly multi-lobed shape. Smaller concave medallions inserted between them serve to fill the empty spaces. Bands, chased with floral motifs and bordered with twisted wires, are inlaid with cabochon emeralds mounted in bezels, similarly accentuating the contours of the base and the lid.

The rock crystal, overlaying illuminated, gilded white paper, is inlaid with rubies and emeralds mounted in relief in round collars striated to give the impression of a double collar. Some of these stones have been left almost in their natural state; others, such as the big emerald in the heart of the central medallion on the side, are cut in facets. The spacing of the gems allows for the illuminated decoration to be visible: supple stems and little flowers treated with the delicacy and precision of the decoration on the *tuğra* (cf. no. 3) are glimpsed through the jewels.

The rock crystal medallions and the gold bands are attached by small silver-gilt nails with lobed heads resembling gold flowers. The underside of the base is covered with a gold sheet which has a punched decoration of five *mandorlas* with a diamond-shaped trellis enclosing little flowers.

The inside of the pen box is made of lacquered wood and adorned with a medallion filled with clouds on a ground of clumps of blossoming plants. On the left, three receptacles, their lids inlaid with rubies, are set in a small fixed sheet cut in the form of an arch. The field is decorated with *rūmī* arabesques and *ḫaṭāyī* flowers treated in black and gold tones which evoke niello, and is studded with rubies and lozenge-shaped diamonds. The right tray, which is intended for the pens and seems to be later in date, is removable and fitted with a chain, the other end of which is fixed to the gilded lid.

At the end of the central bar which divides this tray into two compartments is set a sand caster. The tray can be lifted out; under it is a compartment used to store documents.

The shape of this pen case is classical, common in the fourteenth and fifteenth centuries, used in the Iranian world as well as in Mamluk Egypt and Syria.

The originality of the decoration makes this an exceptional piece. The faceted cut of some of the stones was used by Ottoman lapidaries only in the second half of the sixteenth century, and therefore allows us to date the work to this period.

Bibl.: Türkoğlu, O., 1985, p. 13; Kõseoğlu, 1987, no. 59

Photograph Jacqueline Hyde T.B.

135 PLAQUE FROM HORSE'S HARNESS DECORATED WITH ARABESQUES

Turkey, second quarter of the sixteenth century
Engraved mother-of-pearl inlaid with gold, black paste, rubies and turquoise; gilded silver; 6.5 x 8.5

Vienna, Kunsthistorisches Museum, Waffensammlung, C.152b
Registered in the inventory of the collections of Schloss Ambras in the Tyrol in 1603

This mother-of-pearl plaque is possibly from a horse's harness, on which it would have been attached to leather, velvet or metal. The techniques employed, the motifs used and the fineness of its decoration invite comparison with the belts (nos 103 and 104).

The plaque, oval-shaped and festooned, is entirely backed by a sheet of gilded silver. The arabesque motif is arranged on two levels, one encrusted in black, the other in gold in low-relief and punctuated with leaves, flowers, cabochon rubies and turquoise.

Bibl.: Sacken, L. Freiherr von, 1955, pp. 292–93; Grosz, A. and Thomas, B., 1936, 101, no. 15

Photograph Jacqueline Hyde M.B.T.

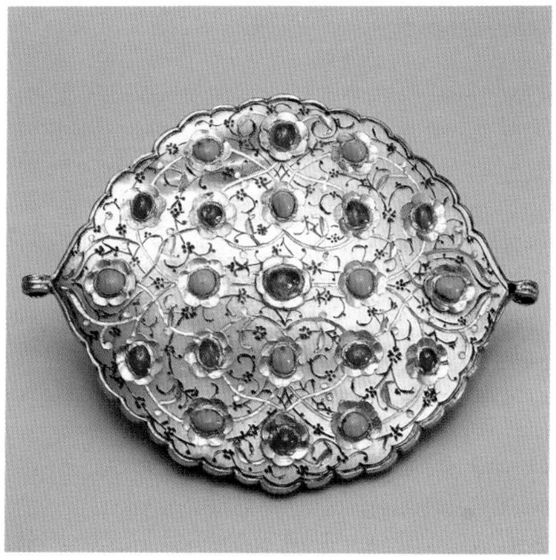

APPENDIX

GLOSSARY

'ACEM: in Arabic; barbarians, non-Arabs; but often applied by the Turks to Iranians
AÇEMOĞLAN: Person recruited under the *devşirme* system
AĞA: Title given to high-ranking people such as the commandant of the *janissaries* or the head of the palace eunuchs
AKÇE: "Small white"; silver coin used in everyday commerce
ALTIN: Main gold coin of the Ottoman empire
AMIR: Military chief or governor (equivalent to the Turkish *bey*)
ARABESQUE: Sinuous foliage interlacing, animated by an uninterrupted rhythmic movement
ARZ ODASI: Audience chamber
ASKER: Person of the military classes
BAB I-HÜMAYAN: Imperial gate leading into the first courtyard of the Topkapı Palace
BAB Ü-SELAM: "Gate of Safety", leading into the second courtyard of the Topkapı Palace
BAB Ü-SAADE: "Gate of Happiness", leading into the third courtyard of the Topkapı Palace
BASMALA AL-RAHMAN AL-RAHIM: "In the name of God, the mild, the merciful"; the opening text of all the *süra* of the Koran except the ninth. Used in the abbreviated form "Basmala" at the opening of all important acts requiring divine protection
BEY (BEG): "Chief" or "Master"; title given to numerous high-level civil and military functionaries and to the chiefs of tribes
BEYLERBEY (BEGLERBEG): "Bey of the Bey"; governor of regions
BEKTASI: Member of a religious heterodox brotherhood controlled by the state, to which the *janissaries* were affiliated
BĪRŪN: "Exterior"; outer services of the palace (in the two first courtyards)
CALIPH (Ḳalīf): Successor of the Prophet Muḥammed and head of the Muslim community
CAMI: Large mosque
ÇATMA: Cut velvet, usually enhanced with gold and silver thread
CEDVEL: Frame of a text
CELI: Monumental script
ÇINTEMANI: Decorative motif of Far Eastern origin, combining a group of three points arranged in a triangle with two undulating parallel clouds
CUERDA SECA: A technique in which glazes of different colours were used to decorate a ceramic surface separated by a line of greasy material
DEFTERDAR: Controller of finances
DEVŞIRME: "Gathering up"; a system of recruitment of adolescents, usually of Balkan origin, who were converted to Islam and educated in the imperial schools to serve later in the army or in various administrative areas
DIVAN (DĪVĀN-I HÜMAYŪN): Imperial Council, comprising the highest dignitaries of the state, which met four mornings each week in Süleyman's time
DIVAN (DIWAN): Poetry anthology
DĪVĀNĪ: A cursive script, the standard script used for *fermans*
EHL-I ḤIREF: Corps of palace artists and artisans
ENDERŪN: Interior services of the palace including the harem
ENGOBE: In Ottoman ceramics, a fine layer of siliceous material put on the clay under the glaze to form a ground for the painted decoration
EṢNĀF: An organisation of merchants or artisans
FETVĀ: A written answer to a legal question usually issued by the Şeyhülislam
FERMAN: Decree validated by the *tuğra* (the Sultan's monogram placed at the beginning of the text)
ĞAZEL: An elegiac genre of love poetry
GAZI: Fighter for the Faith
GRAND VIZIER: "Absolute representative of the Sultan"; second-highest person in the state
ĞUBARĪ: Minute script
ḤADĪTH: Collection of sayings and deeds of the Prophet
ḤĀN: Turkish title given to high-ranking people, and part of a sovereign's title
HAN: Caravanserai
ḤAREM: Sacred place, reserved or protected
ḤAREMLIK: Part of a house, especially of a palace, reserved for women; often abbreviated to "Harem"
HASODA: Private chamber
HASSEKI: Official favourite
ḤAṬĀYĪ: "Of Cathay: Chinese"; plant design of Chinese inspiration made up of lotus flowers and peonies on a background of wreath-like coils and scrolls
HAZINE: Treasure
ḪIL'AT: Ceremonial kaftan, more ample than the usual kaftan and made of sumptuous fabrics (often fur)
IC OĞHLAN: Pages or servants assigned to the palace
'IMĀRET: Hospice
JANISSARY: See YENIÇERI
KADĪ: A judge
KADĪ'ASKER (KAZASKER): Army judge
KAFTAN: Over-garment of which there are several varieties distinguished by length, sleeve-length, fastening and fabric
ḲĀNŪN: Secular legislation of the empire
ḲANŪNI: "The lawgiver"
KAPIKULU: "Slaves of the Gate"; the elite of the army, comprising corps of *janissaries* and cavalry
KAPUDAN PAŞA: Commander-in-chief of the imperial fleet (grand admiral)
KATIB: Secretary or scribe
KEMHA: Very luxurious silk fabric or garments
KILIÇ: Sabre with a curved blade
ḲIT'A: Cut out script
KUFIC: Arabic script of generally angular, regular letters on a single base line
KÜL (ĞUL): Slave
KULLIYE: Building complex, often run by a VAKF
MANGIR: Copper coin used for everyday transactions
MAŞRAPA: Drinking receptacle in the shape of a tankard or pitcher
MATARA: Ewer or canteen for water
MATRAK: Game of throwing long sticks, invented by Nasuh, who became known as Matrakçi
MEC: Sword with straight, narrow blade
MEHTER: Military band placed under the authority of the standard-bearer (620 men in 1567)
MIḤRAB: Niche in the wall of qibla indicating the direction for prayer, i.e., the direction of Mecca
MILLET: Nation; specifically an ethnic or religious community: Greek, Jewish, Armenian
MI'MAR BASI: Chief architect
MINBAR: Stepped pulpit, placed on the right of the MIḤRĀB, from where the sermon is given during the solemn Friday prayer
MÜCELLID: Bookbinder
MUḤAQQAQ: Type of cursive script
MUSAVVIR: Painter
MUZEHHIB: Illuminator
NAKKAŞ: Painter and decorator
NAKKAŞHANE The scriptorium of the 16th century Ottoman sultans
NASKHĪ: Type of cursive script
NIŞANCI: Chancellor
OCAK: Corps of *janissaries*
PERI: Imaginary creature ("fairy")
QIBLA: The obligatory orientation of prayer
RAḪLE: Folding book-stand
RE'AYA: "herd": people not belonging to the military class
REIS: Naval commander
RESSAM: Designer
RŪMĪ: Decorative motif of fringed palmettes and half-palmettes, often bifurcated and curved at the ends, usually integrated within a network of arabesques
SAF: Large prayer-rug decorated with multiple niches
SANCAK: Province (subdivision of a large

cat. no. 129

region) governed by a SANCAK BEY
ṢĀZ: A swash feathery leaf much used in sixteenth century Ottoman decoration
SEJJADE: Small prayer-rug
SELAMLIK: Part of a house or palace reserved for men
SERASKER: Chief commander of the army
ŞEHZADE: Imperial prince
ŞEYHÜLISLAM: Head of all religious, theological and legal dignitaries
SHARĪ'A: Muslim law based on the Koran and the HADĪTH
SHĪ'Ī: Supporters of 'Alī who asserted his descendants" right to lead the Muslim community; divided into several sects (including zaidīya. Duodecimens, Ismā'īlīya)
SILAHDAR: One of the Sultan's entourage; sword-bearer
SIPAHI: Horseman; owner of a TIMAR
SÜLÜS: A type of script
SÜRA: Chapter of the Koran
TIMAR: Land, the revenues from which are kept in exchange for military or administrative services
TOPHANE: Arsenal
TUĞRA: The Sultan's monogram used to validate documents
VAKF: The endowment deed of a pious foundation
VALIDE SULTAN: Mother of the Sultan
YENIÇERI: "New troops"; *janissaries* recruited by DEVŞIRME
ZIMMI: Non-muslim subjects, who had to pay a special tax

GUIDE TO THE TURKISH ALPHABET

Note on transliteration

To adapt modern Turkish into English, supplementary letters are used. Some of the letters, with an approximation of their sounds in English, are:

vowels

i (like 'er' as in painter)
ö (like 'ur' as in occur)
ü (like 'oo' as in juice)

consonants

c (like 'dg' as in journey)
ç (like 'ch' as in choose)
ğ (silent, but slightly elongates the preceding vowel; thus *tuğra* sounds like 'tourer')
ş (like 'sh' as in sugar).

For the transliteration of Ottoman (pre-1928) Turkish, the modern Turkish alphabet is supplemented by diacriticals (marks above or below letters) to represent letters of the Arabic or Persian alphabets. These are difficult even to approximate in English, but they include: long vowels, ā, ī, ō, ū; consonants, ḍ, ṣ, ṭ, ẓ, ', ḥ, ẖ, ẕ (dh), s̱ (th), j (zh), ñ (ng).

In the transliteration of modern Turkish letters, the assistance of H. Avni Karslioğlu, Consul of the Turkish Consulate-General in Sydney, is gratefully acknowledged.

SELECTED BIBLIOGRAPHY

AKALAY, Zeren, "Tarihi Konularda Ilk Osmanli Minyatürleri", *Sanat Tarihi Yilligi*, vol. II, 1969, pp. 102–16; Akalay, Zeren, "Tarihi Konularda Türk Minyatürleri", *Sanat Tarihi Yilligi*, vol. III, 1970, pp. 151–66; "Klasik Türk Minyatür Resimlerinin Öncüleri", *Sanat Duniamiz*, vol. VII, 1976, pp. 14–23

ALLAN, James and RABY, Julian, "Metalworks", pp. 17–71, in *Tulips, Arabesques & Turbans*, ed. Yanni Petsopoulos, London, 1982

ALPARSLAN, Ali, "Islam Yazi Cesitleri: 2 Aklâm-i Sitte", *Sanat Dünyamiz*, vol. 32, 1985, pp. 35–46

ALTINDAĞ, Ülkü, "Topkapı Sarayı Müzesi Osmanli Saray Arsivi Katalogu", *Fermânlar*, vol. I, 1985

ARSEVEN, Celal Esad, *Les Arts décoratifs turcs*, Millî Egitim Basimevi, Istanbul, 1952

ATASOY, Nurhan, "1558 Tarihli Süleymanname ve Macar Nakkas Pervane", *Sanat Tarihi Villigi*, vol. 3, 1970, pp. 167–96; "Nakkas Osman'in Padisah Portlereri Albümü", *Türkiyemiz*, vol. 6, 1972, pp. 2–14

ATASOY, Nurhan and ÇAĞMAN, Filiz, *Turkish Miniature Painting*, Istanbul, 1974

ATASOY, Nurhan and RABY, Julian, *Iznik, the Pottery of Ottoman Turkey*, Alexandria Press, London, 1989

ATIL, Esin, "The Art of the Book", in *Turkish Art*, ed. Esin Atil, Washington, New York, 1980, pp. 137–238; *Süleymannāme: the Illustrated History of Süleyman the Magnificent*, Washington, New York, 1986; "The Age of Süleyman the Magnificent", Washington, 1987

AUER, A., "Das Inventarium der Ambraser Sammlungen aus dem Jahr 1621, l. Teil: Die Rüstkammer", *Jahrbuch der kunsthistorischen Sammlungen*, v. LXXIX, 1984

BABINGER, Franz, "Drei Stadtansichten von Konstantinopel, Galata ('Pera') und Skutari aus dem Ende des 16. Jahrhunderts", in *Österreischische Akademie des Wissenschaften. Philosophisch-Historische Klasse*, LXXVII, 1959, pp. 3–21

BARKAN, Ö.L., "Istanbul Saraylarina Ait Musahebe Defterleri", *Belgeler*, vol. 13, 1970, pp. 1–380

BEAUFORT, Ch. and GAMBER, O., Katalog der Leibrüstkammer, v. II: *Der Zeitraum von 1530 bis 1560*, Busto Arsizio, Bramante, 1990

BERLIN-DAHLEM CATALOGUE, 1971: Museum für Islamische Kunst, Berlin-Dahlem, *Katalog 1971*, Staatliche Museen Preussischer Kulturbesitz, Berlin, 1971

BILINGEN, Emine, "Topkapı Sarayı Hazinesinden 16. Jüzyila ait kemer parçalari", in *Sanat Dünyamiz yapi Kredi Kültür Yayini yil 14*, sayi 38, ilkabar, 1989

BLOCHET, Edgar, *Musulman Painting XIIth-XVIIth Century*, Methuen & Co, London, 1929; *Catalogue des manuscrits turcs de la Bibliothèque nationale*, v.I. Paris, 1932

BOEHEIM, Wendelin, "Urkunden und Regesten aus der K.K. Hofbibliothek", *Jahrbuch der Kunsthistorischen Sammlungen des allerhochsten Kaisershauses*, Band VII, 1888, pp. XCI-CCXIII; *Album hervorragender Gegenstände aus der Waffensammlung des allerhöchsten Kaiserhausest*, v.I, 1894

BRUNHAMMER, Yvonne, *Tapis d'Orient*, Massin, Paris, 1957

ÇAĞMAN, Filiz, "The Place of the Turkish Miniature in Islamic Art", in *Turkish Contribution to Islamic Arts*, Istanbul, 1976, pp. 90–117; "The Miniatures of the Divan-i Huseyni and the Influence of Their Style", in *Fifth International Congress of Turkish Art*, ed. Gèza Fehér, Budapest, 1978, pp. 231–59; "Turkish Miniature Painting", in *The Art and Architecture of Turkey*, ed. Ekrem Akurgal, Oxford, 1980, pp. 222–48; "A Flask in the treasury of Topkapı Palace. An evaluation of its form and function", vol. III, pls 80–83 in *Ars Turcica: Akten des VI internationalen Kongress fur turkische Kunst*, Munchen, vom. 3 bis. 7, Sept. 1979; Maris, Munchen, 1987

ÇAĞMAN, Filiz and TANINDI, Zeren, *Topkapı Sarayı Museum: Islamic Miniature Painting*, Istanbul, 1979; *Topkapı: the Albums and Illustrated Manuscripts*, ed. J. Rogers, London, 1986

CARSWELL, John, "Ceramics", in Petsopoulos, Yanni, *Dir. L'Art decoratif ottoman: tulipes, arabesques et turbans*, Denoel, Paris, 1982, pp. 73–119; "The Tiles in the Yeni Kaplica Baths at Bursa", *Apollo*, July 1984, pp. 36–43

CECEN, Kâzim, *Süleymaniye suyollari*, Istanbul, 1986

CIĞ, Kemal, "Hattat Aḥmed Ḳaraḥiṣārī", *Tarih Dunyasi*, vol. 1/6, 1950, pp. 234–35

DAVIDS, Samling, Copenhague. *The David Collection: Islamic Art*, Davids, Samling, Copenhagen, 1975

DEMIRIZ, Yildiz, "Türk Sanatinda Bahar Acmis Meyva Agaci Motifi", in *I. Milli Turkoloji Kongresi 1978 Tebligler*, Istanbul, 1980, pp. 382–400; *Osmanli Kitap Sanatinda Natüralist Uslupta Ciçekler*, Istanbul, 1986

DENNY, Walter B., "Blue-and-white Islamic pottery on Chinese themes", *Boston Museum Bulletin*, vol. LXX, no. 368, pp. 76–99; "Turkish tiles of the Ottoman Empire", *Archaeology*, vol. 32, no. 6 (1979, Nov./Dec.); "Ceramics", in *Turkish art*, ed. Esin Atil, Smithsonian Institution, Washington, 1980; "Les Textiles", in Yanni, *Dir. L'Art décoratif ottoman; tulipes, arabesques et turbans*, Denöel, Paris 1982, pp. 121–69; "Dating Ottoman Turkish works in the Saz style", *Muqarnas*, vol. 1, 1983.

DERMAN, M. Ugur, "The Turks and the Art of Calligraphy", in *The Turkish Contribution to Islamic Arts*, Istanbul, 1976, pp. 53–83

DUDA, Dorothea, EI[2] *Encyclopédie de l'Islam*, Nouvelle éd. Leyde, E.J. Brill, G.P. Maisonneuve, Paris, 1960; "Khurrem", S.A. Skilliter; "Khair-al-Din Pasha", A. Gallotta; "Hafside", H.R. Idris

ELLIS, Charles Grant, "The Ottoman prayers rugs", *Textile Museum Journal*, 2, no. 4, Dec. 1969, pp. 5–22

ERDMANN, Kurt, "Neue Arbeiten zur türkischen Keramik", *Ars Orientalis*, vol. 5, 1963, pp. 191–219

ETTINGHAUSEN, Richard, "Die Bildliche Darstellung der Ka'ba im islamischen Kulturkreis", *Zeitschrift des deutschen Morgenländischen Gesellschaft*, vol. 87, 1934, pp. 111–37; "Les Siècles de l'Islam", in *Les Trésors de Turquie*, Skira, Genève, 1966

FARIS, N.A. and ELMER, R.P., *Arab Archery*, Princeton, 1945

FEHER, Geza, *Türkische Miniaturen aus den Chroniken der Ungarischen Feldzüge*, Budapest, 1976

GAMBER, O., *Waffe und Rüstung Eurasiens*, Brunswick, 1978

GLUCK, Heinrich and DIEZ, Ernst, *Die Kunst des Islam*, Berlin, 1925

GÖNÜL, Macide, *Turkish Embroideries, XVI-XIX Centuries*, Istanbul, n.d.

GOODRICH, Thomas B., 'Atlas-i Hümayun: a Sixteenth-Century Ottoman Maritime Atlas Discovered in 1984', *Archivum Ottomanicum*, vol. X, 1985, pp. 83–101; 'Some Unpublished Sixteenth Century Ottoman Maps', in *Comité International d'Etudes Pré-ottomanes et Ottomanes VIth Symposium Cambridge*, Turcica, vol. IV, 1987, pp. 99–103

GROSZ, August and THOMAS, Bruno, *Katalog der Waffensammlung in der Neuen Burg*, Wein, 1936

GRUBE, Ernst J., 'Herat, Tabriz, Istanbul: the development of a pictorial style', in *Paintings from Islamic Lands*, ed. R.H. Pinder-Wilson, Cassier, Oxford, 1969, pp. 85–109; 'Painting', in *Tulips, Arabesques and Turbans*, ed. Yanni Petsopoulos, London, 1982, pp. 193–212

GUEST, G.V., *Shiraz Painting in the XVIth Century*, Washington, D.C., 1949

HERODOTUS, 'The Persian Wars', F.R.B. Godolphin, New York, 1942

HOBSON, R.L., 'Chinese porcelain at

Constantinople', with contributions by Sir Percival David and Bernard Rackham, *Transactions of the Oriental Ceramic Society*, vol. II, 1933–34, pp. 9–21
IVANOV, Anatol A., 'A Group of Iranian Daggers of the Period from the Fifteenth Century to the Beginning of the Seventeenth', in Elgood, R. ed., *Islamic arms and armour*, Scolar Press, London, 1979, pp. 64–77
JACOB, A., *Armes blanches de l'Islam*, Paris, 1975 (ABC du collectionneur); *Les Armes blanches du monde islamique*, Paris, 1985
KARABACEK, Josef von, 'Zur orientalischen Altertumskunde IV — Muhammedanische Kunststudien, 5. Tauschiertes Eisenschwert des Osmanen-Sultans Suleiman I. Turkei, Jahr 1527. Kais. Schatzkammer, Konstantinopel', in *Sitzungsber. der philos.-hist. Klasse der K. Akademie der Wissenchaften*, CLXXII, I, 1913, pp. 29–33, figs 238 and 239
KARATAY, Fehmi E., *Topkapı Sarayı Müzesi Kutuphanesi Farsca Yazmalar Katalogu*, Istanbul, 1961, 2 vols; *Topkapı Sarayı Müzesi Kutuphanesi Arapca Yazmalar Katalogu*, Istanbul, 1962–69, 4 vols
KONYALI, Hasan Celebi, *Topkapı Sarayı: Uzerine Yapilmis Eski Haritalar*, Istanbul, 1936
KORAN: *The Holy Qur'an Manuscript in 953 H/1546 by Aḥmed Ḳaraḥiṣārī for Sultan Süleyman the Magnificent* (facsimile ed.), Rome, 1980
KOSEOĞLU, Cengiz, *Topkapı Sarayı: obj. sous la dir. de J.M. Rogers*, ed du Jaguar, Paris, 1987
KRAHL, Regina and AYERS, John, *Chinese ceramics in the Topkapı Sarayı Museum*, ed. John Ayers, Sotheby's Publications, London; Istanbul Sarayı Museum, 1986: (1) *Yuan and Ming celadon wares*; (2) *Yuan and Ming porcelains*; (3) *Quing Dynasty porcelains*
KUHNEL, Ernst, 'Die Osmanische Tughra', *Orients*, vol. 2, 1955, pp. 68–82
KURTOĞLU, Fevzi, Türk Suel Alaninda Krokilere Verilen Deger ve Ali Macar Reis Atlasi Istanbul, 1935
LANE, Arthur, 'Ottoman pottery of Iznik', *Ars Orientalis*, vol. 2, 1956, pp. 247–81; *Later Islamic pottery: Persia, Syria, Egypt, Turkey*, Faber and Faber, London, 1971
LATHAM, J.D., *Saracen Archery*, London, 1970
LONGQUAN GINGCI, ed. Zhejiang Sheng Qinqponqye Ting et al., Beijing, 1966
LUBENAU, Reinhold, *Beschreibung der Reinhold Lubenau*, Konigsberg, 1912–30, 5 vols
LUCHNER, L., *Denkmal eines Renaissancerfürsten, Versuch einer Rekonstruktion des Ambraser Museums von 1583*, Wein, 1958
MACKIE, Louise W., 'A Turkish carpet with spots and stripes', in *Textile Museum Journal*, vol. 4, no. 2, 1976, pp. 4–20; 'Rugs and Textiles', in *Turkish Art*, ed. Atil Esin, Smithsonian Institution Press, Washington, D.C.; H. Abrams Inc., New York, 1980, pp. 299–373
MAHIR, Banu, 'Osmanli Sanatinda Saz Uslubundan Anlasilan', *Topkapı Sarayı Müzesi Yilik*, vol. 2, 1987, pp. 123–40
MAYER, L.A., *Islamic Armourers and their Works*, Geneva, 1962
MELIKIAN-CHIRVANI, A.S., 'Four Pieces of Islamic Metalwork', in *Art and Archaeological Research Papers*, London, 1976
MIGEON, Gaston, *Musée du Louvre, l'Orient musulman*, A. Morance, Paris, 1922, 2 vols
MINORSKY, Vladimir, *The Chester Beatty Library: A Catalogue of the Turkish Manuscripts and Miniatures*, Dublin, 1958
MISUGI, Takatoshi, 'Topukapi Serai no Chugoku jiki, parts 1–2', *Mizue*, nos 2, 3, 1967; *Chinese Porcelain Collections in the Near East*, Topkapı and Ardebil, Hong-Kong, 1981, 3 vols
NAMIKAWA, Banri, *Chinese Ceramics in the Topkapı Sarayı Collection*, Tokyo, 1974 and NIKAMI, Tsugio, CIG, Kemal
ÖGÜTMEN, Filiz, *XII-XVIII. Yüzyillar Arasinda Minyatür Sanatindan Önekler. Topkapı Sarayı Minyatür Bölumü Rehberi*, Istanbul, 1966
ÖZ, Tashin, *Turkish textiles and velvets: XIVth-XVIth centuries*, Turkish Press; Broadcasting and Tourist Department, Ankara, 1950; *Turkish ceramics*, Ankara, 1957
POPE, Arthur Upham, *A Survey of Persian Art*, New York, 1964–65 (new edition), 12 vols
RABY, Julian, "Diyarbakir: a rival to Iznik", *Deutsches Archaologisches Institut, Istanbuler Mitteilungen*, vols 27–28, 1977–78; Krahl, R, *Veir*, 1986, vol. I
RABY, Julian and LJÜCEL, Ünsal, "Blue-and-White, celadon, and white wares: Iznik's debt to China", in *Oriental Art*, vol. XXIX, no. 1, 1983, pp. 38–48
RADO, Sevket, *Türk Hattatlari*, Istanbul, n.d.
RENDA, G., "Traditional Turkish painting and the beginning of western trends", in *A History of Turkish Painting*, Istanbul, 1987, pp. 16–86
REYHANLI, Tülay, "The Portraits of Murat III", *Erdem*, vol. 8 (1987, May), Ankara, pp. 453–78
ROGERS, Michael, "A Group of Ottoman pottery in the Godman Bequest", *The Burlington Magazine*, 1985, March, pp. 134–45
SACKEN, Eduard Freiherr von, *Die vorzüglichsten Rüstungen und Waffen der k. k. Ambraser-Sammlung in original Photographien herausgegeben und beschrieben nebst biographischen Skizzen*, Wien, 1859–62, 2 vols
SADEQUE, S.F., *Baybars I of Egypt*, Lahore, 1956
SANDARS, H., "The Weapons of the Iberians", in *Archaeologia*, vol. 64, 1912, pp. 231–58
SERTOĞLU, Midhat, *Osmanli Tüklerinde Tuğra*, Istanbul, 1975
SKELTON, Robert, "Characteristics of later Turkish jade carving", in *Fifth congress of Turkish Art Budapest*, 1975, Akademiai Kiado, Budapest, 1978, pp. 795–807
SKILLITER, Susan A., *Life in Istanbul 1588. Scenes from a traveller's picture book*, Oxford, 1977
SOHRWEIDE, Hanna, "Dichter und Gelehrter aus dem Osten im Osmanischem Reich (1453–1600)", *Der Islam*, vol. 46, 1970, pp. 263–302; "Der Verfasser der als Sulaymân-nâma bekannten Istanbuler Prachthand-schrift", *Der Islam*, vol. 47, 1971
SOUCEK, Svat, "The Ali Macar Reis Atlas and the Deniz kitabi: their place in the genre of portolan charts and atlases", *Imago Mundi*, vol. XXV, 1971, pp. 17–27
SOUSTIEL, Jean, *La Céramique islamique: le guide du connaisseur*, Office du Livre, Fribourg; Vilo, Paris, 1985
SÖYLEMEZOĞLU, Nerkis, "An illustrated copy of Hamdi's Yusuf we Zuleykha dated A.H.921/1515 A.D. in the Bayerische Staatsbibliothek in Munich", in *Near Eastern Numismatics, Iconography, Epigraphy and History*, ed. D.K. Kouymjian, Beirut, 1974, pp. 469–78
SPUHLER, Friedrich, *Oriental carpets in the Museum of Islamic Art, Berlin*, Faber and Faber, London, 1988
STAATLICHE MUSEEN PREUSSISCHER KULTURBESITZ, BERLIN; *Museum fur Islamische Kunst*
STCHOUKINE, Ivan, *Les Peintures des manuscrits Safavis de 1502 à 1587*, Paris, 1959; *La Peinture turque d'après les manuscrits illustrés. Ire partie: de Süleyman Ire a Osman II*, Paris, 1966
TANINDI, Zeren, "Islam Resminde Kutsal Kent ve Yöre Tasvirleri", *Journal of Turkish Studies*, vol. 7, 1983, 1984, pp. 407–37; "Rugani Turk Kitap Kaplarinin Erken Ornekleri", in *Kemal Cig'a Armagan*, pp. 223–53; "13–14. Yüzyilda Yazilmis Kuranlarin Kanuni Doneminde Yenilenmesi", *Topkapı Sarayı Müzesi Yillik*, vol. 1, 1986, pp. 277–94
TATE, H., *Jewellery*, London, 1983
TEZÇAN, Turgay, "Topkapı Sarayı Müzesindeki Turk migferleri", *Sanat Dünyamiz*, vol. II, 5, 1975, Sept., pp. 21–27; *Topkapı Sarayı Müzesi*, 9: Silahar, Istanbul, 1983; "Turkish Bows and Arrows", in *Ilgi*, Istanbul, 1977
THOMAS, Bruno, "Aus der

detail from another page (f. 24a) of cat. no. 55

Waffensammlung in der Neuen Burg zu Wein: orientalische Kostbarkeiten", *Bustan*, vol. 4-5, 1963-64, pp. 121-26

TUNCAY, Hülya, "Ceramic lamps in the Topkapı Palace Museum", *Sanat Dunyamiz*, vol. 4, no. 12, 1978; *Topkapı Palace Museum*, 4: Cin Kösk, Istanbul, 1980

TÜRKOĞLU, Sabahattin, "Saray Ku umculugu", *Sanat Dünyamiz*, vol. II, no. 34, 1985, pp. 12-17

ÜNAL, Ismail, "Cin Porselenleri Uzerindeki Türk Târsiati", *Turk Sanati Tarihi Arasturma ve Incelemeleri*, I, 1963, pp. 674-714

ÜNVER, A. Süheyl, *Hattat Ahmed Ḳaraḥiṣārī (A well-known Turkish calligrapher Ḳaraḥiṣārī Efendi, 1469-1556)*, Istanbul, 1948

VAN BERCHEM, M., 1912, oir: exposition Munich 1910, article: "Arabische inschriften"

VAN DE WAAL, E.H., "Manuscripts maps in the Topkapı Sarayı Library, Istanbul", *Imago Mundi*, vol. XXIII, pp. 81-96

VEINSTEIN, Gilles, "L'Empire dans sa grandeur", in *Histoire de l'empire ottoman*, dir. Robert Mandran, Fayard, Paris, 1989, pp. 159-266

WOODHEAD, Christine, "An Experiment in official historiography: the post of Sehnameci in the Ottoman Empire, c. 1555-1605", *Wiener Zeitschrift für die Kunde des Morgenlandes*, vol. 75, 1983, pp. 157-82

YERASIMOS, Stephane, "Les Registres de la Suleymaniye", in *Dossiers Histoire et Archeologie*, no. 127, 1988, May, pp. 46-49

YUSUF, Ali A., *The Holy Qur'ān*, London, 1975

ZIMMERMAN, Ernst, *Altchinesische Porzellane in Alten Serai, Meisterwerke der Turkischen Museen zur Konstantinopel, Bd II*, ed. Halil Edhem, Leipzig, Berlin, 1930

EXHIBITIONS

DUSSELDORF, 1973
Heftens-Museum; *Islamiche Keramik*, Dusseldorf, 1973

LONDON, 1976
Hayward Gallery; *The Arts of Islam*, The Arts Council of Great Britain, 1976

PARIS, 1977
Grand Palais; *L'Islam dans les collections nationales*, Réunions des musées nationaux, Paris, 1977

ISTANBUL, 1983
Topkapı Palace Museum; *The Anatolian civilisations III, Seljuk/Ottoman*, the Council Europe XVIIIth European Art Exhibition (S.I.), Turkish Ministry of Culture and Tourism, 1983

LONDON, 1983
British Museum; *Islamic art and design 1500-1700*, J.M. Rogers, British Museum Publications, 1983

FRANKFURT, 1985
Museum für Kunsthandwerk Essen, Villa Hugel; *Turkische Kunst und Kultur am osmanischer Zeit*, Verlag Aurel Bongers, Recklinghausen, 1985, 2 vols

LOUISIANA, 1987
Art from the world of Islam 8th-18th century, Louisiana, 1987, Louisiana Revy, 1987, vol. 27, no. 3

WASHINGTON, 1987
National Museum of Art; Chicago, Art Institute; New York, Metropolitan Museum, 1987; *The Age of Sultan Süleyman the Magnificent*, Esin Atil, Museum of Art, Washington; Harry N. Abrams, New York, 1987

BERLIN, 1988
Grosse orangerie, Schloss Charlottenburg; *Schatze aus dem Topkapı Serail das Zeitalter Suleymans der Prachtigen*, Staatliche Museem Preussischer Kulturbesitz, Berlin, 1988

JAPAN, 1988
Exposition itinerante, Japan, 1988-89. *The Splendour of Turkish civilisation: Ottoman treasures of the Topkapı Palace*, ed. Tokyo National Museum, the Middle Eastern Culture Centre in Japan, Asahi Shimbun (S.I.), 1988

LONDON, 1988
British Museum; *Süleyman the Magnificent*, J.M. Rogers, R.M. Ward, British Museum Publications, 1988

PARIS, 1990
Grand Palais; *Soliman Le Magnifique*, Galeries Nationales du Grand Palais, 1990

CONCORDANCE

MAJOR PREVIOUS EXHIBITIONS

Cross-reference list by catalogue number

cat.no. 1990	Institution Inventory Number	PARIS 1977	ISTANBUL 1983	FRANKFURT 1985	WASHINGTON 1987	LONDON 1988	BERLIN 1988	PARIS 1990
1	TKS GY 1400				1	8	7	1
2	TKS H 1563							5
3	TIEM 2401							15
4	TKS E 7816/2				3			16
5	TIEM 2316							18
6	TKS EH 71		E14					128
7	TKS EH 60							123
8	TIEM 400							126
9	TKS YY 999				9a	15a	19a	122
10	TKS EH 227				13	19	23	125
11	TKS EH 266							124
12	TKS A 21		E55		15	21	25	129
13	TKS EH 222				16	22	26	127
14	TKS EH 77							130
15	TKS 2/2896				21	27	31	133
16	TKS 2/2086		E204					134
17	TKS 2/2095							233
18	CK 41/2				166	129	137	116
19	MDL 5547	582						117
20	CK 41/16		E154		195		160	121
21	MDL 7509							146
22	TKS D 43/25							143
23	TKS YY 159							141
24	TKS R 917				22	37	41	135
25	TKS 2/2274				55	64	66	137
26	TKS 2/4736							138
27	TKS 13/1183							108
28	TKS 13/1182							109
29	TIEM 774						132	110
30	TIEM 804						133	111
31	TIEM 6							113
32	TIEM 107							115
33	NGV AS107/1986							
34	TKS 2/74		E217		95	88	89	57
35	TKS 2/83		E218		96	89	90	58
36	TKS 1/10989				103	95		60
37	KHM C5-C5A				104a-104b			61
38	TKS 1/463				88	85	86	62
39	KHM A 1337							63
40	KHM A 1341				90			64
41	RS EL-ARD							65
42	TKS 1/294				89	86	87	67
43	KHM C 152a-b				93			70
44	RS EL-ARD							71
45	KHM C 208				94			72
46	TKS 1/2571		E227		101	93	94	73
47	TKS 1/2441		E105		100	92	92	75
48	KHM C 159							78
49	TKS 2/1187		E219		84	87	88	79
50	RS EL-ARD							
51	TKS 2/3776		E85		86	83	84	80
52	TKS 2/715				85	82		81

cat. no. 1990	Institution Inventory Number	PARIS 1977	ISTANBUL 1983	FRANKFURT 1985	WASHINGTON 1987	LONDON 1988	BERLIN 1988	PARIS 1990
53	TKS 2/2879		E77	Vol. II 8/1	107	97	97	82
54	TKS H 644							84
55	TKS R 1272				38	42	46	92
56	TKS 17/348		E75		44	49	51	93
57	TKS H 1517 f.235r							94
58	TKS H 1517 f.360		E71		41c	45c	47c	95
59	TKS H 1592							97
60	MDL 7449	583						156
61	CK 41/155		E33		170		141	179
62	TKS 15/6086				163	150	158	184
63	MDL 7456							171
64	MDL 3919-102							169
65	MDL 2402	59						181
66	MDL 6643							175
67	MDL 7590	593						194
68	MDL 5960	594		Vol. II 2/19	188			294
69	MDL 7595				198			296
70	MDL 7880-70	598						298
71	MDL 7880-82							87
72	MDL 7880-61							88
73	MDL 7880-28	599						283
74	MDL AA403	601			205			286
75	TIEM 816							288
76	TIEM 817		E168					289
77	MDL 3919/2287				206			199
78	MDL AA405							302
79	MDL 3919-56 & 57							305
80	TKS 25/3216							158
81	TKS 23/1625		E94		50	62	64	159
82	TKS 2/2856				57	66	68	236
83	TKS 2/2836		E215					237
84	TKS 2/2873		E96		56	63	67	228
85	TKS 2/2842							186
86	TKS 2/3831				64	71	72	185
87	TKS 2/8		E211		61	68	69	189
88	TKS 2/3826							229
89	TKS 2/3832		E207		66	72	73	232
90	TKS 2/3825		E206		54	63	65	226
91	TKS 2/3725							235
92	TKS 2/2085				63	70	71	230
93	TKS 2/1372-3							238
94	TKS 15/668		E131		71	77	77	239
95	TKS 15/2944				70	76	76	241
96	TKS 15/2762							242
97	TKS 15/2767		E214		69	75	76	243
98	TIEM 419				80	60		104
99	TIEM 421				81	59	61	105
100	TIEM 416				82	60	62	106
101	TKS 2/2912		E84		83	61	63	251
102	TKS 2/1801		E81			78	79	252
103	TKS 2/575		E120		78	56	58	253
104	TIEM 482				77	55	57	107
105	TKS 2/627 2/628 2/629							255
106	TKS 2/635		E90					256

cat. no.	Institution	PARIS	ISTANBUL	FRANKFURT	WASHINGTON	LONDON	BERLIN	PARIS
1990	Inventory Number	1977	1983	1985	1987	1988	1988	1990
106	2/636 2/638							
107	TKS 13/92 13/93				112a-b	102		244
108	TKS 13/100				121a-b	109a-b	108	245
109	TKS 13/145							246
110	TKS 13/46		E102		114	105	105	248
111	TKS 13/38		E136					249
112	TKS 13/72				115	104	104	193
113	TKS 31/50		E109		132	120	118	100
114	TKS 31/53							101
115	TKS 31/54							102
116	TKS 13/1446		E134					272
117	RS EL-ARD							
118	TKS 31/169		E132					273
119	TIEM 36						131	274
120	TKS H 2168 f.15r		E178					192
121	TKS H2135 f.14r							191
122	TKS H 2163							201
123	TKS H2169 f.37r							202
124	TKS H 2162 f.8r							204
125	TKS H2168 f.14v		E177					205
126	TKS GY 323/158							212
127	TKS EH 416				6			213
128	TKS H 2177							214
129	TKS YY 846							215
130	TKS H 802				33a-b	35a-b	39a-b	216
131	TKS EH 522		E66		17	23	27	190
132	TKS 2/894				68	74	75	206
133	TKS 2/2111		E205		67	73	74	208
134	TKS 2/22		E209		62	69	70	209

TKS	Topkapı Sarayı Müzesi, Istanbul
TIEM	Türk ve Islam Eserleri Müzesi, Istanbul
CK	Arkeoloji Müzesi Çinili Köşk, Istanbul
MDL	Musée du Louvre, Paris
NGV	National Gallery of Victoria, Melbourne
KHM	Kunsthistorisches Museum, Vienna
RS El-Ard	Collection Rifaat Sheikh El-Ard, Riyadh